Cios

Life in Afrikanderland as viewed by an Afrikander

A story of life in South Africa, based on truth

Cios

Life in Afrikanderland as viewed by an Afrikander
A story of life in South Africa, based on truth

ISBN/EAN: 9783744755184

Printed in Europe, USA, Canada, Australia, Japan

Cover: Foto ©ninafisch / pixelio.de

More available books at **www.hansebooks.com**

LIFE IN AFRIKANDERLAND

AS VIEWED BY AN AFRIKANDER

A Story of Life in South Africa, based on Truth

BY

"CIOS"

LONDON
DIGBY, LONG & CO., PUBLISHERS
18 BOUVERIE STREET, FLEET STREET, E.C.
1897

PUBLISHER'S NOTE

In all times of stress and struggle, it is not from our friends and supporters, but from our enemies and opponents, that we receive the best and most practical instruction If an evil or a peril exist, it is surely best to know it; and if serious treason be hatching in dark places, publicity may easily rob it of its main strength and neutralise its virulence. Further, in order to rightly understand racial conflicts—of all the most bitter—we must put ourselves in our adversary's place in order to arrive at just conclusions. We are quite aware that in issuing this uncompromising attack upon British supremacy in South Africa the writer is viewing everything from an entirely anti-English standpoint, but surely it is of great practical importance that we should be accurately informed as to the way in which our adversaries regard us. More practical instruction can be obtained thus than in any other manner. The intense hostility of the writer to England is manifest, and a perusal of these pages is calculated to be of real service to those to whom, as to ourselves, the solidarity and permanence of the British Empire is a primary consideration.

Dedication

To my mother do I dedicate this work, who, I am sure, had she lived to read it, would have approved the sentiments expressed herein, and would have thoroughly sympathised with the earnest object for which this work has been written, viz., the ultimate triumph of TRUTH.

CIOS.

PREFACE

To the Reader,

Gentle Reader, I have written this story in the English language—a language learned by me, as a foreign language, for the chief purpose of placing before the English reading public a true and faithful version of the character and life of an Afrikander. So many libels and false stories have of late been spread in England and all over the world about the Boers by enemies of the people inhabiting the Colonies and States of South Africa, that I could not resist the temptation to write something in which the truth and nothing but the truth would be told. I have made the attempt; whether it is to be successful or not, the reading public must decide.

In this story there is no plot (excepting the Great Complot). It is simply a story of everyday life, with little or no embellishment. Yet I trust the reader, in lands far away as well as those living here in my own beloved native land, will find sufficient to interest him to lead him on to the end of the book. At the least, there was subject-matter enough to write about without going out of the paths of Truth. My only difficulty was not to be led away by my subject and make this work too large for a first attempt in literature.

The incidents and adventures related, as well as anecdotes by old Burghers of the South African Republic, are all based upon truth, and were learned by the writer from the parties themselves. The sad death by lightning of poor Daniel is true, word for word, even to the premonition he had of his death, and occurred only as late as the beginning of this year (1896); and many will recognise the family as described by the writer.

The writer has mostly made use of Christian names, as all the characters used in this story are real and living; and it would serve no purpose to publish real names, while substituted names would only be misleading. Where politics have been drawn into the story, the reader may rely upon the truth only having been told of events, as well as prevailing opinions as expressed by representatives of the different parties. The latter part of the book is largely devoted to the events of the New Year (1896) which occurred near Krugersdorp, Johannesburg and Pretoria, and its results as gathered by one who took note of everything on the spot, and may be relied upon as being true in every detail. If I have succeeded in convincing a portion of the public of the truth, I shall rest well satisfied.

THE AUTHOR.

CONTENTS

BOOK I

BOOK II

LIFE IN AFRIKANDERLAND

BOOK I

CHAPTER I

A DEATH-BED SCENE

A DEATH-BED is always a sad scene, but doubly so when it is that of a parent surrounded by his or her children, and trebly so when those children are young and helpless.

Let me introduce the reader to such a scene for a moment, for 'tis good now and again to be drawn near to death, if only for a moment, for it brings us face to face with the fleeting and uncertain nature of life, and admonishes us to be prepared.

Behold, then, a pale weak figure, in a white draped, old-fashioned, four-post bed; that figure is the figure of a dying man, that man the father of three children a boy and two girls, who are standing around the bed clinging to their mother.

'But if father is going away, where is he going to, mother?' said the boy, the eldest of the three. Alas! he did not realise what was taking place. He had been told that his father was going away; but he could not realise that he would see him no more on earth, and that he would be left alone to fight the battle of life, with only a poor, poverty-stricken mother to stand between him and starvation.

'Dear Stephen, he is going to heaven. God has called him and he must go.'

'But may we not go with him, mother?'

'No, my child, we may not go till God calls us.'

'But when will He call us, mother?'

'I do not know, dear; we must be prepared to go whenever He calls; it may be to-morrow, or it may not be for years.'

'But when shall we see father again, mother?'

'When God calls us to heaven, too, dear.'

'Come near, Stephen,' his father called to him in weak and trembling tones. 'Steve, my son, I want to say a few words to you before I leave you. First I want you to take care of your mother and sisters as much as you can. Your mother will be weak and unprotected, and when you are grown up, you must work and support her and your sisters as best you can. Then I want you to promise to always fear God and look to Him for aid in time of need, and serve Him to the best of your ability in time of prosperity. And lastly, I want you always to be faithful to your country and your people. Remember that here we are a vassal race as yet. But thank God there are two bright spots in South Africa where our people are free, and acknowledge only one King—God—the King of kings. And if ever the time should come that you may be able to aid in bringing our people nearer to being a one and united people—free—under God's guidance, do your best. Do you promise?'

'Yes, father, I will do my best.'

'I know, child, you can hardly understand these things yet, but when you are older you will understand what I mean. Your mother will write my request down for you, and when you are grown up and are a man, you will understand. Now kiss me all of you. May God bless you and be a father to you all. Amen.'

CHAPTER II

BOYHOOD

SEVEN years have passed, our young hero has grown considerably. He is now twelve years of age. Behold him once more. He is kneeling near to his mother and sisters. The mother is praying. 'Oh, God,' she prays, 'have mercy on our dear people. Oh, Jesus, they are of our blood and our race, and they have done no wrong as a people. Oh, Christ, they have fled into the wilderness to worship Thee in quiet and in peace. Oh, God, they have done naught but they have done it in Thy name. Oh, Lord, they have struggled against famine and troubles untold. Oh, Jesus, they have bled and fought against the heathen and Thou hast always succoured them. When death faced them Thou saved them and said, "Live, and be a *people*." Oh, God, Thou wilt surely not desert them now. Lord aid, even though victory seems impossible to human minds. Thou art the God of battles, and to Thee all things are possible. Oh, Lord, in Thee do we and they trust, now and evermore. Amen.'

They rise, and Steve goes up to his mother and stands leaning fondly against her.

It is January 1881. It is the time of the Transvaal struggle for independence and freedom.

Daily alarming telegrams arrive, and tear the hearts of relatives and friends of the poor struggling immigrants in the Transvaal. The killed and wounded of the Boers are always given in hundreds. We *now* know how lying these telegrams were. But the friends of the Boers did not then know what was true or not.

Steve nestled near to his mother and said,—

'But, mother, cannot we go and help our people in the Transvaal? Surely it is not so far away but we can reach them, and fight by their side? And,' drawing himself up to his full height, 'if needs be, we can die with them.'

'My dear, you are far too young to talk about fighting and dying in battle; but it is impossible, even if you were old enough, to do so. There is many and many a heart here that beats in unison with our race, fighting for freedom in the Transvaal, and would gladly take up arms for them. But, alas, we are bound hand and foot, and are surrounded by the enemy. We cannot leave here a day's march, but the English Goverment will stop our people from going to help their friends in the Transvaal. We are surrounded by enemies. No, child, we can only pray and trust in God.'

'And will God help them if we pray for them, mother?'

'Yes, child, for their cause is just, and God always helps in a righteous cause.'

CHAPER III

A CONTROVERSY

'STEVE, you are talking nonsense.'

A group of boys were standing talking, warmly arguing about the all-absorbing topic of the day—the Transvaal war.

'I should like to know why I talk nonsense more than you?'

'Why, you say that the Transvaal Boers can fight against England and win. I should like to know how a few Boers can fight against England, when we have already more soldiers on the Transvaal border than there are Boers to fight, and there are as many more coming out from England, with ever so many cannon. And when these arrive, what will your Boers do then? You are talking nonsense, I say!'

'I am not talking nonsense, for mother says that, if we pray to God to help our people, He will surely do so, and then they will win; for God is stronger than England and all the world besides.'

Steve's opponent smiled derisively, as if he thought Steve was talking nonsense worse than ever—as if people could swallow such childish superstitions in the latter end of the nineteenth century, that God fights the battles of nations; these things are too antiquated! But, thought he to himself, I might as well fight it out with him on his own ground, and with his own weapons, so he said,—

'But, Steve, the English people will also pray; and why do you think God would answer your people's prayers more than the prayers of the English?'

'Because God only answers our prayers when we pray for a righteous thing; and our people's cause is righteous; the cause of the English is unrighteous, for they seek to oppress a weaker people than themselves, who have done them no harm.'

Steve's simple faith in his mother's teachings and in the promises of his God, had given him the victory in this schoolboy controversy. His opponent could only smile in a depreciating sort of way and walk off.

CHAPTER IV

INDEPENDENCE GAINED ONCE MORE—YOUTHFUL PATRIOTISM

THOSE were anxious times for all true South Africans—the time of the Transvaal war of independence. At first, nothing but cooked telegrams came, which made out that the Boers wherever met were being defeated. But later the truth leaked out, as it is ever bound to do, viz., that the Boers were wondrously victorious in every battle that had been fought. The accounts of

Bronkorstspruit, Laingsnek and Schuimhoogte were received with mixed feelings in the town of G——n, in the Cape Colony, where Steve and his mother lived. Mixed, in that they were received by all Afrikanders and Republicans with joy and thanksgivings to Him, to Whom alone they ascribed the victory of their brethren; but with anger and almost with unbelief by the Imperialists. *They* could not believe it, for how was it possible for those cowardly (?) Boers (who, it had been predicted, would run away at the first cannon shot), to defeat the thoroughly armed and disciplined troops of England, why it is impossible! *They* believed that such simple faith as Steve's *was* childishness. But what was their consternation when the disastrous news —to them—of Amajuba came, capped by the tidings that peace had been concluded favourably to the Boers. They called shame on England for at last recognising the injustice that they were perpetrating on a quiet and peace-loving people.

Public opinion in England, and all over the world, had shown the Imperial Government the error of their ways at last. They had to make peace after being defeated, and promise the Boers their independence back again. But the Imperial Government seemed to say, 'Never mind the defeat and shame, we will show the Boers a trick or two yet. We will appoint a Royal Commission, and force a convention on the Boers to our own liking, and they shall feel the Lion's paw in another way.'

Yes, England was magnanimous (?) enough to *give* (?) the Boers their independence back, but not the independence that had been taken from them.

Oh, no, English diplomats are not such fools! They took gold from the Boers; they gave them brass in exchange. They took their independence, independence in every sense of the word, from them; independence without conditions, such as was recognised by the Sand River Convention, but they gave back a false municipal independence, only a shadow of the independence possessed before.

'Bah!' thought these English diplomats, 'how will these ignorant Boers know the difference?' Alas, England, England, where was thy boasted *honour* and magnanimity then? Thou protector of the weak and injured, remember there *is* a God, Who weighs the nations, as well as individuals; and the time may arrive, when thou mayest see that dread hand-writing on the wall with those fatal words, 'Mene, mene, Tekel, Upharsin, —Thou hast been weighed, and thou hast been found wanting, and thou shalt be swept from off the face of the earth. *Stop*—before it is too late, and use the power and wealth that God has granted thee, to a better purpose than that of enslaving and oppressing a weaker people.'

'Twas a glad day for Steve when he stopped before the notice board of the local paper one day and read the news of the Transvaal victory at Amajuba, and that peace and freedom were promised to the people of his father. He ran joyfully to his mother and cried out, 'Mother, mother, God has heard our prayers, the Transvaal has won, and our people are *Free*.'

'Is that true, my son?'

'Yes, mother, I have just seen it on the notice board,' and then Steve told her all he had read on the board.

His mother, God-fearing and grateful, made him kneel at her side, and poured out praises and thanksgivings to God Almighty, Who had thus wrought a miracle to save His people.

Does England realise that the Boers are a God-fearing people, who have never heard of materialism, Atheism and other blaspheming *isms?* still less do they believe in such. No, they believe simply, and with the faith of a child in God and His word:—'If your faith is no larger than a grain of mustard seed, ye shall say to that mountain "*Go*," and it *shall* go, "*Come*," and it shall come.' The Boers had *faith*, and they moved not mountains, but they moved—England.

While the war was still going on, and the ultimate end of the war was yet uncertain, Steve, to show his patriotism, and to prove that he was not ashamed to be called a Boer (which name was generally used by the English as a name of contempt and reproach), got up an association amongst all his young Afrikander friends. In this association there was only one rule, and this rule was, that no member was to speak to another member without using as a name of endearment the name '*Boer.*' Each one was to be honoured when addressed by another member by being called 'Boer'; and for some time the English schoolmates of these young patriots were surprised to hear remarks such as these, 'Hillo, "Boer," are you going for a swim this afternoon,' or, 'I say, "Boer," let us go and have a feed of grapes at Tante (auntie) Sannie this evening.' And even to this day, when these young men are grown up and are scattered over the country, when corresponding with each other, they are in the habit of beginning their letters in this way,—

'My dear old Boer, I received your last letter,' etc., and they have lived to see the name of Boers not only not to signify shame any longer, but to be honoured by friends and foes.

Steve was over jealous of the good name of his people, and lost no opportunity to stand up for them.

Our young hero had one staunch English friend, that is English in that his parents were English, but he was Afrikander born, and he was an Afrikander at heart. He was named Gus Turner. These two young friends were standing together amongst a group of other boys one day arguing on politics as usual. Why shouldn't they?—their parents talked nothing else all day.

A young man named Jim M'Murphy was speaking sneeringly. He was strongly built, and considerably larger than Steve. He was saying,—

'It is all humbug these Boers having beaten our soldiers. They are all cowards!'

'You lie!' cried Steve in his anger; and before he

knew what was going to take place, he was sprawling on the ground, with a bloody nose from an unexpected blow. But Steve was not the boy to accept punishment unreturned, so he jumped up and hit his assailant on the eye, which spoilt the sight of that eye for a day or two.

'Well done, Steve,' cried Gus; 'do it again.'

But he had no time to do it again, for at that moment one of the teachers appeared on the scene and put a stop to further fighting. But M'Murphy had not done with him yet; a black eye was not to be taken tamely by an Englishman from a Boer!

That night, when Steve went home from the evening preparation class at school, he was surprised to see a crowd of street arabs outside the school door. These youngsters were composed of Kaffirs, Hottentots, and bastards of all colours. To explain their presence, we must state that M'Murphy's father kept a grocery store; among other good things, he retailed sugar sticks. Jim M'Murphy was his fathers' assistant when not in school, and thus had full access to his father's stock of sugar sticks, and he used these sugar sticks as payment to his regiment of young ragamuffins, who were to assist him in having his revenge on Steve for the black eye given him. What he really intended doing with Steve, when he had captured him, has never been revealed; but as soon as Steve had walked a few paces from the school door, pushing his way through the crowd with the assistance of Gus Turner, and wondering what in the world was up to call such a crowd together, he felt his jacket pulled violently from behind and heard M'Murphy's voice calling out,—

'Here he is.' In a moment two or three more had hold of him before he knew any evil was intended him. But when he saw how the wind lay, he wrenched his arms free and struck out right and left, always seconded by Gus Turner, who stuck to his friend like a man. But although Steve's arms were now free, M'Murphy still had hold of his jacket, and he could not reach behind himself to strike at the coward behind his back. But he was not at a loss yet. He spun round and round as fast as he could, and here was M'Murphy revolving round him, standing straight out behind Steve's back, somewhat like the snake that had hold of Paddy's clothing when Paddy was running round the house.

Going round at the speed that Steve was spinning, even M'Murphy had to let go! and the sudden cessation from his circular motion caused him to lose his balance, and sent him squirming on the ground. M'Murphy's army was now closing up to take Steve and his companion prisoners by force of numbers, when the teacher once more appeared on the scene, being attracted by the noise, and scattered M'Murphy's army (like chaff before the wind) with his great knobby stick.

Steve and Gus took advantage of this diversion in their favour to clear round the first corner, but soon found the whole crowd on their track once more. There was nothing for it now but to run to avoid being captured. But the enemy could run too, and half-a-dozen of the best runners amongst the enemy were soon overtaking the two fugitives. The foremost one was just laying hold of Steve's coat, when Gus Turner dropped down right in front of him, tripped him, and sent him head over heels to the ground, and two more of the enemy, being just behind, followed suit. But Gus was up again in a moment, and once more he and Steve ran for it. Gaining a good few paces by the confusion caused by the tripped enemy, Gus Turner's home, which was the nearest, was soon reached. Once protected by the shadow of his castle, and sure of a safe retreat, the two fugitives stood at bay, and taking out their catapults, a boy's most offensive weapon, sent a shower of buck-shot into the ranks of the approaching enemy, who first halted in a crowd at a short distance, but finding themselves thus bombarded by the hidden battery of the two boys standing in the dark shadow, the enemy soon scattered and dispersed, leaving Gus and Steve in possession of the battlefield.

CHAPTER V

YOUTHFUL PRANKS

IT is not our purpose to give a full history of the boyhood of our hero. We would rather hurry on to give an account of his life as a man. But we hope our readers will not think it tedious, if we give an episode or two of his boyhood's life, which will enable the reader the better to understand and sympathise with him in his aspirations and ambitions.

Steve was by no means a paragon of goodness at all times—no boy ever is. He loved mischief as much as any other boy. We do not believe in the perfect hero. Every boy and man, as well as girl and woman, has his or her faults. Steve's greatest fault was a keen sense of the ludicrous, which often led him into mischief; besides he loved mischief for its own sweet sake. He, one night, nearly had to sleep in the lock-up through his mischievous pranks. He and a companion, thinking it a pity not to make the best use of a fine moonlight night, proceeded to prepare for a game of *snake*. To the reader, who has never had the pleasure and excitement to play snake, I will explain how it is done.

A dark coloured strip of cloth is obtained in the shape and size of a fine large healthy snake. To one end of this artificial snake the end of a thin and almost invisible string is tied. The longer the string the safer the operation is.

Well, Steve and his companion manufactured just such a snake. They laid the snake on one side of the street in the regulation way. That is in the shape a snake is supposed to delight in assuming, viz., curled up in a zigzag form. Then they took the further end of the string to the opposite side of the street, crept through a hole in the hedge, taking their end of the string with them, and watched their opportunity. Presently a man came down the street, walking jauntily along as if he feared neither man nor devil; but as soon as he is in a line with the snake the fun commences. The first thing our peaceful citizen is aware of is a snake entangled with, and curling between, his legs, in a most lively fashion (operated by the string of course). Who is going to fight a snake of such a size in the uncertain moonlight, and unarmed too? Not he! no fear! So the only result was a yell, a whoop, and a mighty jump, and our peaceful citizen disappears round the first corner with long record-beating strides, leaving the destruction of the snake to the next comer. Of course, as soon as the victim is out of earshot, Steve and his companion are holding their sides, laughing at the jolly fun. The snake is soon replaced and the fun recommences. After sundry victims had afforded copious fun to the mischievous operators, they began to think it rather slow waiting for customers, so they started walking up the street in search of the slow-coming victims. The fun was lively and brisk for some time, but they reached the summit of their enjoyment when they frightened a troop of servant girls, accompanied by their beaux, out for a walk. The troop scattered all over the street, howling, yelling and screaming, fit to wake the dead. They did wake someone from his sleep, who was not quite dead yet—the night watchman. Now this night watchman was not a bird to be caught by chaff twice. *He* had seen this trick before. He caught up the snake, and, following the line up, soon came to the hiding youths. But if he thought that he was going to gain promotion by catching these night-birds he was mightily mistaken, for these slippery gents crushed their way through the hedge lining the street into a garden, and climbing hedge after hedge, from one garden into the other, until they came to another street, easily escaped, and walked quietly home, minus their snake, which had fallen into the hands of the watchman. Of course this spice of danger made the fun all the greater.

Steve and his friends had one grand playground. It was on the edge of the town on the river bank. There they would congregate of an afternoon and indulge in all the different kinds of games dear to a boy's heart. Steve was one of the youngest of the boys who met here, and therefore was not as yet initiated into all the crafts of the band. One night, while playing cricket at this spot, Steve's cousin and namesake—a boy easily led astray and into mischief, vacillating and weak principled, of which more will be seen further on—came to him, and, after leading him on one side, said in English (which, the reader must understand, is a foreign language to Steve, his mother's tongue being Dutch, or rather Afrikander, and he was only just beginning to learn English at school).

'I say, Steve, do you want to smoke?'

'Smoke? Smoke? What is that?'

'Rook, rook!' replied his cousin.

'Oh, rook! I don't know. Is it nice?'

'Oh, yes; come and try.'

Of course the policy of his elder companions in asking Steve to join them was to make him participate in their stealthy practice, and thus incriminate him, to prevent him from getting them into trouble by telling anyone about it, by which means their parents might come to hear of it, which, of course, would mean severe punishment to them. Steve's cousin led him into a dense bush on the river bank, which he had never explored as yet, therefore he was surprised to see his cousin part the bushes and lead him into a large but thoroughly concealed opening among the bushes. The overhanging branches made it a nearly rainproof retreat. Here Steve found about half-a-dozen members of the secret smoking club. After a look round, our hero was offered a smoke, which he accepted, and was soon puffing away at—what does the uninitiated reader think? —a piece of ratan, which was one of the first stages in learning the art of smoking in this particular band; the porous wood of the ratan, or cane, serving as a good conductor of the smoke from the burning end. Of the whole band gathered here, only one was advanced enough to indulge in the real article, viz., tobacco; the rest were all smoking one, or another, of the different substitutes for tobacco known to the rising generation. I suppose the manly reader who has been brought up in a proper and an enlightened manner has learned to smoke with the usual cigarette, made up of Turkish, or mixed tobacco. But these youths, sons of more or less poor parents, being allowed no pocket money, had to satisfy themselves with the best substitutes for tobacco they could discover; and they showed a rare genius in discovering different cheap articles to serve their purpose, amongst which were such things as pumpkin stalk, cane, leaves of various trees, and various similar rubbish. All this is vulgar is it not? Yet I can assure you it is not as bad as it sounds. It produces plenty of the chief thing desired—smoke!

But to resume. Steve did not remain satisfied for many days with these insipid and weak substitutes; so when his cousin, who was the only one who smoked tobacco regularly, offered to allow him a few puffs at the real thing, he accepted readily enough, and smoked like all novices generally do, viz., smoked as if his life depended upon his finishing the pipe as fast as possible. All went well until he had finished the pipe, for while he was yet smoking, he had thought it not at all as nasty as it had been described to him. But when he had put the pipe down (which was made of two joints of reeds, one about an inch in diameter serving as the bowl, and another one with a tiny opening serving as the stem) he began to feel the effects. He felt as if the world were whirling round and round on purpose to make him sick. He made his way to some water the best way he could, plunged his head therein and washed out his mouth, but nothing would take away that awful feeling which most readers who are also smokers know to be the effect of the first pipe of tobacco. It was only after having lain down on the grass for an hour or so, with closed eyes, vowing innumerable vows never to touch tobacco again, that he got well enough to go home, amid the teasings and jokes of his companions. But I must state here that Steve did not keep his vow never to touch tobacco again. Who does not make these vows when learning to smoke, and who does not break them? Steve tried again and again, and after having broken his pipe and renewed his vow not to smoke again for some dozen times, he succeeded at last in smoking without getting sick, and to-day he can smoke his pipe against any man.

CHAPTER VI

A CHARACTER SKETCH OF OUR HERO

STEVE was not fond of school. He liked studying and learning, but he wanted to select his own studies, and hated to be forced to learn what he did not wish to study. He was passionately fond of books, with hardly any distinction. He would never allow a book to pass out of his hand without first reading it, if he could help it. If he got hold of a book he would read it. If he had no time, he would make time. While walking in the street, he would be holding the book in front of his nose, while carefully feeling his steps, or while taking his hurried meals, or when other people were soundly sleeping at night, and even in school he would find time to read; and read books, too, which no teacher of any self-respect would have tolerated. But what did Steve care for the opinion of his teacher as to what books he should read? A book was a book to him, to be used and to be made the most of possible. He would smuggle the book into school under his coat, and while his teacher was thinking that Steve was studying his lessons most diligently, that young man would be deeply interested in some book of travels, or something of the kind. Not that Steve did not learn his lessons. He did learn them, but it did not take him long to do so; reading his task over once or twice was quite sufficient for him to know as much of it as he cared to know. His object was not to be at the top of his class. No, his nature was too retiring to allow him to render himself as conspicuous as all that. If he did happen to come up top by accident, he made his way down to the bottom again as fast as he could. His friend, Gus Turner, was also fond of being at the bottom of the class, but not from choice, but perforce because his mental abilities did not allow him to get up higher, and he always did his best to keep Steve near him, for he found Steve useful to prompt him when his own knowledge of questions asked, failed him. Steve always obliged his friend as best he could, both in supplying answers as well as in keeping near him at the bottom of the class. One day he was caught in the act. The teacher had come down with a question right from the top of the class, and no one could answer the question asked, until he had come to Steve, who thoughtlessly answered it correctly. 'Go up top,' said the teacher. But Steve quietly kept his seat. He was not going to leave his friend at the bottom while he went to the top! The teacher soon noticed this, and asked him why he did not go up. He replied that he did not care to do so. 'Go to the bottom then,' commanded the angry teacher. Steve did so. What did he care? His friend was at the bottom; he had been just above him, now he was just below him. What difference did it make?

I have said that Steve was fond of reading; he was also fond of *thinking*—day-dreaming, His great delight was, when he had the time for it, as on Sundays, for instance, to go out for a walk into the veld, and find a shady grassy spot on which to lie on his back, looking up into the sky, to *think*—think about all sorts of things, past, present, and future. He did not fear to try and think out problems which had puzzled greater and more matured brains than his. There was one great mystery to which his thoughts generally would come back again and again. He could generally find some solution to all questions that cropped up, but this particular one would not be solved, turn it over as he would. This mystery was—*Space*.

CHAPTER VII

THOUGHTS AND FLOWERS

WHILE thus lying on his back, gazing up into the bright South African sky, with the sun seemingly floating as an atom in all the immensity of space; and the sun he had learned in his books was ever so many times larger than our earth, and yet it seemed only a speck in space. 'Space, space, what is space? Where does it begin? Where does it end?' And then he would fly on in imagination from world to world, from star to star, from sun to sun, but his imagination could not find even a probable ending for space. He had never read anything on the subject to help him. He had never read any book in which he had seen what others thought of the subject, so he had to puzzle his own poor brain, eternally thinking, thinking ever on it. *Surely*, SURELY there must be some answer to this problem. Surely there MUST be a beginning to space as well as an end, otherwise how can it be, and yet it *cannot* have beginning or end. He felt as if he should get mad trying to think it out; and when he got so far as to feel his brain reeling in endeavouring to pierce beyond the mystery of space, he would jump up and shout and laugh, and run about looking for his favourite wild flowers in order to forget this maddening thought, but it would come back to him whenever he was alone and thinking.

Speaking about flowers—that was another of his passions. He was never so happy as when tending his few flowers. He was famous for the beauty of the wild flowers he generally gathered in the mountains when he had time. He used to think a half-holiday well spent if he could take a walk into the mountains to gather a beautiful bouquet of his favourite wild flowers. As has been suggested before, he was of a retiring nature, and greatly disliked crowds. At any festival in town, when everybody, including his own family, would all eagerly gather together to enjoy themselves by seeing and being seen, he would rather go for a walk in the veld, where his thoughts were his only company—and good company he always found them. Or he would find a comfortable nook and read a book, during which occupation he would forget the rest of the world and be happy.

CHAPTER VIII

STEP-CHILDREN

STEVE'S mother had married again a few years after his father's death. She would have preferred remaining unmarried, as she considered it would have been more faithful to the memory of her dead husband; but she found herself too poor to educate her children unaided, and bring them up as she would like to do. It was not a happy marriage, which is usually the case where there are step-children to cause jealousy—the more so when the step-parent is not of the best-natured and gentlest character. Steve's stepfather respected and, in his way, loved his wife; but he disliked Steve, because that youngster was a manly and proud little fellow, and rebelled against his stepfather when the latter treated him unjustly, or ill-treated his little sisters: which his stepfather often did, more out of spite to Steve than from any other reason.

He used to make Steve work (out of school hours) in the garden, chop wood, carry water, and, in fact, he invented work for the poor boy if there was no work really wanting to be done. Poor Steve did all this most patiently and dutifully, even though he lost his play hours; for he did not really care much for the usual boyish games of his companions. All he cared for was to secure a candle end to read his beloved books by at night, when everybody else was sleeping, or to take his walk into the veld on Sundays, after church time. Amidst the beauties of Nature, which he loved with the love of a true child of Nature, he was happy. He was patient and enduring amidst the petty persecutions of his stepfather, for his mother's sake, while it only concerned himself. He did not even complain when his stepfather one day found him stealing a glimpse into a new book which he had borrowed from a friend and cruelly took it from him and cast it into the fire. His stepfather could not have done him greater personal injury if he had tried for a month to find the way. But Steve took it quietly and patiently, even though it was a borrowed book and it would take some of his few most-treasured books to satisfy his friend from whom he had borrowed the volume. Steve was accustomed to these daily persecutions from his stepfather.

But there were times when even his stepfather was awed into fear of him—that was when Steve considered his sisters ill-treated. To give an instance.

Steve's mother had a son by her second husband, seven years old at this time—a child who, perhaps, would have been a good boy if he had been left to his mother's care and training. But his father utterly spoiled him by giving him his desires and wishes unstinted, no matter at what sacrifice or how foolish those wishes were. If it was the most precious article belonging to his stepbrother or sisters, if he asked for it, he was to have it. Steve had long rebelled against this, especially on behalf of his sisters, but always to no effect. In fact, he made himself only the more hated by his stepfather. He did not dislike his little half-brother; he wished to treat and love him as his mother's child, but the child's father made this an impossibility for Steve, through his continual injustice. The result was that the boy was perfectly spoiled, and, whenever he saw his brother or sisters have anything new, he used to cry for it until his father made them give it up to him.

One evening the whole family was sitting round the table, waiting for evening prayers, at which the mother always insisted that everyone should be present. Steve's sister, Dora, had that day secured at school a pretty little picture book; she was sitting looking at this when her little stepbrother, who was sitting next to her, snatched at the book and tore a leaf. She, of course, pulled the book away from him, which made the spoiled child set up a fearful howling. His father got up and gave poor, innocent little Dora a severe slap on the cheek, which made the poor child turn blue from pain in a moment. Steve could not stand this. He was now sixteen years of age, and could not quietly see his little sister treated in such a cruel and unjust way.

He rose, pale from anger, and, striking his fist on the table, which made the different articles thereon jump again, said in a voice hard and firm,—

'By God, if you strike my sister again in that way, I shall kill you. Do you hear?' And his voice sounded and his expression looked so threatening, that the coward (all blusterers are cowards) felt awed and afraid. He had not the courage to brave Steve in his anger. He looked down and did not say a word more.

CHAPTER IX

FAVOURITE HEROES

When Steve was fifteen years of age he was taken from school and placed in an office at a small—very small—salary.

His education was not completed yet by far. He could read *well*, write fairly well, of arithmetic he knew sufficient for the ordinary wants of business life; his grammar was only sufficient to help him to speak English fairly correctly, with a mistake only once in a while. In orthography he was proficient enough to write a fairly well spelled letter. In history he excelled—that was his favourite study, no matter whose history it was. Bible, secular, English, Dutch, Italian, but especially South African, French and American history, he studied; the latter two because they were Republics, for he was a thorough Republican, and wished to know everything about Republicanism.

He loved to read the story of Napoleon. He gloried in Napoleon's genius, in his wonderful victories. But he grieved over the follies of the *Emperor*. The General Bonaparte, even the first Consul was his admiration—but the Emperor was a monster to him. He could not understand that a man, who had displayed such wonderful genius as Napoleon had done, could make such foolish mistakes as Napoleon had made as Emperor. He could not understand that such a man should care for the empty pomps and vanities of a throne. To his mind Napoleon would have been a *greater* man by far if he had remained only a Consul or President of the French *Republic.* Why a man who had done what he had done for France, and who had striven to the end to live and work only for the people, who wished to live for posterity as a man who had won the *hearts* of his people (such a man would be nobler and grander by far than one like Napoleon proved in the end) had only used his country and people to work for his own glory and vanity, puzzled Steve.

On the other hand, he considered George Washington by far a greater and nobler man than Napoleon. For Washington had lived and fought *only* for his country, and had proved to be nobly unselfish to the end. *The States*, in his opinion, really did "lick creation" as a great and free country.

The history of his own country he simply devoured. He never lost an opportunity of getting hold of a book which treated in any way of South Africa. If the book spoke favourably of his country and people, he was pleased and happy. If the book libelled his country—as so many books really do—he was grieved, but treated it with the contempt it deserved, and took his revenge by extracting any information he found in it.

CHAPTER X

OUT OF SCHOOL

As we stated in the last chapter, Steve was taken from school before his education was at all fairly completed and placed in an office. This was done against the wishes of his mother; but his stepfather said he could not have him eating the roof off the house and live a lazy, good-for-nothing life any longer—he must work and earn his living.

William Waitz (which was the name of Steve's stepfather) wanted to make a mechanic of the poor boy, but his mother, who understood his nature, would not allow this. *She* knew this was altogether against the wishes and abilities of her son, and she insisted that he should be placed in an office. Her influence—and a good woman's influence, even on a bad man, always makes itself felt—gained for Steve the victory, and he was not placed with a mechanic, which he would have hated. He desired opportunities to improve himself mentally, and how could he improve himself so as a mason or bricklayer?

Steve knew his education was by no means complete, but he did not mind leaving school, for he ardently desired to earn his own living and to be independent: besides, he did not intend to leave off studying, only now he could choose his own subjects for study. History—political and natural—astronomy, geography, books on agriculture, horticulture, tree culture, apiculture, all were welcome to him; he would as readily read and study the one as the other, and on many a night, when his stepfather sent him hungry and starving to bed as a punishment for doing nothing in particular, he would console himself and forget his hunger in reading some book or other. It was nothing unusual for him to be caught by the daybreak stealing into his little room, his candle still burning, and he deeply immersed in his book.

CHAPTER XI

HOPES

For the first couple of years Steve's earnings all went into the pockets of his stepfather. But during the third year Steve simply refused to give up more than three-quarters of his salary, for his father supplied him only with the barest necessities in clothing, and he considered he was entitled to a small portion of his earnings to buy such things as he wished for, such as books, etc.

The first thing Steve did, when he found himself absolute owner of a portion of his earnings, was to subscribe to the local library, even though he sadly wanted a new suit and a new pair of boots. But to be able to select his own books to read from such a stock of books as the library contained, he would have sacrificed almost anything.

He first of all inquired for all books dealing with his beloved South Africa ; and if he could find any dealing with the Transvaal or Orange Free State, he was doubly happy. The Transvaal and the Free State were to him as two shining stars in an otherwise dark sky ; they were the two states in which *his* people were *free*. Ah ! how he used to long to go to the Transvaal and live where he could feel free, and say, 'Here I am a man, for here I can look everybody in the eyes and feel I am his equal, and not subject to a foreign race.' His plan was firmly made up to go to the Transvaal as soon as ever he could manage to do so. The time did arrive at last when he could go.

CHAPTER XII

THE TRANSVAAL IN PROSPECTIVE

STEVE had always watched with absorbing interest the progress of events in the Transvaal. He had seen with intense pity the struggle of the Republican Government to make ends meet, and to prevent financial ruin. But he always trusted that all would come right ; and it was with a joy almost greater than if his own fortune was in question that he—at last—saw the rising fortunes of the South African Republic. He saw the reported discoveries of gold at Barberton; which already gave a great stimulus to commerce and trade; and then, as if Providence had determined at last to make the Transvaal prosperous and rich, far beyond the dreams of avarice, the grand discoveries at the Witwatersrand followed those of Barberton, which in turn were augmented by further discoveries all over the district. Miles of main reef were traced out, companies with enormous capitals were promoted, and a time of great prosperity and successful speculation followed. Fortunes were made and lost in a week, a day, an hour. The Government revenues rose by leaps and bounds, and they had no longer to almost beg for the loan of a few thousands. Capitalists were only too eager to advance money on such safe securities as could be offered.

Government officials, who before had to work for the love of country and people only, now received their rewards; from the highest to the lowest they were able to now receive their salaries at the end of the month. And when the finances of the country were placed on a sound and safe footing, the Volksraad did the right thing at the right time by advancing salaries all round.

The reported rich finds, so marvellous and so rich at the Witwatersrand, were soon noised all over the world; and people flocked from all quarters of the globe to the goldfields. They came, saw, and were satisfied—even as the Queen of Sheba was—that all the riches of the Rand had not been reported to them.

A township was laid out and given a name—Johannesburg. Who has not heard of it? Johannesburg became the ninth wonder of the world. It rose, as if in one night, and became a great and well-built city, such as can be found no where else in South Africa, and, in certain senses, nowhere else in the world!

Beautiful buildings, strong and lasting, rose, as if by enchantment, one after the other, proving that confidence was not wanting in the stability of the goldfields.

Johannesburg differed greatly from other goldfields in other countries. In Australia and California, when a goldfield was first rushed, tents and tin shanties prevailed. Here, buildings in brick and stone were prominent everywhere. In the former, law and order was noted for its absence; here, everything was done most orderly and lawfully, which showed once more the ability of the Boer Government to govern even such a community, and that not by display of force. Comparatively few police were kept; only sufficient for watching the individual criminal and vagabond that even such a law-abiding goldfield will attract.

It was, and is, a marvel to many how order and law were kept and administered by such a weak show of police. I believe it was simply the conscious strength and stability of the Government which was felt, if not seen, by all parties, combined by the promptness of the Government to remove all just causes of complaints, and to give aid where aid was required. No honest and just memorial was ever refused by Government. The only request which could not be granted was the Franchise, the justness and fairness of which is open to question, and appears altogether in a different view when seen either by the one side or the other. But of this we shall see more anon.

CHAPTER XIII

THE NESTLING PREPARING FOR FLIGHT

WELL, Steve thought these things all tended to realise his dream of becoming a Transvaaler.

One thing only troubled him; would it be right for him to desert his mother and sisters? After long thinking, he decided to leave it to his mother to decide for him, so he went to her and said,—

'Mother, you know I have always wished to go to the Transvaal; you know what my father said on his death-bed; that I must do all I can to make our people one strong nation, and I can do more for them in a country where they are free and independent. From there I can work as if entrenched in a castle, and who knows, some time we might be able to *free* our people in this country too? But on the other hand, father also said I must look after you and my sisters; do you think I ought to stay here? do you think I can do more for you staying at home, or can I do as much or more by going to the Transvaal, and work and try and make enough money to be able to help you and my sisters in time of need?'

'My son, the thought of losing you is dreadful, and that alone could induce me to keep you here; but my love for you is above being selfish; I can only wish for what is best for you, and if you think you can do better in the Transvaal, let not the thought of me or your sisters, keep you back. We can get on, and we shall write to you every week, and if we need you, or aid from you, we shall not fail to let you know. I would not thus give you up so easily, but I know your heart is set upon going; I have expected it for a long time. I believe I can trust you to keep your name and heart pure even thus far away from me; and God will watch over you.' She wept. Even though she appeared to give him up so easily, to go far away from her, not to see him again, perhaps for years, perhaps never again on earth, her heart was torn to the very roots. But she was an unselfish mother, and would not sacrifice her son's well-being and future prospects to her love.

'But, mother, will father be as good to you and sisters when I am away as when I am here, for, without vanity, I may say I think he fears me just enough to forbear from ill-treating my sisters, and when I am away he may feel no such restraint.'

'Better, I think,' replied his mother, 'for I really believe it is the antagonism he feels for you that makes him bad-tempered and cruel sometimes. I think if you are away, and ceased to irritate him, he will be a better stepfather and wife to us.'

'Mother, you have decided for me. I go as soon as I can hear of an opening!'

CHAPTER XIV

COUSINS

STEVE'S cousin and namesake had proceeded to the Transvaal some months before this.

We have mentioned the young man before as Steve's tutor in the art of smoking. A few words as regards him will not be out of place here, as we may hear, off and on, of his doings, as affecting Steve. We have said before that he was a vacillating young man; a fact which he showed in every act of his life. Years before he surprised Steve's constant young heart, during the Transvaal war of independence, by declaring—while the issue was as yet uncertain—that the English would give the Boers such a licking as they would never forget. He declared the Boers were cowards. He was one of those that took up the saying, that the Boers would run away at the first cannon shot. He changed his mind when the Boers were successful. *Now* he composed songs, in which he celebrated the victory of the Republicans in glowing terms, and abused the English tyrants enough to suit the taste of the most fiery Republican. Such was his nature. He was inconstant to his friends, he was inconstant to his sweethearts (mind the plural), he was inconstant to himself!

Like all such natures, he was a braggart and boaster. When he was amongst strangers he was a Crœsus in wealth, a king in power. Amongst his friends, he had always seen and done things wonderful to relate. But not one of them seemed ever to have the luck to be present when he saw and did these things. But his acquaintances knew him, and generally treated his stories with derision and contempt. Their ironical questions and looks appeared to his vanity questions and looks of belief and wonder.

He was not actually ill-natured or unkind. He had his tender spots. Real pain and grief greatly affected him, and brought pity into his heart, and at such times he was always amongst the first to render aid. In this respect only he resembled Steve. In all else he was his direct opposite. His vanity, love of boasting, and wish to thrust himself into a prominent part of whatever was taking place, together with a weakness to be on the side of the stronger party, was the bane of his life. The worst of him was that he did not seem to realise the shame and dishonour of deserting his party when it seemed to be on the losing side and taking up with the stronger.

Steve hated these faults in his cousin, and tried to reason sense and honour into him. But, being several years the junior of his cousin, his opinions were considered as childish, and disregarded. So Steve could only view his cousin's backslidings with patience and grief; which he did; as he was thrown into daily contact with his cousin through force of circumstances. In one thing or another he had to do with him every day, and really bore him a sort of cousinly affection, but this was unaccompanied by any respect.

CHAPTER XV

THE RISING GENERATION

WHEN Steve's cousin left for the Transvaal a sort of correspondence was kept up between them. Steve took advantage of this to write to his cousin and ask him to look for a situation for him.

At this time, through the force of circumstances—the want of proper schools, the struggle for existence against poverty, native troubles, and other difficulties—the youth of the Transvaal were seldom educated enough to take their proper places in the civil service of their country, or in the commercial, law, or other offices, so that the Government were forced to employ Hollanders, young educated Afrikanders from the Cape Colony and elsewhere, in the civil service; and merchants, as well as other employers, were forced to do the same, the only difference being, that for Government service a knowledge of official language—Dutch—was absolutely necessary for applicants, while private offices were not always particular, especially commercial offices. Hence the abuse the Government has had to suffer on account of employing so many of their Hollander brothers. These disabilities on the part of born Transvaalers are gradually disappearing through the fostering care of Government. Schools are State-aided in an instituted manner now, and young Transvaalers are continually entering Government service more and more every day.

CHAPTER XVI

THE APRON STRINGS CUT

FOR the reason given in the last chapter, it did not take Steve's cousin long to find a good situation for him; and when Steve received the letter in which his success was told, and bidding him come up without a day's delay, his joy was unbounded.

His preparations did not take long. By selling everything that he had which he could not take with him, and scraping together every penny he had, he just managed to get together sufficient to take him to Pretoria—his final destination. Why linger over Steve's leave-takings from friends and relatives? why should we restrain him with our presence when he bids good-bye to mother and sisters? why visit with him for the last time the haunts of his childhood? Many of us do not require to be told what took place, many of us have gone through it ourselves, have cast a lingering look on a beloved walk, or favoured spot, have given the last pressure to the hands of dear ones weeping, have felt the choking sensation which prevents the voice from saying the last word we fain would say, but must leave unsaid through emotion.

Steve was on his way to Eldorado; to the land of freedom and wealth; to the land where were centred all his hopes and ambitions for the future.

It was the first time he had left home for longer than a week; but in spite of his regrets to leave home, mother and sisters, he felt happy. He left as if he was a man at last. Free. He was going to fight the battle of life unaided; he asked for naught but a fair field and no favour.

Ah, Nature looked doubly glorious that morning as he rode through the surrounding hills and valleys and felt the genial sunshine and breathed the pure free air.

We will not accompany him any farther. We will leave him travelling on the top of the coach, enjoying his freedom and the beauties of Nature, as viewed from his lofty perch, free to indulge in his day-dreams and build his air castles unstinted for material; his rich imagination supplied all. The future is his; we will meet him in Johannesburg.

CHAPTER XVII

FIRST VIEW OF JOHANNESBURG

A COACH halts in front of the coaching office, Johannesburg, a young man gets down and bustles about to secure his luggage, for here the coaches change, a new one has to be taken for Pretoria.

Of course this young man is no other than Steve. He arranges for his luggage to remain at the office until the Pretoria coach leaves, which will not be until three o'clock in the afternoon; it is only 10 a.m. now. He thinks the best thing he can do is to have a look round and see as much as he can of the place while he has the opportunity. He turns to a young man—whose acquaintance he has made during the journey on the coach, and who was returning to Pretoria, after spending a short holiday at the sea-coast—and said,—

'I say, Harrison, what are you going to do while you wait for the coach?'

'I am sure I don't know. Kill time as best I can, I suppose.'

'Suppose you act as guide and mentor for me in viewing the place. You know the place—I don't—and you might take me to the places most worth seeing during the few hours we have. Come, be charitable this once, and help a green un.'

'All right, old boy, I am always willing to be unselfish, and besides it will do as well as anything else to kill time and keep me out of mischief.'

He took Steve all over the principal streets to Hospital Hill, and gave him a bird's eye view of all the surrounding places; and a sight worth seeing, too, it was to a young man that had just left a quiet provincial town. It was all bustle and vigour wherever he looked. It seemed as if there was an electric power in the air which forced everyone to do and act; no lingering or looking backward here, on, on, seems to be the watchword, or be left behind, to catch up never again. Even Steve seemed to feel this mysterious influence stealing over him as he stood gazing on the busy throng ; he felt as if he would like to rush into the midst of them and to push and elbow his way until he was amongst the first, to stay there. For the moment Steve forgot his natural inclination to be reserved and quiet ; he felt as if he could push and rush on with the best of them.

But other thoughts soon came crowding on ; thoughts of pride and joy that he at last had the privilege to see the place fully which was so famous all over the world for its riches.

And this place belonged to his people—to the Afrikanders. Here they were free, and the equal of other races. Here they had the right to work out their own destiny. Ah, it was something to be proud of ; this youthful but mighty and growing city ; these surrounding and undulating plains, underneath whose green grass has lain concealed for ages past untold wealth. Wealth which was laid and preserved by Providence for the purpose of helping the people of his race to rescue their country from poverty and financial ruin.

Ah, God has been good to us. He means it well with us. We have a right to hope that he shall lead us on right to the end, if only we can remain true to Him as a people.

He spoke something of the latter thought to his companion, who was an Englishman, and who supposed Steve to be an Englishman too, from his pure accent, as he had learned to speak English very well, and with a purer English accent than is generally acquired by Afrikanders, through being in daily contact in his six years of business life with Englishmen. His companion replied,—

'My dear fellow, do you think that this rich mining country will long remain in the possession of the Boers? If you do you are mightily mistaken. If the Boers do not themselves soon begin to see that they are unable to keep all these Uitlanders in order, and ask the British Government to take the government of the country over, then England will take it over whether they consent or not?'

Steve felt a pang shoot through his heart.

'But how can England take their freedom from them? They have once tried to do so, and the Boers fought for their country and liberty and got it back. How can England take it now again?'

'My dear fellow, you must remember that at that time this country was only a poor, worthless desert and England did not consider it worth while fighting for?'

'Take that for granted; but even then, do you think England would be so unjust to take the country from the Boers again, just because it turns out to be richer than she thought; that would be disgraceful.'

'But England has, through her capitalists, thousands of pounds sterling—and soon it will be millions—at stake in the goldfields of the country; she is bound to look after the money her subjects have placed in this country.'

'Let us put it plainly,' said Stephen. 'You have a house, I have a thousand pounds; I wish to find a safe hiding-place for my money, I think your house just the place; I hide it there, without your request or permission. But, on after thoughts, I think my money would be much safer if I had possession of the house instead of you. I arm myself; I go to you and say, "You clear out of this, my money is not safe while you remain in possession." You refuse to go. I put a bullet through your brain, carry you out, bury you, and take full possession. My money is safe now, no more need be said—might is right. That is about how you place the case.'

Harrison shrugged his shoulders, and replied doggedly,—

'You do not understand these national affairs; it is otherwise than with individual personal affairs.'

'I hope I may never understand it, if it means dishonour,' replied Steve.

After this they wended their way to view a mine or two, from the outside, as they felt they could not spare the time then to go inside a mine. There was very little to be seen from the outside—a large shed-like building, hauling gear over a seemingly bottomless pit, surrounded by heaps of quartz and débris. Steve could hardly realise that this apparently hard, common stone, called quartz, really represented the great wealth of the mines. He had hoped to see, at least, some visible gold, but he was disappointed. It was just hard, flint-like stone, without a particle of yellow metal visible; and yet he was assured the gold was extracted in paying quantities from this stone.

After this they returned to town, to seek some refreshments, and came to a large building in course of erection.

Steve saw a couple of children playing close by, under the scaffolding; he took no particular note of them, but stood admiring the architecture of the building.

Suddenly he heard a cry of horror behind him; he saw a gentleman and lady standing with upheld hands, with a horror-struck and transfixed expression, looking at the children near to him; he turned, and what he saw sent a thrill of horror through him. He loved children, and would rather bear pain himself a thousand times than see a child in pain, wherefore he felt the danger of a child all the more. What he saw was this: A little girl was standing under the scaffolding, innocently looking at a beautiful doll another girl was carrying in the street, without seeing the terrible danger that was threatening her. Above her a tremendously heavy beam, which was securely tied at one end, was slipping down on the opposite side, a workman was holding the dangerous end. A rope was tied round it, and he was holding with all his might to prevent its falling; but the weight was too much for him. He dared not take breath to call out for help, the waste of the least breath, or the least bit of strength taken from the effort of holding the beam, would precipitate its fall. But it was slipping—slipping. 'My

God,' thought he, 'will no one see and take away that child.' Someone saw. The cry of the mother of the child and the look of horror on her face had drawn Steve's attention to the danger. He saw all we have described in the flash of an eye. Not a moment did he hesitate or think what he should do. He never lost his presence of mind in danger. Like the arrow from a bow, he flew right under the threatening beam, the fall of which meant death to any living creature that might be under it. He seized the child by the dress, and came out on the opposite side of the beam. He felt a shock against his shoulder, as if some heavy object struck him. He felt himself whirled round several times by the shock, and thrown against the wall. The thunder, as of a falling mountain, sounded in his ears. But he held the child firmly in his arms; she was safe. The beam had fallen, if Steve had been a fraction of a second later, or the beam had fallen a fraction of a second sooner, both he and the child would have been crushed. As it was, it just grazed his shoulder. He was unhurt save for a severe bruise on the shoulder.

Of course, a crowd collected in a moment. The mother and father had rushed over from the opposite side of the street where they had been standing. The mother was hugging and kissing the child; the father was wringing the hand of Steve, with protestations of gratitude and service. A re-action came for the mother; she felt faint and could scarcely speak her gratitude to Steve. So her husband hurried her to a carriage with the child, and going to Steve said,—

'My friend, you have done a brave action; you have saved my child, on whose life the happiness of my wife and myself depends. I am your friend and debtor for life; here is my card. Let me see you this afternoon, and if there is anything I can do for you, I trust you will let me know it. I would not leave you now, but I must take my wife home.'

'Thank you, sir,' replied Steve; he was thankful to

be prevented from saying more by being pushed and pulled away by the crowd.

He hurried to find his companion (who had seen and heard all), and said to him, 'Come on, Harrison; we have no time to lose, if we do not wish to lose our coach!'

'What, are you going away without accepting the invitation of your new-found debtor? I would not, if I were you. He might do something good for you. Let me see his card.'

On seeing the name on the card, he whistled in surprise.

'I say, young fellow, your fortune is made; I wish I were you. Why, man, the name on this card represents the most successful speculator and company promoter on the Rand. Why, a tip from him is worth thousands. Of course you will change your mind and let the coach take care of itself, and go and see him as he requested.'

'Of course not; I do not like this fuss and bother about nothing. I do not wish to be paid for doing a humane action. Come on, let us be off.' And in spite of his companion's repeated advice not to lose such an opportunity to make his way in the world, Steve boarded the coach and left for Pretoria.

Quixotic? Yes, I suppose so. Unworthy the nineteenth century? No! I think the nineteenth century is unworthy of such Quixotism. Such an act is only worthy of the time of knight errantry, when men acted only for the honour of the thing, and every deed was not valued in £ s. d. But then Steve lived in that time in a sense—in a shell; his shell was composed of books, in which such creeds are still taught and tolerated, even though they are derided and laughed down in actual life—that is, in ultra-civilised life, which really means 'live for self, and self only; nothing for nothing, and everything for *gold*.' But Steve was unacquainted with this creed as yet; let us hope that he will never become the slave of such a creed.

CHAPTER XVIII

PRETORIA AND ITS LIFE

The writer of this has never admired the works of Rider Haggard; they are too untrue—untrue to Nature and the probabilities of life, and certainly untrue to facts, which are grossly exaggerated. But even in winter a strayed swallow is seen in our country. On the barest plain a tree is met occasionally, and in Haggard's work I once came across something with which I can cordially agree. It is long ago since I read it, but it so surprised me that I have always remembered it. Yet it is so long since I read it that I am not quite sure in which of his works I saw it; but if I am not mistaken the thing is in *Jess.* The passage I refer to is where he says that Pretoria is the prettiest town in South Africa; and if Haggard thought so in the days when he knew Pretoria, when the streets were swamps, covered with grass, and it was a danger to venture out of doors after dark for fear of breaking a limb in some concealed hole, when no better building—or hardly better—than the house which Jess inhabited existed in the town, what must we say of it now, when the streets have been rebuilt (more or less), when beautiful buildings—the best and grandest in South Africa—have been raised; merchant princes have erected palaces, beautiful stores rival European houses, and Government has covered a block of ground with a pile of buildings of which even Pretoria can be proud. Even Nature herself has been improved upon, if I may be allowed to say so. Plantations of trees have been planted, where formerly bare plots of ground existed, beautifully laid out ornamental and flower gardens enchant the vision. A block of tares, which grew only a crop of grass formerly, is now laid out in a beautiful park, worthy the name, with a large fish pond in the centre, and even a substantially built bandstand has been added lately. All in all, Pretoria more than deserves the name so often applied to it, 'Pretty Pretoria'; it really deserves to be called beautiful Pretoria.

No wonder, then, that Steve, who possessed a keenly appreciative eye for the beautiful, was enchanted with the view which met his eye when he entered Pretoria through the *poort*, from which emerges the road leading into it from Johannesburg, and he felt—like so many others have felt before and since—that once having seen Pretoria, a man may travel the world over, but he would ever feel a longing to be back in Pretoria. Many have felt this longing when in foreign lands, and have come back. Steve found his cousin waiting for him at the halting-place, and was soon introduced into his room at the quiet boarding-house, which had been secured for him at his request.

After a few days spent in resting after travelling for days in a cramped and crowded position, and becoming acquainted with the town in which he had resolved to make his home, Steve took his place in the office where he had secured the much-desired situation.

It did not take Steve long to get well into the mysteries of his work and the good graces of his employer and fellow-clerks. What pleased him most was that he came in daily contact with the Burghers of the district, which gave him the opportunity he had desired, viz., of studying the men whom he looked upon as heroes, in that they had dared so much and suffered so much, and had come out of the ordeal safe and victorious.

He found them distrustful at first, although kind and respectful. The stranger you are to them, the more civilly and kindly you are treated, but always with great reserve. But by studying them, and being always friendly and cordial towards them, he soon gained their confidence, and many was the pound of butter and biltong, varied now and then by a dozen of eggs, a couple of fowls, and at Christmas time even a lamb, that he received from them as tokens of friendship.

He found that the better they knew you, and the more they liked you, the more they joked with you and teased you. They are very fond of teasing, which has led foreigners to take them in earnest, and spread all sorts of reports, repeating for fact what the Boers said when they were only what is vulgarly but expressively called chaffing them. They especially delighted in doing this to 'green uns,' but always with the utmost good nature, and only when they liked such a 'green un.' They would never do it to one whom they disliked or distrusted. By the good grace and good nature with which Steve received all this banter, he got to be greatly liked, and was soon considered as being quite one of them, and was known to them far and wide. We shall see a great deal more of them in connection with Steve's adventures and life amongst them, and shall delight to study their character with him with the view of understanding better this much maligned people.

In this way Steve spent several years of quiet life. He applied himself vigorously to his work, so that, as we have said, he soon gained the confidence of his employers, and speedily obtained promotion and increase of salary, which enabled him, while saving considerably, to send many a present to his mother and sisters.

In the boarding-house where he lodged, he found quite a pleasant party, composed of many nationalities, amongst whom he struck up many friendships irrespective of language. He found himself a fellow-lodger of his cousin; his former travelling companion, Harrison; another Englishman, a colonial named Keith, and a young Afrikander named Theron, who formed his particular circle of friends, and they generally managed to be together when any excursion or picnic was undertaken.

Although, as we have said, he did not really *agree*

with his cousin, he felt that in common gratitude towards him for having obtained a situation for him, and as a duty due to cousinly affection, he was bound to include him as one of his friends.

In the boarding-house, the boarders were in the habit of forming themselves into a sort of free and easy debating society, for want of better recreation in the long evenings. That is to say those who did not care to spend their evenings in bar-rooms and billiard saloons, which formed Pretoria's principal places of amusement at this time. Of course it goes without saying, that Steve kept clear as much as possible of these places, for he was accustomed in his native town to the idea that it was a disgrace for any self-respecting man or youth to be seen going into a bar. What shocked him was for the first time to see a girl serving drink in a bar, surrounded by a coarse and blaspheming crowd of young men. To him women had always seemed as creatures almost divine, too good to be touched without veneration. He thought they should be worshipped at a distance, and that in their presence the most choice and delicate language only should be used. There he saw them treated roughly and disrespectfully, and even handled as if they were only coarse, common, everyday human beings, and worst of all they seemed to be pleased with such treatment, and even to invite it by their actions.

'Surely,' thought he, 'these girls must have mothers and fathers, who grieve over their disgrace and degradation; and many of them must have brothers—what must their feelings be to see their sisters in such a position? And he would utter a silent prayer for God to keep his sisters innocent and pure. Of course Steve's horror of bars and barmaids gradually lessened, and he afterwards even went so far as to accept an invitation from a friend now and again to 'Come and have something cooling this hot weather,' or, 'something warming this cold day?' (for alcohol seems to have the power to cool on hot days and *warm* on cold days); but he never allowed himself to acquire the habit of frequenting these places, and when he did enter them, he always treated the barmaids with the utmost respect; for, said he, 'The question is not, whether they are ladies, but whether I am a gentleman.'

Through his always keeping from bad places, and only going to places where he was sure respectability was guaranteed, he soon got into a good circle of society in Pretoria. He was received and welcomed in the best families, but his pride kept him from taking full advantage of this. He was too poor to meet them on equal terms, and rather than meet them as an inferior, even though it were only in purse, he would rather not meet them at all, except in a casual way now and again. For Steve was proud, and, what is more, he was proud of his pride. 'For,' said he, 'if it were not for my pride, I would do many a wrong action which now I am too proud to do.' He was never too proud to do a good action. He would stop and speak to the poorest beggar on the street if he could do good by it. He would walk alongside of a poor, ill-dressed person in the street, were his clothes ever so much patched; his hat so old that it hung over his eyes; he would never think of his dress, if it were a hard-working, honest man. But he was too proud to be seen in the company of a well-dressed, idle, good-for-nothing, bar-frequenting, prostitute-hunting man. He was too proud to speak or know a flighty, forward woman. And who shall say that he was wrong?

CHAPTER XIX

A DEBATE

As we have said before, Steve and his fellow-boarders sometimes constituted themselves into a sort of debating society, in which the public questions of the day were generally discussed. Let us follow Steve into the drawing-room, which he is just entering as a heated debate is on.

'Hullo, Keith, at it again as usual, running down the powers that be of the land we live in,' remarked Steve on entering. 'What is the use of knocking your head against a rock; for I tell you this Government is as firmly established as a rock. Have you ever seen a big old mastiff walking along the street, calm and self-contained, a troop of curs following, barking and snapping at him, without the mastiff taking the least notice of their noise or snaps. Well, Oom Paul is the mastiff, the newspapers that abuse him and petty pot politicians (I hope the shoe won't fit you) are the curs; there you have my opinion.'

'So you think it currish to stand up for your rights, and agitate for it?'

'By no means.'

'What do you mean then?'

'I think it currish to be perpetually barking and snapping at a man, as so many of the Jingo imperialistic papers and private amateur politicians are continually doing. You do not see it because you do not wish to do so; but just watch the actions of the Government, no matter *what* they may do or decide upon doing, but it is reviled and cried down. They may do something with the most honest intention of pleasing the Uitlanders, but some sinister intention is found, or supposed to be found, lurking behind it. No contract is given out for some public work, no matter if the man be the best workman and has sent in the lowest tender, but somebody is sure to have taken a bribe from the contractor to work into his hands, and so with everything, just because it is a Boer Government; any stick will do to beat a dog with, or—a Boer official.'

'Well, all the same, it is hard lines that an educated Englishman should submit to laws made by ignorant, uneducated Boers; we won't submit to it. Rule Britannia, Britannia rules the waves, Britons never, never will be slaves; there you have my opinion.'

'My dear fellow, no one wants you to submit to it. I don't believe you got an invitation from the Boer Government to come here and live under their laws. All you have to do is to submit to it or leave. No one will prevent you or ask you to come back. I do not say this because I wish to make myself nasty, but, in common fairness, you must consider what is right. Here you come into a free Republic, inhabited by a quiet, peace-loving, God-fearing people. They have obtained their country after herculean struggles against enemies from within and without. Again and again they had to fight for country and liberty, and at last they seem to be safe, and wealth comes to them. Strangers from afar come unto them. (Strangers, besides, who are of the people who have persecuted and chased them from their old home, "into a new country, and out again"; and still are they threatened by the Government of these self-same strangers.) They share their wealth with these strangers, they give these strangers the protection of their laws, on an equal footing with themselves. But these gold-hunting strangers are not satisfied with this. It is not enough for them to share with the original owners of the soil—no, they want to be *masters!* And because the owners of the soil will not walk quietly out of their country and give everything up to the would-be usurpers, they are reviled, libelled and abused. You are an Englishman, an Englishman's boast is supposed to be *love of "fair play,"* where does your love of fair play come in here?'

'But if they wish to share with us, why do they not share the franchise with us?'

'That is it—you are asking for the handle of the knife. You know very well that if the franchise is given to every Tom, Dick and Harry, the Uitlanders will get hold of the handle, and if the Boers should try to pull it out of their hands, they will cut their fingers. You are asking them to simply commit political suicide. No, old man, a thing obtained, as their liberty was obtained, will be more cherished than to be thus lightly given up. Now, if your intentions were honest and fair to the Boers, you would quietly wait your hour until the stipulated time expires, when you may legally become a Burgher; and if the time appears rather long, I have perfect confidence that, if the Uitlanders will only show the Government that they wish to become peaceful, law-abiding citizens of the Republic, anxious to advance the honour and prosperity of the country of their adoption, which they can only do by working with the Government, and ceasing to show their prejudice to everything that is *Boer*, then I am sure the Government will soon shorten the time of probation, and take them into the fold of full burghership.'

'Yes; but we are not going to humble ourselves and beg for a vote; no, by Jingo! sooner than that, we will fight for it, and take by force what is refused us when we ask for it. Besides, even though we are not strong enough to take the Government by force, we only have to get up a row, and start some sort of revolution, and ask the British Government to step in, and of course England will say to your President, "You cannot keep the peace, we will have to come and keep it for you," and the trick is done, *wacht em beetje*.'

Such reasoning disgusted Steve, as I am sure it would many an honest and fair-thinking Englishman. However, he replied,—

'All I can say is that, if England does this, her glory shall pass away from her; such injustice will be tolerated by neither God nor man, and England shall raise such a cry of shame as has never been heard before. She shall feel something like the man who opened a hive of angry bees, and when the bees are stinging and buzzing about his ears, she shall be sorry she ever opened that hive. But I must say I have more faith in the honour and justice of your countrymen than you seem to have.'

Such discussions as these were the order of the day, and the sample given above may be taken as a fair example of the opinions of the two parties in the country. We shall leave the debaters now, but on some future occasion we shall take advantage of the privilege of historians to visit them again.

CHAPTER XX

A HUNTING WE GO

After a few years stay in Pretoria, Steve and his four special friends made up a party for a sort of picnic and shooting expedition combined.

They procured a roomy Cape cart and four horses, laid in a stock of tinned provisions for three weeks, and started one sunny morning in August.

It was a beautiful day, and our friends enjoyed the sunshine and fresh air greatly, after their long confinement in town and office. Steve's cousin, as usual, took a leading part. He was driving. After a halt for breakfast and again for dinner—which was doubly relished for being partaken of in the open air—they went on at a good pace, so as to arrive in time, before dark set in, at a certain farm, the owner of which was known to Steve.

'Well, I declare this is grand,' remarked Steve as he lay back in the cart, comfortably settled and puffing away contentedly at his pipe. 'I do enjoy driving at a good pace, with the wind fanning your chin—oh—ah—her—goodness gracious, where are we going to? I must remark here, and at once, that I *don't* enjoy a journey to the centre of the earth, where you seem to be taking us, cousin mine. What in the name of goodness do you mean by driving us in here?'

'But I am in the path.'

'My dear fellow, don't you know that when you come to a place like this, the farther you are out of the path the safer you are? Let me instruct you now, once for all, that while you are driving this company, when you come to a black-looking, soft, soapy, muddy hole like this, turn out of the path, and cross where you see the longest grass, and if a cart or waggon has never ridden there before so much the better.'

For the benefit of the reader, who is unacquainted with Transvaal roads, we will describe the sort of 'black, soft, soapy, muddy hole,' as Steve called it. In certain patches of the country stretches of a black, soft soil are found, something like what, I imagine, an Irish bog to be from descriptions that I have read of it. When rain has not lately fallen, it is hard and firm enough, but where a stream runs through it, *then* you have to be careful. Those who know what they are about, generally take good care to cross where no one else has crossed before, and where grass is growing, where the grass itself and its roots form a pretty safe bridge across. But where waggons or carts have been in the habit of crossing, the grass and roots have been cut up, down you go, horses and all, up to the nave and over. In just such a hole our young hunters now found themselves. The horses were up to their bellies in the soft mud, and could find no foothold to work themselves and the cart out. The cart itself was simply floating on the mud, the bottom of the cart lying like a boat on it, while a little of it ran in and blackened the tan-coloured shooting boots of the occupants. What were they to do now? To leave the cart meant a mud bath, and such mud!—black, sticky, oily mud!

I am afraid they would have made up their minds to spend the night in their uncomfortable position; but always when danger seems to be greatest, help is near at hand.

Fortunately for them, they were in sight of the farm-house where they intended spending the night; and the kindly old Boer and his two sons were soon seen coming along with half-a-dozen oxen yoked to a long chain.

The chain was soon fastened to the harness of the leaders, which the rescuers could just reach, and the oxen pulled out cart and horses. But what a state they were in; the nice tan-coloured harness was painted black as far as the mud reached, so were the horses and cart. But fortunately night was coming on, and the entry of the visitors to the *werf* did not look so disreputable as it otherwise would have done.

CHAPTER XXI

A BOER AND HIS FAMILY

THE farmhouse at which our young friends arrived in such an unclean state, was a really fine villa, had only lately been built, and was as comfortable and commodious as any town-built villa, and as good looking too. A verandah surrounded the house, affording a shady seat at any time of the day; a convenience which is greatly valued in this country, especially in December and January, when it is too hot and close to remain indoors with any sort of comfort.

The rooms inside were comfortably furnished, each spare bedroom being provided with a feather bed, wash-hand stand, chest of drawers, surmounted by a mirror, and a couple of chairs. Of course the bedroom of the father and mother of the house was the bedroom *par excellence*, and was furnished in style. The dining-room possessed an expanding dining-table and a suite of morocco covered chairs, also mahogany sideboard, and a few pictures—sea views—mounted in gilded frames, adorned the walls.

But the room on which the most money and care had been lavished was the sitting-room. An upright piano in one corner faced an American organ in the opposite corner; a thick carpet covered the floor, on which was distributed a satin-covered drawing-room suite and table to match; a whatnot and book cabinet occupied the two corners not filled by piano and organ; innumerable vases, ornaments and nick-nacks completed the decorations, as far as the furniture was concerned. As to the walls, they were reserved for the family portraits—grandfathers and grandmothers, both paternal and maternal-fathers and mothers ditto; and then came two grand life-size portraits of the present head of the family and his wife, flanking a family group of the whole existing family.

The house overlooked a fine valley, through which flowed a rivulet of bright clear water, from which was irrigated the grand orchard and ornamental trees which occupied the whole stretch of ground lying between the rivulet and the house. This orchard was the pride and care of the mother of the house, who was assisted by a 'Cape boy' (bastard), who in turn was assisted by two or three Kaffirs in the care of the orchard. She had taken particular pride in ordering fruit trees and vines of the best and latest varieties, as well as roses and flowering shrubs and ornamental trees, such as her neighbours had never seen before, from the Cape and Natal. Of course, the father of the house had enough to do, even with the assistance of the sons, in looking after the numerous lands lying lower down the fertile valley, and then he had the care of the large herd of cattle and sheep grazing on the surrounding hills; besides which cares, he had lately been busy planting timber and fodder trees. Lately he even had to do without the assistance of his two sons, as one was studying for some profession in Edinburgh and the other at Bloemfontein, O. F. S., while he himself had lately been elected a member of the Volksraad, and was thus obliged to spend four months of the year in town, assisting at the council of the nation.

This particular farmer had not always been so well off as now. When he first married he had this farm—inherited from his father—a couple of hundred sheep, a dozen or so of cows, a waggon, and one span of oxen. He and his wife went to live on this farm with no capital whatever to work this uncultivated and houseless farm. He set to work, built a *hartebeest house* (mud house), composed of three little rooms—kitchen, dining-room and sitting-room combined, and a little bedroom. Together they worked and economised, saving every penny they could, made *kraals*, planted trees, sowed the lands, made irrigation furrows, and tended their flock of sheep, until they got fairly well off and saved enough even to buy another half farm adjoining theirs.

The discoveries of gold came, gold was found on the lately bought half farm, and was sold for £20,000 cash, with a quantity of shares in the company buying it. Thus prosperity came, and our former struggling, hard-working Boer, who had to put his own shoulder to the wheel and work hard himself, if he wanted anything done, could take matters easy and enjoy himself.

What did he do now—live on the fat of the land and let others do the work? No. Just here I want to point out a peculiarity which I have noticed in our Dutch farmers in the Transvaal.

In the boom for gold farms, many a formerly struggling farmer has suddenly found himself a rich man, selling his farm, or one of his farms, for from £10,000 to £100,000 or more, and yet, amongst them all, I do not know of one of them that has given up his former simple mode of life and leads a retired easy life. They may build a larger, finer and more comfortable house, furnish it better, be more lavish in their hospitality, but their former occupation is never given up. Still they sow their lands, still they tend their flocks, still the season's yield of wool is taken to town, and from the proceeds thereof the household requirements are provided. A progressive farmer will spend some of his thousands to improve his farms, his implements and his stock, but his occupation is kept, with few exceptions. Even members of the Government, who formerly farmed, keep their farms going, visiting them now and then, even though they could not attend to them themselves. Even so with the particular farmer we have been describing. His wealth increased his responsibilities and cares, but in nowise decreased his work.

We have given this description of a farmer of the wealthier classes; we would give his name, but it would serve no purpose, it might only displease him, as he, in common with most of his race, dislikes publicity. Let it suffice that the description given is from life.

CHAPTER XXII

A TALK ON BEES

STEVE and his friends were received with the greatest cordiality; first, because Steve was known to the family and liked by them, and secondly, because hospitality is natural—in fact, seems born in a Boer. You will arrive at a farmhouse—poor or rich—you are one of the so-called hated nation—a *rooi nek* (nickname given to Englishmen because their tender skin causes their necks to blister and turn red in the hot South African sun, literally meaning 'red nek')—unknown; at the door you meet a youngster just able to talk. You will dismount. This premature young man will come up to you with an air of—*playing the host* about him, will take hold of your hand, give it a shake, and say,—

'Wil Oom nie afzaal nie?' (Will uncle saddle off?)

Yes you will.

'Well, then, uncle can walk just right in and have a cup of coffee; I will see to the horse.'

Well, as I said, our young friends were well received.

and soon found themselves seated around a supper table, as well laid and as well provisioned as man's heart could desire in such a locality. Roast beef, stewed guinea-fowl, leg of venison, stuffed with bacon and baked vegetables, salads, etc., custard pudding, blanc mange, fresh butter, cheese, etc., washed down with coffee, and such coffee as only a *Tante* knows how to brew, and that Java coffee too. After supper, the party adjourned to the sitting-room, where they were soon followed by the *Tante*, after she had seen to the servants getting their food, and the remnants of the supper had been safely put away.

'Now, Stephaans,' said she to Steve, 'you or your friends must come and look at a bee-hive that a *winkelier* (shopkeeper) made me buy in town last week. It is one of those new-fangled patent things. Its inside is full of pieces of wood—goodness only knows what for. They say it is better than just an empty box for the bees. I don't understand it. Do you or any of your friends understand it?'

Now Steve saw a chance to distinguish himself in the way he liked to do—by being useful. Apiarian books had been among his favourite studies, so he knew all about it, having always kept one or more hives for study and also for—honey.

'Well, *Tante*, if you will send for the hive, I shall explain all about it to you.'

The hive came, and Steve surprised even his companions by the learned dissertation he gave on bees and bee-keeping. He surprised the simple old gentleman and his lady almost into disbelief, when he told them the queen was the mother of all the bees in the hive; that she was only a fully developed female bee, reared from the self-same egg from which the worker bee is raised, and that she is only made a queen by over feeding and by giving her more space to grow out in in the cell. That the drones, or, as they called them in Dutch, *water-carriers*, are not water-carriers, but that they are, in fact, great, lazy, good-for-nothing male bees, who love to live on what the females earned in the fields, and absolutely refuse to do any work (as so many of their sex, even in the human race, delight to do); that, in fact, they were unable to do any work—not being built that way; but were only called into existence to be husbands to the young queens, which may be raised during the season for the purpose of sending out swarms, and thus obey the command of the Creator when He said, 'Go forth and multiply.'

But their surprise reached its climax, when he told them that he could make the bees manufacture a queen for themselves, should they be queenless, by simply giving them eggs or larvæ to make her from; that, in fact, he could force them to make as many queens to his order as he liked by simple manipulation, and that he could thus make three or four swarms of bees out of one in a season. He tried to explain to them all this, and by explaining the why and the wherefore, he soon got them to believe and understand him. He also showed them how to fix and wire the wax foundation in the frames, and thus spare the poor bees a lot of work; also told them how, by the use of an extractor, they could extract all the honey from the combs without breaking the comb, and thus save the bees the time and expense of wax to rebuild it. 'All you have to do is to replace the empty comb in the hive, when the bees refill it.'

The Oom and Tante were especially pleased when it was explained to them that by the use of the modern hive they were spared the cruel necessity of destroying any of the young bees or brood, when taking the honey out, or, as it is truthfully called, *robbing the hive*, and that the honey reserved for the use of man was pure, without young bees or pollen (bee bread).

From bee-keeping the conversation drifted to gardening, vegetable and flower, as well as fruit culture, in all of which Steve was an adept. He told the Tante of so many new modes of grafting and pruning, that she exclaimed he talked like a book.

In this way it happened, that Steve gained the friendship and respect of all the country people he came across. He could talk to them of things they understood and which interested them—matters concerning their everyday life.

CHAPTER XXIII

GOOD SHOTS

AFTER a good night's rest and a hearty breakfast, our friends once more resumed their journey, being anxious to get farther away from town, where there would be a greater probability of getting something to shoot at.

About three o'clock in the afternoon they reached another acquaintance of Steve's, and were received with an almost effusive welcome.

The family consisted of Oom Ignatious, Tante Letta, Ignatious, junior, eldest, Daniel, second eldest, and Lettie, junior.

Oom Ignatious (pronounced Engnaas) was a spare, slightly grey old man, with a slight stoop in the shoulders, partly from hard work and partly from a weak chest. He was a kindly old man, uneffusive, but always had a smile and a kindly word for friend or enemy. He never lost his temper—at least, not visibly, whatever his inward feelings might be; when annoyed he hardly showed it. He always remained civil and kind, but was ever firm and strong in upholding what he considered right.

Tante Letta was fat, fair, and forty. Her estimated weight was three hundred pounds. She had never been weighed; when asked, she objected on the ground that it was only desired to '*drijf de spot met mij*' (to make a laughing-stock of me). But with all her weight she was a good old soul. Everybody loved the old lady for her goodness. She could never do enough for you to show her hospitable inclinations. She was always bustling about, causing wonder and surprise to all how she could remain on her feet all day in spite of her great weight. When you did manage to persuade her to sit down and have a chat, she simply charmed you with her kindly, smiling, fat, double-chinned face.

The two sons were both big giants of young men, straight as a die, broad-shouldered, deep-chested, healthy-looking and strong, handsome in face and figure, with curly light brown hair, clean-shaven cheeks, but wearing light handsome moustaches. Finally, as to moral character, they were their father and mother's children in deed as well as name. But little Lettie was the angel of the house. I can't describe her with sufficient power to place her before the reader as I knew her. I will attempt, but I know it will be a failure, and will give the reader only a bare idea of her looks. Tall, slender, with a graceful willowy carriage, what a poem in her walk, in her every movement and look! What sweetness in those large star-like eyes, gleaming like dark-coloured diamonds under the long-lashed eyelids. The lines of the face, the shape of nose and chin, I cannot describe, I simply give in; I know not to what style it belonged; I only know they were—*Beautiful.* The mouth I can and will describe. *It was made to kiss.* The long hair was worn loose, and flowed in waves down to the waist in a dark, massive cloud. The dress was a loose, simple gown, fitting the form sufficiently close to show the perfections of the figure; smart costumes would only mar such a figure.

Steve will never forget the walk he took alone with Lettie to the flower garden that afternoon; to him she was the fairest flower that ever he had seen.

Reader! to prevent any future disappointment, I must here state that Lettie is not going to be the heroine of this story; that Steve is not going to marry her, or even to fall madly in love with her. He admired and liked her, but after this visit she passes out of his life; we shall hear no more of her. I have tried to place her before the reader as I still see her in my mind's eye, as a type of the better class of Boer girls, whose figure has not been spoiled by bad taste and knowledge of dressing, and, alas, by hard work too. For many a poor farmer is obliged to help himself with the labour of his girls for want of servants; and thus their shoulders become bent through constant stooping and hard work, and their figures spoiled and ruined.

I have been told of a certain farmer who ploughed, sowed and reaped his lands with the aid of four girls; while one tended the sheep, one the oxen, one led, and one drove the span of oxen pulling the waggon. And thus he had to do all his work with only the assistance of his daughters. He had been blessed with a troop of girls, and not one boy. And as to native labour, since the gold mines are offering such high wages, the poor farmer must consider himself lucky if he can get any at all; while many cannot afford to pay a price sufficiently high to keep their boys from going off to the gold mines. Thus it is that we see so many ill-figured Boer girls. But for all that, I do believe that amongst the Boer women are to be found some as handsome as any in the world. The faint attempt at a description of Lettie is not drawn from the imagination, but is exactly as she was known to the writer.

It was amongst this family that our party of hunters now found themselves.

As I have said, they were welcomed most heartily, their horses were soon stabled and themselves led into the house and refreshed with coffee and cake.

Oom Ignatious, not having had the luck as yet to sell a gold farm, had to content himself with a moderate-sized farmhouse of the old Dutch style, mainly built by himself and friends. It consisted of a dining-room, hall and sitting-room combined (nothing unusual), three bedrooms—one bedroom for the old people, one for Lettie, and one for the boys—and a kitchen—five altogether.

Oom Ignatious's wealth consisted of his oxen and sheep

and in what he managed to raise from his lands, on all of which he contrived to live comfortably without any waste or want, but without having much surplus over at the end of the year.

When Oom Ignatious heard that they were out for the purpose of killing something, he told Ignatious, junior, and Daniel to leave the work they were at and show them the haunts of certain *oribe* and steenbuck that they knew of.

Our party of greenhorns failed to bag anything in spite of repeated attempts. The young Boers showed them buck after buck quietly grazing in the long grass, but, standing or running, our young friends missed every shot. At last Keith said, 'These young fellows are laughing at us, the bucks are too far away, you can't hit them at such a distance.' The young Boers, who knew a few words of English, understood this, but said never a word, and kept on making themselves as agreeable as possible to Keith with their scant knowledge of English.

At last, they were on their homeward way, no game in their bags, when suddenly Ignatious pulled Keith by the arm, enjoined silence, and pointed to a distant rise in the level plain and said,—

'Do you see that *oribe* lying there against the butt?'

'Where? I do not see anything but grass.'

'There, don't you see where I am pointing?'

'No, old chappie, you do not come it over me, there is nothing there.'

'Well, give me your gun.' He had left his gun at home not to spoil the sport of their guests.

Keith gave him the gun with the remark that it was only a waste of ammunition. Ignatious knelt on one knee and rested his arm on the other, took aim and fired, something bounded in the air at the spot pointed out and fell down again and nothing more was seen. Ignatious quietly handed Keith his gun back and led the way towards the spot. Daniel was holding Steve's gun in his hand admiring the workmanship of it, when, as they approached the spot, a buck was seen running from it. Everyone shouted, 'There it goes,' and ran in a slanting direction as if to intercept it when a shot was heard. Once more the buck bounding into the air several feet, fell down to rise no more. It was Daniel who had fired this time and killed the buck on the run. They went towards it, cut it up, took out the intestines and shouldered it, when Ignatious said, 'Now let us go and get the other one.'

'Which one?' said Keith.

'Why, the one I shot.'

'But this is the one you shot at?'

Ignatious laughed quietly and said,—

'The one I shot will never run again; I shot him just behind the shoulder.'

Keith stared at him and thought he was being fooled again, so did not say anything more, but followed Ignatious, only to be led to a dead *oribe*, shot dead through the heart—the bullet had penetrated the buck just behind the shoulder, as Ignatious had said he intended it to do.

Keith thought to himself, 'I wish I could fire a shot like that, and be as sure of it too. Why, it was three hundred yards away if it was one.'

CHAPTER XXIV

ANOTHER TRY

AFTER a pleasant evening and a good supper, our party went to bed, Steve and Theron occupying the bed of the old people, while Harrison, Steve's cousin and Keith took possession of the boys' room; those who were thus ejected, satisfying themselves with a *shake down* on the floor of the dining-room and kitchen respectively. At whatever sacrifice, the guests must be made comfortable!

It had been arranged that the visitors should have another try at those *oribe*, but this time under the guidance of the old man himself, as the young men had arranged to leave after breakfast for the *kerk plaats* (farm on which a church is built, and where periodical services are held).

They would have stayed to oblige their guests, but two fair ones expected them there; the arrangement had been made to meet there, and even the claims of hospitality could not induce them to disappoint two loving hearts.

Everyone on a farm is too busy before breakfast to go shooting; the sheep had to be counted out of the kraal and sent to the veld, cows had to be milked, and all the work of the farm had to be set going and to be seen to first; therefore the party could not leave till after breakfast for the veld.

Ignatious and Daniel had to ride out to an outlying station before starting for their own particular trip. After breakfast, Steve was standing talking on the stoop to Lettie, waiting for his party to get ready. Ignatious and Daniel had just saddled their horses, and were saying good-bye to Steve and his party, as they would very likely be still away when Ignatious and Daniel returned from the out station, when they would immediately leave for the *kerk plaats*.

'What fine fellows these brothers of yours are,' remarked Steve to Lettie. 'You ought to be proud of them.'

'So I am. I only hope that if ever I marry, I may get a man as good as they are for a husband.'

'Daniel is going to get married soon, is he not?'

'Yes, within three months, probably. Do you think he looks sickly, or unhealthy?'

'No; on the contrary, I think he looks remarkably healthy and strong. Why do you ask?'

'Because, a few days ago, I came into his room; he was looking at the photo of his intended; tears were in his eyes. I asked him, "What is the matter?" He replied that he loved her so much, and that yet she would never be his wife. "What! never your wife!" I said, "and you are going to be married in a few months to her; what do you mean?" He replied that *he felt it in his heart;* he did not know why, unless *he should die before the time came.* And then he told me that I was to take his Bible, if he should die, and his sweatheart his new hymn book, and other things he told me to give to mother and father, as well as something for Ignatious. The foolish boy, as if he were going to die so soon; the idea is ridiculous; and yet, if he should die, I don't know what we should do without him.'

'Oh, you need not fear for him, he is strong and healthy enough to outlive us both.'

No more was said, and Steve did not think much of what was said, but he had reason sooner than he could have thought, to recall this conversation.

At last they started, and all hoped to have better luck than the day before. Steve was a fairly good shot at a target, in fact he was (like most South Africans) a born shot; but he had never had a chance to practise rifle shooting at a distance at real game, but he was a good hand at bird shooting with a shot-gun. Ever since he was a boy of twelve, he used to scrape his pennies together to buy powder and shot, and go pigeon-shooting with an old muzzle-loading shot-gun, which had formerly belonged to his father, and a good hand he learned to be at it by such practice. It was one of the few kinds of sport he enjoyed; he loved shooting. For the above reasons, Steve longed to bring down a real antelope of some kind, but he was doomed to disappointment. The game was too shy, and kept at a distance, requiring a really good shot to bring them down. Theron was the only one to kill that day. After a long walk in the hot sun and among the trees, Theron succeeded, by taking a good steady aim (and being told what sight to put on by Oom Ignatious) at a buck standing broadside on, unaware of their presence, in bringing it down. Oom Ignatious refused to shoot, as he said he did not like to spoil their sport, but inwardly he thought that, after the previous day's occurrence—of which he had been told by Steve—it would be too unkind to humiliate the poor young greenhorns by a display of his accurate aim, for he knew that with him to shoot was to kill. The sun was hot and heavy, thunder-clouds were beginning to rapidly cover the sky, so it was determined to return home as fast as possible before the heavy storm, which was surely coming on, broke on them.

CHAPTER XXV

A TERRIBLE THUNDER STORM

READER, have you ever taken note of the signs of a heavy African thunder storm coming on? Have you felt the awful depressing heat, which seems to make the heart feel too faint and languid to beat? Have you noted the awesome, mysterious twilight that seems to settle over the earth? A moment everything appears to be alive and joyous; birds are singing, cattle bellowing, all nature murmurs a pæan of gladness for *life*. In another moment everything seems to hide itself and hush its breath. Not a murmur is heard, not a leaf rustles, not a breath of wind is felt. It is the calm before the storm. Now the suspense seems to be agonising; it gets darker and darker. Suddenly the leaves seem to rustle out of very fear, as if they longed to break the silence, for they rustle, and yet not a breath of wind is felt. Then gradually you hear an ever-increasing roar at a distance. My God! what a crash is that! It is the first clap of thunder that breaks over your head, seeming to strike near you, all around you; you feel that you are not safe, you long for shelter, for company, for somebody to share your terror. Such a thunder storm seems to make cowards of the bravest. It is an invisible enemy; an irresistible danger seems to threaten you, to surround you, to search you out, hide where you will. If you never prayed before, you feel as if you would like to pray now. Deny it if you will, hide it if you might, look as brave as you can, yet I tell you you *do* feel awed when the thunder of heaven seems to speak to you with the voice of an angry God.

After that first clap, the silence is broken, the storm is on you. Clap after clap of thunder strikes around you. The lightning seems to blind you. The trees bend to the ground before the great force of rushing air, and those that will not bend must break, and come crashing down, crushing everything underneath them, and obstructing the paths and roads.

The rain seems to come down, not in drops, nor in sheets either, but in one continuous mass. You can hardly draw your breath because of the wind and rain; and in a moment you find yourself wading in six inches, ten inches, twelve inches of water on the level plain. Woe to the flock of sheep that finds itself in the least hollow or depression between two butts or rises of the rolling plain. They are drowned where a few moments before they stood on dry veld, seemingly safe against any flood. Such was the storm our friends found themselves in now. They could do nothing but pull their hats over their eyes and plod and wade wearily along. Wet to the skin in a moment, their clothes clinging most uncomfortably to them, the house seeming to recede farther and farther away as they struggled on; even the much-prized buck which Theron had shot was dropped and left lying in the veld. Their only desire was to get home; to get at least a roof between themselves and this terrible thunder.

Thank God, it is passing over at last. It did not last long, but while it did last it was terrible!

Now it gets lighter and lighter. The blue sky peeps out gradually larger and larger on the western horizon—the direction from which the storm had come—at last, even the sun comes out again. And everything peeps forth again. The lambs begin to play, the calves gallop and frolic about, the birds sing merrier than ever; and the trees—they can only weep tears of joy that the cruel wind does not bend them down so cruelly any more. Now the storm is raging towards the east, its distant rumbling is heard, and the clouds look piled up in black and blue masses in that direction.

Now our party is able to walk again; the water has gathered in the hollows and rivulets. By choosing high ground, progress can be made.

They were nearing the house when they saw a man approaching towards them in a slanting direction. What can be the matter with him? Surely such a storm was sufficient to sober the most intoxicated man on earth? And yet ,this fellow must be drunk. See how he staggers; sometimes he drops on to his knees, and clasps his head between his hands, and even at this distance they can hear him sob as if his heart was breaking. He rises once more, sees them approaching now near by, he crys out aloud, stretches his arms towards them in a supplicating manner. They hear the agonising words escape from him. Oh, my brother? The old man turns as pale as death. He recognises his eldest son, as did the rest. Oom Ignatious rushes forward; he reaches his son just as he drops down in a dead faint. His father lifts him, holds him in his lap, and cries,—

'Oh, my son, my son, what has happened? Oh, my God, see how he is scorched! Oh, horrible, his clothes are crumbling as if burnt; his skin comes off. Oh, my God, have pity upon a poor father, and spare my son.'

The young man opens his eyes once more and murmurs, 'My brother, my brother.'

'Where is your brother, Ignatious?'

'Over there,' he replied, pointing to a round hill commanding the rest of the valley.

'I'll go to him,' said the old man. 'Is he hurt, too?'

'No, father, you must not go. Steve will go with his friends. You must go with me to mother to prepare her for the terrible tidings.'

'What terrible tidings? Ignatious, that you are wounded?' queried the old man.

'No, father. I am terribly scorched, but I may yet recover; but poor Daniel—oh, my father, that I should live and he die when we were side by side.'

'What—dead!—dead!—my Daniel dead? You cannot know what you are saying; you are delirious from your wounds.'

'No, my dear father, I fear me he is dead. Take courage; you must be strong and help us to comfort mother; come.'

The old man seemed to make a strong effort, rose and helped to raise Ignatious.

'You are right, my son. Your mother must be our first care; come.'

He begged Steve, with tears in his eyes, to go and find Daniel while he went home with Ignatious, who could scarcely stand.

'I will send a cart or waggon at once to bring him home, if you will only wait there and do unto him as if he was your own dead brother.'

Steve and his four companions went, and what a sight met their eyes!

CHAPTER XXVI

'TIS THE WILL OF GOD

THE hill on which they found themselves was the highest point of the rolling plain. On it were scattered masses of ironstone. Whether there was any kind of metal present in the soil of the hill, or whether it was because it was the highest spot in the neighbourhood, Steve could *not* determine, but he later on learned that this was a favourite spot for the lightning to strike down on.

What they saw was this—

Two horses, dead and all twisted up as if they had no bones in their bodies, indescribably horrible to see. Entangled with one horse, a man's body was seen. When they lifted him up by the arms, his head dropped backwards between the shoulders, as if his neck was composed of only skin and soft flesh. His hat and most of his clothes were carbonised, and his flesh, where exposed, was scorched and burnt in crooked lines. But let us draw a curtain, 'tis God's work; His ways are inscrutable.

The body was conveyed, in a waggon (sent for the purpose), home.

When the body was carried into the house, the mother of the dead man cast off all restraint and threw herself in a passion of weeping upon the corpse, and had to be dragged away by main force from the awful sight of the mutilated body of her son.

To cut a gruesome story short, the body was buried the following day at midday. Steve and his companions came over from a neighbouring farm, where they had gone the afternoon of the accident, as so many relatives and friends had come to assist the bereaved family that they thought it well to leave and relieve the house of the care of stranger guests.

Poor Ignatious was in a precarious condition; his life

was despaired of for some time. But he recovered in the end. But poor Tante Letta; the shock was too much for her; she nearly followed her boy to the grave, and was delirious for months afterwards. Oom Ignatious spanned in his cart, on the doctor's advice, and rode from neighbour to neighbour for weeks, every day giving his wife change of scene and faces. By this means, she gradually recovered a shadow of her health and reason. But the beautiful motherly smile, which formerly dwelt on her face, was gone for ever. She is now the tender care of little Lettie, and is waiting patiently for the time when her God will call for her, and take her to her beloved son. God comfort the poor old lady!

CHAPTER XXVII

A DANGEROUS FORD

THE day of the funeral was Sunday. Steve and party took leave of the sad household, and the following day went farther on.

Keith was moved by the kindness and godliness of the family he had just left. 'These Boers are not such a bad and uncivilised people as they are made out to be by their enemies; in fact, I wish Englishmen were more like them. What surprises me in them is their quiet, simple, unboastful manner, and their extreme kindness to strangers such as I am.'

'You will find exceptions to every rule,' Steve replied. 'You will find boasters and bad people amongst them as amongst all other peoples. But, as a people, they are true Christians, leading a life as near as they can to what their Bible teaches them their lives should be. Their Bible is their law, and by that standard they act and judge all things. It is true they have some prejudices, likes and dislikes, which is to be deplored;

but even in that they injure no man. They have the making of a great people in them, and I am proud to be of their race.'

During the Monday, our friends moved on quietly, their conversation was hushed, they spoke of serious matters; and the usual lively and sportive conversation prevailing amongst a party of young men out by themselves, was entirely absent.

The road they were travelling ran through a vast plain, black as night. The fire, prevalent at this season, had burnt up every blade of grass. The farmers usually burn the grass down just before the first summer rains come on, so as to have the grass come out young and tender for their flocks. And as soon as rain has fallen, and the grass is growing, they move out of their winter quarters in the bush veld, and come back to their houses on the high veld, which, during the winter, are left under the care of, perhaps, one member of the family, or a native servant whom they can trust, or is left to take care of itself.

The party travelled on all day, and came only at midday to a house, where they could obtain a little soaked mealies for their horses. All the other houses they had come to were deserted, as the families were still in the bush veld, and they had been unable to procure a mouthful of forage for their horses. They themselves were all right, for they had a good stock of provisions, but the poor brutes were starving.

After the feed of mealies, the horses put a little spurt on again during the afternoon, but soon the want of food again made itself felt.

The young men began to feel anxious. If the horses got no food, they could not pull the cart; and to remain stuck in such a black and uninhabited plain, with no shelter from the hot sun, would be decidedly unpleasant

They had been directed to a farm where they would find good people at home, as well as forage for their horses and game for their guns, and were pushing on to reach this place. But on this bare, black plain many roads crossed and recrossed. It was a regular network of roads running from farm to farm. They became confused as to which road they should take and which leave. They soon realised the fact that they had lost their road, and were going at random. The danger now began to get serious. Their horses were dragging wearily along, and could scarcely keep up a semblance of a trot, and would soon give in altogether. The poor brutes had been in harness most of the day, and that on a mouthful of mealies only. But what could they do? They must keep on to reach shelter for themselves and food for the horses. Night is coming on; 'tis only twilight now, and twilight does not last longer than thirty or forty minutes here. Soon they will be unable to see the road, and will be forced to span out on this barren, inhospitable veld.

'Hurrah! I see a light, and what is more, the dim outline of trees, and I do believe a house,' cried Steve.

'But where the dickens is the road?' cried his cousin. The road seemed suddenly to disappear on the hard, unimpressionable soil. But all jumped down and went in search of a road.

Going a little forward, they discovered that they were by no means out of the difficulty yet. A river lay between them and the light, and what is more no *drift* was visible. The banks were steep, and no cart could pass it, and a deep *zee koe gat* (wallowing pools of sea-cows) occupied the whole visible stretch of the river. They ran up against the stream and soon came to what appeared to be a sort of *drift*. But what a *drift*.

On examination they found it to be an old disused *drift* or ford. Wash-aways of one foot to a foot and a half crossed the steep road, going down into the river. And in the river itself large round stones three feet high lay piled up one against the other on the only place where a cart might have passed. What were they to do now? No other *drift* seemed near. Stay there they could not, and darkness was settling down on the land.

They stood looking in dismay at this *drift*. The opposite side was not crossed by wash-aways, but seemed to be almost one large precipice in itself. But still, with good horses, once there, they might be able to mount it. But how to get there?

'Well, I do not see the use of standing talking here; we cannot stay here—cross we must—let us act!' said Steve.

'But we cannot cross here,' cried Harrison. 'The cart would be smashed! So how can we act?'

'I for one won't drive through here; my life is not insured,' said Steve's cousin.

'And I would not remain on the cart if you did,' said Keith.

'Well, undo the leaders and lead them across. I shall drive the cart over, but with the wheelers only. They seem to be steady and reliable, and fairly lively yet,' said Steve.

The others stared at him, but he remained cool and calm, as all great natures do in the time of peril. He started undoing the leaders, as the others seemed in doubt whether to take him at his word or not, led them on one side, and handed them to Theron, who seemed the most collected of the others.

He got on the cart, spoke firmly but kindly to the horses, took the reins well and strongly in hand, as short as possible, and started down the precipitous road. When he got to the first drop or wash-away in the road, he made the horses climb down first, stopped them, then moved them forward step by step, holding them hard in the mouth, until the cart came on the edge of the drop. When the cart came to the edge, it dropped down, but gently, as the horses at this moment, pulled back firmly by Steve, pressed the wheels firmly against the side of the little precipice, and thus broke the fall, bringing the cart down with only a slight bump, without injuring it in the least.

In this way he climbed down all the dangerous drops, until he came to the river itself.

Here the danger seemed greatest. How to get across those great, big, round stones? But even across these he got, foot by foot, inch by inch, making the horses pull the wheels out against the round sides of the rocks, and back it down gently on the other side. Thus he went from rock to rock. Sometimes the wheels jumped from rock to rock, when they were near enough; sometimes the cart seemed on the point of tumbling over into the *zee koe gat* alongside, when one wheel was on top of a rock and the other down between two others. But the worst of all was the feet of the poor tired horses amongst these great, big, round boulders. Sometimes one or the other would slip down on its knees, only to be picked up gently by the firm hand at the reins; sometimes their feet would stick fast between two rocks, but by moving only one step at a time, and keeping his horses quiet, Steve found himself at last in front of the steep wall on the other side. Now he fully saw how steep it was, and, worst of all, it was heavy sand. Will the poor, tired horses ever manage to get out of this hole? Should the horses lose their footing or give in for a second, when half-way, the cart would drag them down, and all would come down in a broken mass — horses kicking, stones obstructing—and, perhaps, the whole would go down into the *zee koe gat*, which would mean almost certain death to the man finding himself entangled in this mass. But there is no time for hesitating now. He is in, and must get out. It is nearly quite dark now. After giving the horses a moment to breathe, he let go the reins, shouted to them to go, and lashed them until they flew forward in terror, right against the steep wall. Now they are half-way up—my God! they are slipping in the sand! For a moment they seemed to go down. No! up they go again. They pant and bend, but up they go; and at last, the cart stands on level ground again.

Now only Steve discovers that he is pouring wet; the sweat is simply running from him. He is trembling all over from excitement; his mouth is parched. He steps down, quiets the horses, gets a drink from the water canteen, and wipes the sweat from his eyes and is himself again. He is soon joined by his companions, leading the two other horses. They had been standing looking on as if paralysed. They expected to see the cart sink into ruins every moment, and their admiration was unbounded when they saw him guide the vehicle over obstacle after obstacle, safe and sound. When they came up to him, they generously congratulated him, in unmeasured terms, for his pluck and skill; and, to the end of their trip, when they came to dangerous places (which was often enough), they made him take the reins, to the disgust of his cousin.

Well now, at last they could go to the house they had seen at a distance. It is true it is dark and no road visible, but the light still shone and invited them on; and after such a *drift* crossed, surely they can find their way across the level plain, even though it be dark. Steve led the way on foot, and soon they found themselves in front of the house they had seen.

But their hopes appeared dashed to the ground again.

'Seems to me this is a poor show, and it strikes me we will have to camp outside after all.'

They had come to the poorest of poor houses. A low, small mud house. It must be one of the poorest farmers in the district.

The barking of the dogs had brought the inmates out of the house by this time. The following dialogue took place.

'Good evening, Oom.' (Steve spoke).

'Good evening, Neef.' (Nephew).

'Who lives here, Oom.'

'I do!'

'May I ask Oom's name?'

'Certainly, young man; my name is Zarl Venter.'

'Will Oom have a shelter for us to-night.'

'Young friend, I have never turned a stranger away from my door, even though I am poor; and hope I never will. If you are satisfied with the best we have, which is not much, you are welcome.'

'Thank you, Oom; we have food, but we should like a shelter as it looks like rain, and a little food and shelter for our horses.'

'Food and shelter for yourselves, I have already told you you are welcome to the best we have. As to your horses, I have no stable, but those big trees are as good as any stable if it does not rain very much. As to forage, my son has a little; you must ask him.'

'We will pay him for it, uncle.'

'Speak to him yourselves.'

The horses were soon tied up and fed, and our young men found themselves in a low room, barely furnished, with a few chairs and a table. Supper was on the table, and consisted of coffee and bread *ad lib*, nothing more.

The young fellows stared at each other. They were hungry, and only bread and coffee. True, it was nice, fresh, delicious home-made bread; but bread and coffee was no supper for a hungry townsman. True they had plenty of nice tinned meats and fish on the cart, but on its being suggested in a whisper to Steve by his cousin, he shook his head. He had no wish to humiliate the poor old people by bringing food to their table, after they had offered them the best they had. So after their frugal meal, they retired to bed. They slept on the bed of the old couple themselves; who, as Oom Ignatious and his wife had done, slept on the floor to accommodate their stranger guests. The son had a little nest of his own, but one too poor to offer to these city folks.

The four had to make themselves as comfortable as

they could on the large double bed of the old people, by lying crosswise. At any rate, the bed was perfectly clean.

CHAPTER XXVIII

A CHANGE OF ROUTE

THE party rose early next morning, fed the horses, and held a consultation. They learned that they had passed the farmhouse to which they had been directed, far to the right. They were told by Oom Zarl Venter that they would find very few people at home on their present course, as in that direction nearly everybody was in the bush veld with their cattle.

'But if you want game, why don't you go to the bush veld. There you will find lots of game as well as people.'

'But it is too far away from here.'

'Not at all, you can be in the bush veld to-morrow if you choose, tired as your horses are.'

He further told them that they might go as far as Mijnheer Stienberg's place, just this side of Kameelpoort, and the following day pass through Kameelpoort, when they would be in the outskirts of the bush veld, and just in the right place for pheasants and partridge shooting.

'But is there no place half-way between this and Mijnheer Stienberg's place where we might obtain forage for our horses?' asked Steve.

'Yes, there is a place. Old Salas Prinsloo lives there—but—' and the old man smiled, 'he is very *Kwaai*' (bad-humoured).

'Too *Kwaai* to sell us some forage for our horses?'

'Well, you see, some *Smouses* cheated the old man several times, and if you are taken for *Smouses* (traders or hawkers), you must look out and get out of his way;

and he seems to suspect all strangers with a cart laden as yours is for *Smouses.*'

'Well, we will try at all events,' said Steve.

They set out, well directed as to which roads to take and which to leave; and after the previous day's predicament, took good care to go right.

After several hours' travelling, they arrived at a house which, from the description they had heard, they correctly surmised to belong to Oom Silas Prinsloo. They halted in front of the door. An old man with a stern countenance was leaning over the bottom half of the door, surveying them with a threatening and severe cast of countenance. He did not speak.

'Good-day, Mijnheer!' began Steve.

'Good day!'

'Who lives here, Mijnheer?'

'What has that got to do with you?' severely.

'Oh, nothing, Mijnheer. Only I thought Mijnheer Silas Prinsloo must be living here, who, I have been told, would be kind enough to sell us some forage for our horses.'

'I don't keep forage for every cheating Jew of a *Smouse* who may come to cheat me. You had better go; I don't want to buy anything, and my dogs are very *Kwaai* (fierce).'

'We are not *Smouses*, Mijnheer, we are going to the bush veld for a little shooting and want to buy a few bundles of oats for our poor tired horses.'

'And what may your name be?' he asked, still suspecting.

'Stephaans Joubert, Mijnheer.'

'From where do you come?'

'From Pretoria.'

'Where were you born?'

'At G——, Cape Colony.'

'At G——, Cape Colony? That is where *my* parents come from, and my great grandmother was a Joubert. We must be related then, surely?'

'The ice was broken, the old man came out, shook hands, accepted Keith's tobacco pouch, filled his pipe, and assisted to outspan the horses, led the way to the stable, and, hey presto! the horses were contentedly chewing plenty of good oats. The party was invited into the house and coffee brought forth, while poor Steve had for a full long hour to explain the genealogy of his house, and hear that of the host explained; and the old man succeeded in explaining how they were related. Steve did not exactly understand the conversation, but from the old man's use of words, such as cousin in the third and fourth degree 'to my grandmother,' and so forth, he thought it must be somewhere in Noah's time that the relationship commenced. However, as the pretended relationship helped to feed the horses, he did not complain. After an hour's good feed, the horses were once more inspanned, and, much to Steve's relief, his new-found relative was left behind, in spite of urgent appeals from the said relative to spend the day there.

They arrived early in the afternoon at Mijnheer Stienberg's, and were well received by the family. The old man and his wife were emigrants themselves from the Cape Colony, and belonged to the most progressive class of farmers. A good governess was kept for the boys and girls, and the farm work was carried on progressively and at a good profit.

The young men enjoyed a real pleasant social evening with the governess and the girls, who were all good musicians and had splendid voices. The young fellows, who all liked music, joined them in several songs, but enjoyed most to lie back in their easy-chairs and listen to the fresh voices of the girls singing Dutch and English ballads and hymns. Thus they occupied themselves until a late hour, after which they went to bed and enjoyed a good night's sleep. An early start was made the next day, for all were anxious now to reach the bush veld.

CHAPTER XXIX

THE BUSH VELD

AFTER half-an-hour's travel, Kameelpoort was reached, and on emerging on the other side, our friends found stretched out before them hills and valleys covered by trees and bushes. It seemed to them, as they stood high above these valleys and hills, that the earth appeared to sink lower and lower the farther northward they looked. It was really so. They were standing on a range of hills separating the high from the low veld. The high veld is a bare, undulating plain, covered with grass only. The low veld is covered with bush and trees, ranging from low dwarf bushes to the high majestic yellow wood, and other large varieties of trees. The farther north you go, the lower you descend, and the warmer it becomes, so that in mid-winter you have a mild pleasant climate, but in summer only natives and game can exist.

Under the trees and in the open glades a high, sweet grass grows—splendid feeding for cattle and sheep in winter. Thus it is that all farmers do not consider themselves well off before they have a farm or two on the high veld for summer, and a farm in the bush veld for winter pasturage.

After descending into the valley before them, our party reached a stream where were encamped about ten families of farmers, some of whom Steve knew. The usual welcome was accorded them.

We shall describe the winter quarters of one of these families, which are all alike more or less, some better some worse.

If the family has two full tent waggons, so much the better, then they have two bedrooms ready. In each a comfortable *Karlet* (bedstead without legs) is tied, and a feather bed made on it.

Between the two waggons, one or two tents are stretched, one serving as another bedroom, and the other as a dining-room.

In front of the tents and waggons an enclosure is made of marsh or river reeds. In the enclosure thus formed, a floor of mud and cow dung is laid, which makes a smooth, hard floor. On one side of the enclosure a fireplace is made, being a circle large enough to contain all the pots of the family, enclosed by a ridge of mud three or four inches high, to keep fire and ashes within bounds. This is the kitchen, and also the sitting-room of an evening, when all would gather round the fire, and the events of the day would be talked over. This enclosure is always kept neat and clean.

Steve and his party found a good company of sportsmen in the community here encamped. As it was still early, a party was got up to go shooting. They started about four o'clock.

A good bag was made. We shall relate only one incident of the afternoon. Steve found himself with the boaster of the company; he was named William. His stories of his skill in shooting were marvellous. Steve was considered by him as a greenhorn, and thus a suitable party to be stuffed with yarns of miraculous shots that he—William—had at various times made. Steve listened quietly and thought he should like to see a few of these accurate shots. They arranged to shoot turn by turn. The guns were all shot-guns, as they were only out after partridge, koraan and pheasants.

The first of the two to shoot was William. He got a fine shot at two pheasants, as they hid themselves behind a tuft of grass, or thought they did, for they were still plainly visible. William fired and—missed. Of course it was an accident, something the matter with the gun. Steve's turn came next; and a good turn he got. They came to a pool of water; walking quietly up, four koraan were seen standing in a line. William whispered to Steve to let him fire, as Steve was sure to miss, and he would guarantee to bring down, at least, two. Without answering, Steve took aim and fired—and killed all four.

William boasted no more after that in the presence of Steve.

CHAPTER XXX

ANECDOTES

STEVE and William returned home to find the rest of the party gathered in consultation. Keith had strayed from his companion and guide, and could nowhere be found.

He had gone in chase of a lot of guinea-fowl, and had disappeared in the bush, and could not be found again. He was searched for, and shouted for, but in vain.

The present consultation was to arrange plans to go in search of him. Steve and William, on their arrival, were told of the situation, and immediate preparation was made for a search-party, composed of all the males in the encampment. They started westward, and after half-an-hour's brisk walking, and continued shouting and bell-ringing, they heard a gun fired to the north. It was agreed among all present that it was a signal of distress from Keith. A reply shot was fired to let him know they were near. The result was a continuous fire of shots from the direction in which the first shot had been heard.

'Oh, he is all right,' said Harrison; 'he is having a grand old time amongst the guinea-fowl. He is not lost after all, he has only been following the guinea-fowl up, and, I suppose, he has succeeded in driving them into a corner at last, and is killing them one by one at his leisure; at least, that seems to be the case from the number of shots he is firing.'

All laughed, for they understood this to be a joke at Keith's expense, for, of course all knew those shots were mean to guide them to the lost man, and were by no means fired at guinea-fowl.

Although a reply shot was fired now and again to let Keith know that help was coming, he seemed to be determined to let them know where he was, for he kept on firing, apparently as fast as he could pull out empty cartridge cases and put full ones in again.

Guided in this way, they soon came up to the place where Keith was standing. When they came up he looked thoroughly disgusted with himself and everybody else. But he felt *awfully* glad, as he afterwards expressed it, to see them. He confessed to having really been afraid to spend the night in the bush; nameless terrors came before his mental vision, and, said he, 'If I felt so dreadfully lonely and afraid, when I knew I could not be far away from the camp, what must one's feeling be to be really *lost* in the bush? It must be awful—ugh!'

'But how did you manage to lose yourself?' asked someone.

'Well, you can't understand it before you get lost yourself; I always thought I would never lose my bearings, wherever and however situated I might find myself. But when I had given up the chase of the guinea-fowl, and I wanted to retrace my steps, I could not for the life of me determine which way I had come. I was not sure which way the camp lay, and as the sun had gone down, I could not say which side was north or south. I climbed a confounded thorn tree, and after I had perforated myself with thorns, and got as high as I could, I was rewarded for my pains by seeing the tops of other thorn trees, and nothing else. I got down and ran in the direction in which I thought the camp might lie, and after running a distance I thought it must lie in another direction, so I kept running in one direction and another. I was so excited that the sweat was pouring off me in streams. At last I was so tired that I thought I had better sit down and rest, and on a little calm reflection, I saw that I was a fool for running about in this way, and that I was only tiring myself, and probably running farther and farther away from the tents, so I sat down and waited.'

'But I say, Keith,' chimed in Harrison, 'how many cartridges have you left in your belt?'

'Not one; why do you ask?'

'And how many guinea-fowl have you killed?'

'You go and bury yourself!' retorted Keith, who saw whither Harrison was leading him, and that he was trying to raise the laugh against him.

The party returned to the camps, and after a hearty supper of venison, *storm jagers* (dough nuts) and fresh butter, Keith got his spirits back, and joined in the laugh against himself for losing himself so easily; it was considered a good joke by the Boers, who could find their way in the darkest night in the bush and never get lost.

After supper, pipes were lighted, and all the men folks (as well as some of the younger women folks) of the whole encampment gathered around the large fire in one of the largest enclosures to indulge in chat and anecdote. The fire was glorious. Timber was plentiful. Once the fire was burning well, two or three tree stumps were put on, and the fire would keep burning on this solid mass of fuel till next day.

This gathering just suited Steve. He had been in such gatherings before, and loved to hear the anecdotes of the hunting field, as well as the battlefield, told by grey-headed men around the fire of an evening.

After one tale and another had been told by individuals of the junior members, Steve turned to one of the seniors, who was known to be on intimate terms with President Kruger, and said,—

'I suppose even the President was fond of hunting in his younger days, Oom Simon?'

'Yes, he was a noted lion hunter; I have heard a story or two of his doings as a lion hunter, but I have never asked him about the truth of it, so you need not believe it, but I will relate it to you.

'The first was when he and another man were suddenly attacked by a lion one day. They were both unarmed, as they did not expect to find lions or dangerous beasts of prey in the vicinity. The President had his hunting-knife on his hip, and that was all. Suddenly they nearly stepped on a lion lying in the tall grass; the lion sprang up, and before he could get out of the way, the President's companion found himself under the lion, with the teeth of the brute closing in his shoulder.

'The President sprang to his companion's assistance, drew his knife, seized the lion by the throat, and stabbed him in the heart two or three times. The lion then let go his hold, and fell dead.'

'But, uncle, is not that almost an impossible thing to do, to seize a lion by the throat and stab him to death.'

'Under ordinary circumstances it would be almost impossible, but you must know that when a lion bites into the flesh of his victim and feels the warm blood in his mouth, he seems to enjoy it so much that he always closes his eyes for a few moments, and lies perfectly quiet to enjoy himself. If you think *that* impossible, you might think this still more so. The President had one day walked far ahead of his waggon in the hunting field. He had again left his heavy gun in the waggon. He was standing on a rise, waiting for the waggon—coming on far behind—and resting, when he saw two lions, a male and female, coming on full speed towards him from an opposite direction to the waggon. They were charging direct on him, the lion in front, the lioness some distance behind. The President saw it was no time to show funk and run. To run away on foot meant death. He did the best thing he could under the circumstances. He stood up and faced the charging lion, and looked him firmly and fiercely in the eyes. The lion came within a few paces of him, then stopped, looked him in the eyes for a moment or two, hesitated for a second, then turned and ran away with his tail between his legs. The lioness, who had by this time come up, looked after her flying mate in surprise, seemingly wondering at his giving his prey up so easily. Then she looked at the President in a searching way, as if she sought for the danger which had driven her mate away. She caught the menacing eye of the President, stood spell-bound for a moment as if mesmerised, then turned and followed her lord and master.'

'Well, I can well believe that, for I have often heard that the President possessed the power of mesmerism in a natural way, although he only seems to exercise it in an unconscious way. And I believe that if a man does possess such a power, he ought to, with his wonderful firmness of will, amounting almost to obstinacy.'

'No, I do not think he is obstinate,' replied Oom Simon, 'but he never determines upon anything unless he is firmly convinced that it is the right thing to do; and then, when once his mind is made up as to what is right or wrong, he stands by his opinions to the end, even if he falls by them.'

'He must be a religious and serious old man,' remarked Steve in a way, as if he wished to draw out old Simon. 'He never jokes or laughs, it appears to me.'

'That is because, I suppose, you only see him in public. If you see him in private amongst his friends, especially when travelling, he is very fond of his joke. He *is* certainly very religious, he fears his God, and is a true Christian. But he loves a joke nevertheless.'

'I remember once we were travelling together. We were amusing ourselves with conundrums; at last the President said,—

'"I will give you a riddle now. There is a kraal built of high stone walls. A troop of asses wish to get into that kraal, for the lions are roaring around them, and safety is to be found in the kraal. How will they get in? Over the wall they cannot; and through the gate they may not go. How are they to get inside?" said he, turning to old Mijnheer van Heerden, a member of our party.

'"I know not?" replied Mijnheer van Heerden.

'"Then you are as stupid as the asses themselves, for they knew not how to get in either." Of course Mijnheer van Heerden had to join in the laugh too. He was nicely caught, ha! ha! ha!'

'Talking of being nicely caught?' said Oom Hendrik, another senior of the party. 'I once knew a wild fellow who always liked to play practical jokes. His name was Petrus. One day he met a minister, looking gentle, meek and mild, and also a little green, but looks are sometimes deceptive, as you will see. He went up to the minister and said to him, "Mijnheer, do you practice as well as preach the Bible?"'

'"I hope so, my friend,"' was the reply.

'"The Bible says, 'If a man should strike you on the left cheek, turn to him the right cheek, that he may strike that also.'" And he gave the minister a good slap on the left cheek. The minister quietly turned the right cheek to him; he was a little disconcerted at this, but struck it in a half-hearted sort of way, and said, "Yes, I see you do practice as well as preach." But it was the turn of the minister now, who said,—

'"Yes, but wait a bit, my friend, the Bible also says, 'That by the same measure that ye shall measure others with shall ye also be measured by.'" And the minister took his coat off, and set to, and gave Petrus the best thrashing he ever had in his life.'

CHAPTER XXXI

LIÒN STORIES

STEVE saw that the conversation was drifting out of the desired channel, so he turned to Oom Simon again, and said,—

'But did you ever have a narrow escape from a lion, Oom Simon.'

'Well, I had a narrow escape once of being thoroughly frightened. We had been out for a lion hunt during the day. We found one, or rather he found us, for the first we saw of him was when he was mounted on the back of one of our horses. He had bounded out of a clump of marsh reeds, and sprung right on top of the horse, fastening his teeth in the neck of my poor hunting horse. We shot him. I gave him a bullet behind the shoulder, from the left, and my brother one through the loins from the right. We skinned him, and took the skin to camp.

'That night I was standing near the enclosure, when one of the boys suddenly threw the lion's skin close to the dogs standing near to me. The dogs must have thought it was a live lion. They howled and growled as they usually do when a lion is near. And one of them, as big as the lion himself, was so frightened that he ran against me in the dark. It was so dark I could not see, and I thought it must be the lion himself. I can tell you it took my breath away, I got such a *schrik* (sudden fright), and it was some moments before I was sure there was no lion between my legs, but only a dog.'

'I got a bigger *schrik* than that one day,' said Oom Klaas, another old man, who had been quiet up till now. 'I had shot a red buck one day. I hung him up a tree, in the bush, and went for the waggon to take the game to the camp. I came back with the waggon following at some distance, having left my gun at the waggon, as I had only a short time before left the spot, and did not expect any lions to be there so soon. Judge of my surprise, when I came within sight of my game, to see two lions pulling at it. They saw me, and one ran to the right. I crept round the bushes in an opposite direction. I was continually looking round in the direction towards which I had seen one of the lions go, expecting the other one would follow in the same direction, so I did not look in front of me, but always behind, in order to see him if he should charge me from behind. Suddenly something ran up right against me, throwing me right on my back. In a flash I saw it was the other lion, with the red buck in his mouth; he had gone round by the other way, and thus came upon me in this unexpected way; fortunately he had the buck in his mouth. So that he saw me as little as I saw him, thus the result—that we collided in this unexpected way. I can tell you I did get a *schrik*. I could just shout, *Haai you schelm*, as I lay upon my back. But fortunately for me his mouth was occupied in holding the red buck, and so he could not bite, and when the shock came, he was as much surprised and frightened as I was. He dropped the buck and fled.'

There was amongst the company an old man, named Oom Frans (I omit all family names as these reminiscences are all true; and giving fictitious names will serve no purpose). This old man had gone through many vicissitudes. One day he was felling a tree. It was very heavy. The tree fell and caught four of his fingers in such a way that withdrawing them was impossible. He had only one companion with him. Nobody else was within two days' journey. His companion could not move the tree stump a hair's breadth. What to do now? He got out his knife and asked his friend to cut the fingers off. But the man had not the nerve to do so, and refused his friend's entreaties to amputate the fingers. Oom Frans got wild; he lost his temper at such womanishness. He took the knife and cut his own fingers off himself. It was his right hand. The writer has often shaken that stump of a hand, and wondered at the nerve displayed by the old man in cutting off four of his own fingers with an ordinary pocket knife.

This old man now quietly said,—

'I once had a narrow escape from a lion. It is many years ago now—'

Here Oom Hendrik interrupted him by saying,—

'No, Neef Frans, these young fellows are keeping us out of our sleep, and we old folks get up early. Stephaans and his friends are going to stay over to-morrow, I suppose, as Stephaans himself has had too good success with the koraan to leave them without another try, and I expect Mijnheer Keith would like to be revenged on those guinea-fowl. So you had better postpone your story, or we shall have no adventures to tell them to-morrow night. Good-night, all friends,' and off walked the old chap, followed by the rest of the party, who had all been feeling rather sleepy during the last half-hour; for I can recommend to whoever may read this no better remedy for insomnia than a tramp after guinea-fowl, or after a lost chum in the bush.

CHAPTER XXXII

DANGERS OF THE CHASE

THE party took full advantage of their further delay the following day, and a fairly successful bag was made.

In the afternoon all the farmers who could manage to get away from the cares of their folds joined them. Each of the visitors had one or more guides, some of the junior farmers acting as such, so as to prevent any more straying or getting lost. A point was agreed upon where all would meet at a certain hour to compare notes.

The programme was carried out in full. They all

met, and after a rest had been taken, and success or non-success had been communicated, they all left together to return to the camp.

Suddenly they came upon two men lying under a tree. At a distance they took it to be two men sleeping in the veld, but on approaching it was seen that they were lying in too uncomfortable a position to be sleeping.

An investigation was made, when it was found that they were dead.

It was an old man of about fifty years of age and a young man of about twenty years. There was a family resemblance, which hardly left a doubt of their being father and son.

'How can this have happened?' remarked an old man, closely examining the corpses. 'It can hardly be murder, as I find no wound in them; it might rather be poison, for see how discoloured their faces look. What could they have been eating to poison themselves?'

'They have been eating kambaroo, father,' said a young man. 'See, there is half a bulb lying next to them.'

'That is not kambaroo,' returned the old man, examining the bulb. 'This is a poisonous bulb. Nobody who knows kambaroo would eat this bulb for it. The poor fellows must have heard of it, or known it very slightly, to make such a sad mistake. I wonder who they are!'

'I know them, father?' said the young man. 'I found the nine sheep we lost last week at their tent. The sheep had got mixed with theirs in the veld. They are strangers from the high veld, and nobody knows them here. Their tent is about an hour's ride on horseback from here.'

'Poor fellows, I am very sorry for them and their families. Koos, you and Jan go and span in the cart and take them to their tent; and let the *veld cornet* know. If you can do anything for the poor families, do so, and if necessary, you can stay there till to-morrow and assist to get ready for the funeral. We shall all come over to-morrow to see what can be done to help the widow and orphans.'

This was done, and the party returned to the tents saddened at the sight; and the old patriarchs took the opportunity to point out to the younger men how transient and uncertain life is, and that it behoved them to be prepared at all times to meet their God.

Supper was partaken of silently and soberly. At the usual evening service, which few of our genuine old Boers ever omit, an earnest prayer was offered up for those who had that day been made fatherless and husbandless.

After supper, when sitting round the fire, smoking, and drinking coffee, the spirits of the party seemed to rise sufficiently for Steve to remind Oom Frans of his interrupted story of the night before.

'I do not mind telling you the story, Stephaans,' replied the old man, 'but remember we must have no unseemly hilarity after having met death face to face only a few hours ago.

'Well, as I said, it is now many years ago, when one night the lions attacked our camp and carried away a full-grown bullock. The next day we went in search of them. The grass was very high, and we did not see them until we came right upon them. There were eight of them. I was in front of our party, and when I sighted the lions, their leader was in the act of springing towards me. I fired at him as he jumped, and it turned out afterwards that it was a most lucky shot, as I had shot his lower jaw bone away. But the shot did not stop his tremendous spring, and he came down on top of me. I can tell you I have seen some heavy bullocks in my time, but I felt, as I lay under that lion, that he must weigh more than any two bullocks put together; he felt so awfully heavy as he lay on me full weight, as if he meant to crush me for disabling his biting instrument. But I did not know then that I had shot his jaw away, so I expected every moment to feel his dreadful teeth closing in on my flesh. But I felt glad when I heard several shots, and the lion rolled off me in his death agony. Thank God that his jaw *was* shot away. We shot all eight of those lions that day; and our cattle had peaceful nights for a long time after.'

'A lion may be dangerous, especially when wounded or hungry,' said Oom Koos, another member of the community. 'But you have always at least a chance of disabling a lion when he is charging you. The most dangerous animal, however, when infuriated, is a black rhinoceros. There is no stopping the direct charge of a black rhinoceros. The most accurate shot from the front hardly affects him; and woe betide the man who is charged by him, even a horse can scarcely keep away from him in the bush.

'I saw a black rhinoceros once kill a man. We were tracking the rhinoceros in the bush, and had separated for the chase, when suddenly I heard a rushing sound in the bush near by, and a cry for help. I ran as fast as I could towards the spot, and from behind a stout tree, I saw the maddened animal actually dancing on his victim. Poor Neef Piet, he was almost too shattered and soft to pick up for burial; he had a sad death. I shot the beast dead, but too late.'

'It is true a black rhinoceros is dangerous when wounded, or out of temper,' said Oom Hendrik, 'and a wounded or hungry lion is to be avoided. It is also a fact that a tiger is to be dreaded more than the last two, for he is agile and quick, and no coward like the lion. I will bet that the President will never stare a tiger out of face; for he gives no time, he simply charges right out, and almost before you see him. But even a tiger will hardly attack a man after he has once sprung at him and missed, unless wounded, in which case—look out. I have more than once fallen down flat when a tiger sprang at me, when he would go right over me, and then he will just run on, and never think of renewing his attack. But even this trick requires skill and very quick movement. I once saw a Hottentot perform this trick.

He was not quick enough. The tiger caught hold of him with his claws, just above the eyebrows, as he ducked, and tore his scalp right over his head, so that it hung like a cap behind him. We re-covered his bald pate with the scalp, and sewed it on, after which it grew on splendidly, leaving just a slight mark where it had been torn.

'Well, I say these animals are all dangerous; but I always managed to escape them safe and sound in my wanderings and different hunting trips, either by killing them, or managing to discourage them from following me, or avoiding them somehow.

'But has any one of you ever been chased by a wounded wildebeest? I have been; and you may believe me, I would rather face any living creature on earth than a beast like that again. It happened in this way. We had sighted a troop of wildebeest one afternoon early. There were four of us. We rode down upon them and fired. I had killed one of them, when I saw a fine bull with the best pair of horns I had ever seen on the head of a wildebeest before. I desired those horns, and when the herd separated, I followed this particular bull. The rest of the party each followed a beast of his choice, thus we were soon separated.

'I had not followed my fine bull long when I got a chance for a shot, and wounded him. It was a bad shot. I had wounded him in the shoulder, just sufficiently to draw blood without disabling him in the least. I rode off to one side so as to avoid the charge which I knew would come. I looked back, and saw the bull was in full chase of me. I realised my danger. It was not the first time I had shot wildebeest. I put my horse to the highest pace I dared amongst the bushes and trees, but the bull seemed to be able to turn much quicker amongst the trees than my horse could. I saw my only chance was to make for the open country. I did so, and when I had once gained the open veld I soon gained upon my pursuer. I congratulated myself upon being now safe, and was thinking it time to halt again and take a shot at the bull, who was coming on at full speed, two hundred yards behind — for a wildebest *never* gives up a chase while his enemy is still in sight once he has his temper up—when my horse trod in a hole, and threw me over his head as he fell. I fell, but was uninjured. I ran towards the horse to try and pick him up, as he still struggled on the ground, lying upon his left side, when I saw at a glance that his leg was broken. My gun had flown out of hand, and I could not see it anywhere as the grass was rather tall.

What to do now? Not a tree near, and the bull was only seventy yards away. I could see his blazing eyes as he came on towards me. His horns, which had tempted me so, seemed poised ready to toss me up into the air, as only a wildebeest knows how. At this moment I saw a porcupine hole not far away. It seemed large enough to hold me, and, even though it was not deep, it would suffice, so long as I could keep out of reach of those terrible horns. I sprang towards the hole and crept into it. It was just large enough for me to lie in it, with my head pressed into a hole a little deeper at one end and my feet into a similar one at the other end. The hole seemed to have been originally two holes, with the intervening wall broken down, but not so deep as the two original holes. Into these two holes I hung with my head and feet, while my body was resting on the wall between, which was broken down just deep enough to leave my body slightly below the surface of the surrounding ground. The wildebeest bull was on me. I heard him snorting and tramping about where my horse was lying, and by the fall of a heavy body which I heard, I judged that he had completed the ruin of my hunting horse by tossing him. Now I heard him come towards me. I felt his hot breath on my back. What will he do now? I knew I was out of reach of his horns. Will he have sense enough to tread on me, and thus revenge himself by breaking my back? No; he knew a trick worth two of that it seemed. What do you think he did? He started licking me. Any harm in that? Have you ever seen the tongue of a wildebeest? It is as rough as a rasp, and as hard as a horn. At first I did not think much of his scratching my back with his horny tongue, but he had soon worn through my shirt, which was the only upper garment I had on at the time. Oh Lord! what a sensation it was when first his tongue reached my bare body; it was terrible. But you can easily feel what it was like by taking a coarse rasp and rasping your bare body. My God, I shall never forget that quarter-of-an-hour's torture I endured that day. It felt as if he was tearing pieces of flesh out of my bare back. Soon the blood was streaming down my sides, and the blood seemed to make him madder than ever. Every time he tore his tongue through my lacerated flesh a shiver of horror and pain passed through my body. I prayed to God as I had never prayed before to let me die. When the horror and pain became too much for me to bear, I fainted. If I had not fainted I suppose I would either have died or gone mad. When I came to myself I was lying on my side; somebody was pouring water over me and down my throat. My companions had looked for me, had discovered my horse and the maddened bull, and shot the latter. They found me in the hole where the bull had been standing engaged in his fiendish work. They thought I was dead. But I recovered, and lived to dread the sight of a wildebeest. I have the horns of that brute still to-day at home. I have been offered £15 for them as they are such a splendid pair, but I will never sell them, and I will never risk a single-handed fight with a wildebeest bull again.'

Steve and his companions felt their hair almost stand on end as they listened to the horrible tale.

'You were one of our party that day, *Neef Frederick*,' said the old man, turning to a companion. 'Have I spoken the truth?'

'That you have, Neef; I could take my oath on it,'

was the reply. 'And what is more, I one day saw my uncle killed by just such another wildebeest. We also had a chase after an old bull. We were three. We shot and wounded him. He turned and stood at bay, and chased my poor old uncle, and as he was in a line with my uncle from us we dared not fire for fear of hitting my uncle. In a moment he came up to the old man, as his horse was not very good, and rather slow. He caught the horse with his horn between the hind legs, and tossed him forwards, hind legs in the air. As the horse was tossed forward my uncle dropped backwards, and was caught upon the horn of the bull. The horn penetrated just under his chin, in an upward direction, passing out on the top of his head. When we came up we shot the bull. But my uncle was a dead man!'

After a little further conversation on the peculiarities of game and their habits, the party broke up, and all retired to bed.

CHAPTER XXXIII

SCHRIKRIGHIED

AN early start was made the next day to proceed on their trip, as the plan was not to stay at any one place more than two days so as to enable them to see as many places and people as possible.

Early in the afternoon they arrived at the camping place of a party of transport riders, who were spending a month in the bush veld to recruit their worn-out draught oxen. They were a rough-and-ready lot, but a merry and entertaining party withal.

They were very hospitable and kind, taking the young holiday-makers to the best coverts for birds and game. But what amused Steve most of all was that one of the party was one who *schriked*.

Before proceeding, I must explain what is meant by this word.

The dictionary translates *schrik* to mean fright, dread, terror, horror. But this hardly explains what is meant by the term here. Here it is meant to represent a combination of ticklishness and *schrikishness*, if I may be allowed to use the words in such a manner.

In South Africa, one often meets with persons who are thus affected in various stages. Some need to be touched under the arms, when they will shout out as loud as you like, and jump as high as you please. Some will be affected in the same way by being shown certain animals or insects, composing their particular dread, such as a spider, a frog or mouse. To others you need but to suddenly mention their particular objects of dread to make them act as if they were mad.

To others, again, the worst of all—after having once startled them and put them on the *qui vive*, you may stand at any safe distance, and in a sudden, sharp, commanding tone, order them to do or say what you please, and they simply cannot resist doing as you say.

This disease, as one may call it, is generally acquired by being over tickled in your youth, or receiving a bad fright, as the reader may gather from the recitals of the victims themselves further on. To some people it is a serious burden to be thus affected, as the amusement caused by their doing all sorts of ludicrous things at the will of everyone, tempts everybody to make them *schrik*, and the continual shock to the system causes them to tremble all over, and to feel an excess of nervousness not at all conducive to good health. The writer has known a strong healthy young man thus affected, to faint on being tickled under the arms while being held down.

Steve delighted in these comical persons, who *would* be so stupid as to do what you tell them, or say out loud what you whispered to them, simply out of *schrik.* But he always took care not to make an abuse of the amusement; for as soon as he saw his victim getting too excited, he would soothe him and spare him further for the time being.

The victim in this particular instance was named *Piet.* They were sitting having their dinner. Each was holding his mug of coffee in one hand; the kettle was empty; no more coffee to be had unless the kettle was first boiled. One of the transport riders looks round and winks, and says suddenly,—

'Piet, throw that mug away.' Away goes the mug, coffee and all.

Steve sees how the land lies, and joins in the laugh, seeing some fun ahead.

After Piet's cup had been replenished by getting a portion from each of the other cups, he thought, 'Now I shall be able to finish my meal,' when he received the command, 'Jump up, Piet.' He jumped up as ordered, dropping both cup and food this time. He stood looking comically and disgustedly at his nice venison steak lying in the ashes, while the others were splitting their sides with laughing. Steve, of course, laughed as much as anyone else, and more so—it *was* so foolish to throw your food away like that.

After once more sharing food and drink with the others, he was allowed to finish his meal. After dinner, some Kaffir women came to the camp to sell *stamp mealies* (shelled maize). Some were bought and Piet was requested to pay. He took out his purse, opened it, and took out a shilling to pay the girl, when

'Give her the purse,' came the order.

'*De, de*' (here, here), cried poor Piet, forcing the purse full of silver into the hands of the astonished black lady.

He was allowed to take back his purse, put it in his pocket, when once more came the order,—

'Shake hands with her.' He seized the black girl's

hand and shook it heartily, only to drop it in disgust, and call for soap, muttering something about, 'This is too much, shaking hands with the dirty, greasy thing; soap will hardly wash the stinking grease off my hand again.' The others were lying on their backs shaking with laughter, and holding their sides. The black woman had never been so astonished. Never had a white man offered to shake hands with her before.

'Take off your hat to the lady,' once more heard Piet. He took off his hat and made a profound bow to the staring sable woman. The next moment he took off his hat again and tramped upon it, as if the hat was to be blamed for being lifted in greeting to a nigger.

He was allowed to take a breath now, as the others felt it would be fatal for them to laugh any more. Steve felt as if his cheeks would never take their normal position again; they had been stretched out of position so much from laughing.

Presently the oxen came in to be kraaled for the night. *Speelman*—an old Hottentot—the herder, came up to the fire to be rationed.

Steve and his party had not seen Speelman before, as he had been in the veld all day herding the cattle. He was a short, pot-bellied old sinner, with a round bullet head, and a face, all wrinkles, which seemed as if made of elastic when he drew it into his broad, hypocritical smile, as he came towards Baas Piet and asked for some *baccy*.

Piet took out his *span* of tobacco, cut off a few inches, and handed it to Speelman, when one of his friends named Daniel shouted *slang* (snake).

Speelman bounded into the air, and made Piet *schrik* too as he came down again, and catching hold of Piet round the body, hung there, kicking and howling. 'Help, baas, help, *slang*, *slang*. And as he hung and kicked, Piet struggled and shouted, the one seemed as excited and frightened as the other.

The scene was too much for mortal man to stand. Steve fell on the ground, and rolled about on the grass as he laughed. He had to close his eyes. He felt, if he looked longer on the ludicrous scene, he would break something; his sides had already been abnormally strained. When he opened his eyes, Piet and Speelman were arguing the matter out.

'If you hang to me again with those dirty paws of yours I shall kick you?' Piet was saying in disgust.

'But, baas, how can I help it, when Baas Daniel frightened me so? Please give me some other tobacco, baas; mine fell, and I can't find it,' he said supplicatingly.

'Ask Baas Daniel; he made you lose yours, and now he can give you some other?'

'Oh, please, Baas Daniel, give poor old Speelman some other tobacco, I have had nothing to smoke all the afternoon?' said the old hypocrite, as he went and stood in front of Daniel. Piet saw his opportunity was come for revenge. He shouted,—

'Speelman, kiss Baas Daniel?'

Speelman rushed forward and caught hold of Daniel, and tried his level best to approach his already smacking lips to the lips of Daniel. The woods rang with the roars of laughter as the young fellows saw the biter bitten in this unexpected manner. Daniel caught hold of Speelman by the throat, and even then he had great difficulty to keep the dirty smacking lips of the Hottentot away from his, for Speelman had again, for the second time, heard Piet's command to 'kiss Baas Daniel.' At last Daniel succeeded by main force to throw the Hottentot away from him.

At first Daniel was inclined to resent the trick played on him by Piet, but he was told that he had done as much to Piet, or nearly so, in causing Piet to shake hands with the Kaffir woman; and he had to acknowledge the truth of it and join in the laugh against himself.

When Steve recovered from his last fit of laughter, he called Speelman to him, emptied his pouch in his hand, and said,—

'Now, Speelman, tell me what makes you so disrespectful to your baas as to try and kiss him?'

'I can't help it, baas, I am so *schriking*. When I am told to do anything, I do it.'

'But what makes you do so?'

'Baas, when I was a boy I one day fell asleep under a tree. When I awoke, a snake was partly coiled round my neck, and part of it was coiled on my breast; and when I saw and felt it, I *schriked* so I thought I should die. I jumped up and tore the snake from me, and ran away as fast as I could, until I was so tired I could run no more. After that, baas, if you only say *snake* to me, you can make me do whatever you like.'

'Snake,' called out Steve's cousin at this moment.

'Where? Where? Where?' shouted Speelman, dancing and jumping about.

'Stand on your head,' shouted Keith. He hardly expected his order to be executed, and was surprised to see Speelman fall down and stand on his head, kicking his heels in the air, while he shouted, *Slang, slang* (snake, snake).

Steve now interposed, and said that they had had enough fun out of Speelman for once. They ought to let him rest now and take breath.

The rest of the evening was spent in yarning and story-telling generally, after which all went to bed.

CHAPTER XXXIV

STUCK IN THE MUD

THE following day, Steve and his three companions had good sport amongst the guinea-fowl and other birds.

The transport riders had left early in the morning, each with a good load of firewood for the Pretoria market, as their month of inactivity was at an end, and they had once more to begin work. It had been agreed that the party with the cart should start about ten o'clock from the night's camping place, after having had a turn at the guinea-fowl, etc., and as the waggons started at seven, the cart would catch up with them somewhere about noon, when they could once more have dinner together.

As agreed so done. Steve and his companions came speeding towards the drift, beyond which, it had been agreed, the waggons would outspan, and get dinner ready. As they came nearer, they heard an uproar of oxwhips clapping, and men shouting. When they arrived on the scene they saw that one of the waggons was *stuck* in the drift.

All the other waggons had crossed safely, but the last one, the most heavily laden, and having the weakest span of oxen, had sunk deep in the mud of the drift. The water was no more than two feet deep, but the mud was nearly as deep in itself.

The occupants of the cart saw at a glance that there was no chance for them to pass while the waggon occupied the narrow drift. They, therefore, left Harrison in charge of the cart, and went forward to see how matters proceeded. They found the waggon sunk to the nave in the mud. The oxen were panting and struggling to pull through the mud. Their leader was pulled hither and thither as they swayed to and fro in their efforts to pull out. The men, half naked, were struggling about in the water, talking to the oxen, and clapping their whips. But in vain, the waggon would not budge an inch.

The youngsters from town thought this struggling about in the water trying to extricate a waggon stuck in the mud fine fun, so they took off their clothes, and joined the party of transport riders in the water

Steve and his friends soon discovered that the pleasantest part of the fun was to sit, perched on top of the waggon, and watch the efforts of the others to urge the oxen forward.

There was a lull. Another span of oxen had been sent for to hook on in front. Speelman, who had been the liveliest in his efforts to get forward, was standing alongside of the hind oxen. He was almost naked, having just a remnant of a shirt on. He looked like a dusky mermaid of the waters, he moved so rapidly about; he was now under the oxen, now right under the trek chain; he seemed to be everywhere.

'I say, Speelman, did you see any snakes this morning?' asked Steve.

'No, baas, don't want to see 'em,' said Speelman, suspiciously looking about him, as if he expected to see snakes in the water.

'Jump on the ox,' cried Keith; and in a second Speelman was astride of the kicking bullock.

'Stand on your head in the water,' cried Keith again, not expecting to be obeyed in this. But Speelman ducked into the water, head foremost, and only the tips of his legs were seen above water, kicking furiously.

'You shouldn't do that,' said Steve, laughing. 'It is dangerous; he might get drowned.'

He remained down so long, and the kicking became so furious, that Steve became anxious. He shouted to him to get up, but Speelman could not hear him.

'By Jove! his head must be sticking in the mud,' he cried, and jumping down, he seized Speelman by the legs and pulled him up. Assisted by Keith from the waggon, the poor old Hottentot was dragged on to the seat of the waggon. The poor old fellow presented a most comical face when pulled up. He was drawing in great breaths, to get his steam up again, while he spat the black mud out of his mouth. His whole head, eyes, ears and all were thickly coated with the black, sticky mud, while his pepper corn hair had disappeared under a coating of the same black, smooth pomade. It appears that his head really *did* stick in the mud.

'You must not do that again, baas; poor old Speelman would have been drowned if the baas had not pulled him out,' said he to Keith.

As to Keith, he and his companions had been too frightened to laugh at this exhibition of Speelman's funniosities. He gave Speelman half-a-crown, and told him to go and wash the mud out of his mouth at the canteen beyond the drift. At this moment the extra span of oxen arrived, was attached to the front of the regular span, and with a *Trek, trek, haai you schelm, vat zou blik schottet*, the waggon moved forward, and was soon outspanned with the rest on the other side of the drift. The cart followed over, and soon the whole party was partaking of the regular bush veld fare—venison steak, leg of venison, broiled guinea-fowl, and *storm iagers* (dough cakes).

Speelman followed the advice given him by Baas Keith, and after having imbibed a pint of peach brandy, was as merry as a cricket, and was none the worse for his immersion, except, perhaps, that he was a little more pot-bellied than usual from the quantity of water he had drunk while standing on his head in the drift.

After dinner, Steve and his party took leave of the transport riders with mutual expressions of good will and hopes of meeting again.

In this way they proceeded from camp to camp. Many parties of farmers were met wintering with their herds in the bush veld; and all they had to do was to decide at which encampment they would outspan, or at which they would spend the night, which was mostly decided by the party of farmers who could give the most favourable report as to the game in their neighbourhood.

They had various success. One day, perhaps, they had the best of sport, the next day, perhaps, they failed in bringing down a single head of game. But on the whole, they were perfectly satisfied with their trip. We shall relate only one more incident of their holiday trip. It was the last day; that evening they hoped to sleep in Pretoria again. They were speeding along merrily. It was still forenoon, and Pretoria was hardly four hours distant, so they had no doubt of reaching home before night. It had rained severely the day before along the track of country on which they were then travelling. Suddenly they turned into the main road from the warm baths, and now they had reason to regret the rain of the day before—they were in the famous *turf veld.*

They had not proceeded far before the turf began to tell severely on the pace of the horses. At first they slackened their speed only a little, but soon they were going at barely more than a walk. The sticky black soil was coating the wheels to such a degree that the spokes gradually became nearer and nearer to each other, until the wheels had no spokes, but became a solid mass of black turf. All that the travellers could do was to halt and scrape off the worst part of the mud, when for a time they were able to go on again at a slightly better pace. Full advantage was taken of any unbroken veld, where the heavy waggons had not yet cut up the soil into furrows and ridges of soft black soil. But these patches were scarce, as every driver of waggon or cart generally turns out of the beaten track into the grass alongside, and in course of time the quarter or half mile strip of country, which is supposed to be left unfenced along all roads as feeding ground for trekking herds, becomes so cut up that very little choice is left the traveller as to where he shall steer his weary beasts.

The young men were wearily and dejectedly plodding along, dismounting now and again to scrape the wheels, when they came to a waggon standing in the middle of the road—deserted. The oxen were still inspanned and seemed waiting for their owner. No fear of their running away; how could they? Their own feet were invisible, a round mass of black *turf*—twice the usual size of ox feet—was all that was visible where their feet ought to be, while the wheels of the waggon seemed to be made of solid chunks of mud—no spokes, no rims, no naves being visible.

'Well, this is funny,' remarked Harrison; 'a waggon without owner. There is something wrong here; nobody would leave their waggon inspanned like this—untended.'

'Yes, it is queer,' answered Steve. 'But I fancy there is the owner coming on,' said he, pointing to a man visible in the road about half a mile farther on.

'It may be the owner, but he is not coming, but standing, evidently waiting for the party I see farther on.'

'Why, the nearest one is a woman,' said Keith, 'the other one is a man; but I wonder what is the matter with them? They both remain standing on one spot, but they are gesticulating like mad.'

They soon approached the first party they had seen. IT *was* a woman. She was an elderly old lady, very stout in the beams, and one would have thought, even under ordinary circumstances, she must find it difficult to walk any distance. She appeared to be standing on two lumps of turf, but—they were sticking to her feet. Every step she took increased the size of the lump, until at last she was obliged to stop, she could drag her burden (which, unlike that of Christian, was attached to her feet) along no more.

'Well, I'm blessed if it is not old Mrs M'Kwaire,' cried Steve.

'And who may she be?' queried Keith.

'Why, she is Mrs M'Kwaire,' he replied, laughing. 'She is an old lady of Dutch extraction, married to an old Irishman, both characters in their way—very comical and amusing as a rule; it is most amusing to set old M'Kwaire's tongue a-wagging by mentioning *Home Rule*. If you once start him, you may go away for half-an-hour and come back to find him still talking to some imaginary antagonist about Home Rule and the wrongs of Ireland.'

'Hillo, Tante, why don't you ride on the waggon?' cried out Steve, as they stopped alongside of her.

'That is what I would like to do,' she replied, 'but that foolish Pat would get down to pick up a yoke skey lying in the road, when he remained *stuck*, and, as the oxen would not stop, I, like another fool, got down to help him while the oxen walked on with the waggon to where it is now standing. And now I am sticking between Pat and the waggon; I can't get to him, he cannot get to me, and neither of us can get to the waggon.'

The young fellows could not help bursting into loud roars of laughter at the ludicrousness of the scene. They halted as near to the old lady as possible, and helped her on to their cart and drove on to where Pat was standing, talking and swearing all the time.

'Well, old *Stick-in-the-mud*,' cried Keith, 'it seems the mountain *won't* come to Mahomet, and Mahomet *can't* go to the mountain; what does Mahomet intend doing now?' All laughed at this sally.

'Begorrah, sor, ye niver would lave a pore old mon 'ere.'

'No, I am afraid that would be another wrong to old Oireland. Well, Pat, if Ireland can get out of her troubles as easily as you, I would advise you to get back to her, and stand for the first election of president, king, or emperor, whatever your new constitution would call your chief ruler. I think you stand a good chance.'

'Come along, Keith, that is enough for one day, you are getting too humorously clever,' said Steve. 'Give us your hand, Pat, and jump up if you can.'

But Pat could not jump. He had to be dragged into the cart, and was thus able to sit down and scrape his feet clean again.

Pat and Mrs Pat were driven back to their waggon,

and left behind to proceed to their farm, while the party in the cart proceeded on their way to Pretoria, where they arrived just as darkness was closing in.

'There is one thing I would like to remark now that we are home again,' remarked Keith. 'And it is just this. I have been converted. I had always been impressed with the idea that the Boers are half savage, exclusive, inhospitable and unkind to strangers, especially to Englishmen. I have seen my error. I do not believe there is a country in the world where one would receive such kindness, consideration and hospitality as we have received during our trip. I for one reckon myself as the friend and champion of all Boers from to-day.'

'You are right,' said Harrison. 'When we started, I hardly believed Steve's promise of hospitality from all and sundry, and fully expected to have rough times of it, and I have been agreeably disappointed at the kindness shown us by all.'

BOOK II

CHAPTER I

POLITICAL SUICIDE—HERESY

THE day after their return, Steve heard faint rumours of a certain conference which had been held in Pretoria the last few days in reference to territories lying beyond the northern borders of the South African Republic. He had been too busy attending to accumulated work to take much notice, or to inquire about it. But now it was evening and after dinner, and he was comfortably seated in an arm-chair in the sitting-room of his boarding-house. He was listening to the usual after-dinner debate on current topics.

'What is that you are saying about the Transvaal signing its own death warrant, Thomson?' he asked.

'I say that the Transvaal signs its own death warrant in agreeing to waive any rights they may have northward or westward of their present boundary. It means that they are now definitely enclosed by British territory with the exception of the strip of border which adjoins Portuguese territory.'

'And what consideration is promised the Transvaal as compensation for committing political and national suicide in this way?' inquired Steve.

'Oh, they have some verbal promise to the effect that they will be allowed to annex Swaziland *later* on, and some faint hope is held out to them to be allowed some day to secure a seaport in Amatongaland.'

'But if they have Swaziland and Amatongaland beyond, right up to the sea, thus securing a seaport, how can they be enclosed? That means that they would be less enclosed than they are now by British territory.'

'Ha, ha!' laughed Thomson. 'Do you think they will ever get it? No, my dear fellow, I am sorry to disappoint you, but a verbal promise does not count in diplomacy. Swaziland they may get—perhaps—but a seaport—never. It was only a bait held out to the stupid Boers. The bait will be drawn in gradually, until the Boers are enticed into the trap laid for them, when even the bait will be taken from them, and they will be starved out in the trap, until, like a starved and trapped lion, they will have to submit. The joke of the whole thing is that Hofmeyr, the head of the Colonial Afrikander Bond, has been used by Rhodes to accomplish his object.'

'Yes, you are right. But it is not a joke, it is disgraceful, shameful, to be bitten thus by your own dogs. I wonder that a man like Hofmeyr—who is supposed to be a patriotic Afrikander—cannot see what he is assisting to do. Can't he see that he is assisting Rhodes to kill all the national vitality of the Afrikander race in South Africa? Does he not know that round the independence of the Transvaal revolves the whole hope of Afrikander national existence? Is he blind, or is he a traitor? I used to be proud of the Afrikander Bond, but now I am beginning to be ashamed of them, when they support a man like Rhodes. A man who works, firstly, for self-aggrandizement, and secondly, of course, for Imperialism.'

All the Englishmen present laughed at Steve's earnestness and bitterness against Hofmeyr for working thus against the Transvaal. But they were accustomed to his earnest patriotism, and respected him for it.

'Well, old boy, it may be that Hofmeyr has been squared by Rhodes; who knows? Rhodes is known for his squaring propensities. Or it may be that Hofmeyr is wiser than you, and has seen that it is foolish to kick against the pricks, and that it is better to belong to the glorious British Empire, with its traditions of military power and glory, its traditions of wealth in gold and literature.'

'It may be so,' replied Steve; 'but as a leading Afrikander, I would rather hope and believe that he is only blind, and that some day his eyes will be opened, and that he shall see Rhodes as he is. As to cornering the Transvaal, let them go on. Only I would warn our enemies that though we are a quiet and peace-loving people, preferring to till the land and herd our cattle to fighting, yet I say I warn Rhodes and his clique that an Afrikander at bay is fiercer and more dangerous than any tiger or lion at bay, so let them look out.'

'But, Steve, why are you such an intense Republican? why will you not be satisfied to live under the English flag? Then you would have the right to call upon the whole British Empire to protect you. Then you would be a member of the greatest nation on earth. Then you can say, "I am a subject to a queen upon whose dominions the sun never sets." Is not that better than to have a second-rate republic, with no traditions older than say twenty years; with hardly any literature at all; what more would you have than I have said you would have as a British subject?'

'We would be FREE!' was Steve's curt reply.

'Free! what is the good of being free in a country like this? As I have said, you can only hope to have a second-rate republic, the population of which at best is but a mongrel race.'

'A mongrel race!' echoed Steve. 'We *are* a mixed race, if you like, but a mixture of the best blood of Europe. In our veins run the best blood of France, Holland and Germany. We are descended from heroes; our forefathers have been heroes ever since they left their ancestral homes in Europe for religion and principle: and we are heroes to-day, struggling, as we are, for national existence and freedom, and that against the mightiest empire on earth, as you describe it; but justice and right must prevail in the end. A mongrel race, you say? A race, I say, that has the grandest future before them of any race upon earth. Look at them; toiling sons of Nature! Do they not remind you of the rough diamonds dug out in Kimberley? hardy, strong, persevering, unpretending, but God-fearing as they are. Look at the few of them that have received the least bit of polish. Do they not shine enough to blind your eyes as you look upon them? Wait till they have all been polished and rubbed into shape, and then you will see what a race of men God has raised in this wilderness?' Steve's eyes were shining with enthusiasm. He seemed to see in imagination the future he was describing.

'You have made out a very good case for your people as a nation, Steve, but what will you do with all the Englishmen in South Africa if it should become an Afrikander republic, as you seem to wish and hope? Will you drive them out of the country, or will you let them live an Uitlander race for ever here, as this Government is doing now? Will you exclude them from your future great South African nation?'

'Decidedly not. We should be only too pleased to have them unite with us. I don't know why they should remain Imperialistic for ever. In America they did not remain so! *There* they have united with other nationalities; why should they not do so here? Anyone who desires to become an Afrikander, be he English, Dutch, German, French, or even Russian by birth, all we should wish of them will be to have one object with us in promoting the happiness and peace of Republican South Africa.'

'In short, they may be of whatever European nationality they like, but they must be for *Republicanism?*'

'Even so!'

'Now, Steve, you have defeated me at all points, I am almost bound to confess. It is a glorious object towards which you are tending, viz., a great and free *united South Africa.* But why does not your Government, whom you defend so much, make some beginning towards a union of the races by granting the franchise to all Uitlanders in this State?'

'Because the time has not come yet. To grant the franchise now to everyone would be simply killing our future great nation in its infancy. Grant the franchise now to all strangers (of which the great majority are English), and in a year's time this country will be governed, either as an English republic, with capitalistic rulers, or as an English colony, neither of which are desirable, you will grant—from our standpoint. While, if we had South Africa united as a republic, there would be no obstacle in the way of granting the franchise to everybody, as the main object would be attained then, and we would be strong enough to hold our own against any party of either foreigners, Imperialists or capitalists who may seek to overthrow us again.'

'Even there I must say you are right; I am almost inclined to become an Afrikander already. Now I am afraid you will not be able to answer my next question as well. You may think it immaterial, but I think it of great importance, that a people and a country should possess a literature of its own. What have you to say to that?'

'Of course we cannot pretend to possess a varied and extended literature like England has. There can be no question of rivalry as yet. But we are not altogether without a literature of our own. We have our own patriotic songs, and even poems. We have a few authors, too, of whom we need not be ashamed, chief amongst these we count Mrs Cornwright Schriener, whose thoughtful book is read all the world over. Then we have the literature of our mother countries—Holland, France and Germany. We love to read the stories which tell of the vicissitudes of our forefathers in their own countries. We even take a sort of sad delight in reading of the persecutions our ancesters had to undergo for their religious opinions; persecutions which led either to the scaffold, or to banishment. Then, as I have said, we have the literature of Holland and other countries which has been translated into our language. We read all historical, religious, secular poetry or prose; all is grist to our mill, we only seek knowledge, and as we are thoroughly cosmopolitan, we care not from whose experience or knowledge, we can learn.

'Then we have hope of future advancement in this line. Rome was not built in a day, and you cannot expect us to be the only exception to the rule, that it takes time to perfect all things. As education advances, and we begin to feel more and more that we are a people of some account, our national abilities will develop, and we may expect to gradually advance towards perfection in all things, such as national administration, education, literature, etc. Give us time!'

'Well, I am glad to see that you are honest enough to acknowledge your defects, as well as to extol your virtues and natural abilities. I certainly grant the material for developement is there. It was only a week ago I saw a manuscript poem, which was written by a brick-maker, a poor Boer, who, unkempt, ill-clothed and unshaved, appeared to me as if he were incapable of stringing two thoughts together, and yet, as far as I could understand the short poem, which was written in the *Taal*, was admirable and forcible enough, though crude and rough in expression. I fancy if such a fellow had received a fair education he would have done something.'

'Talking about natural abilities,' remarked Theron, 'I saw a couple of gravestones, made by one Joubert of thi district, at his farm, the other day. It was made from a design in a book of patterns supplied to him by a friend It was simply splendid! The angels, vines and flowers, as shown in the pattern, were brought out in grand relief and were most accurately delineated. I do not think the most skilled artisan could improve on it. Then there were a few others made from designs of his own, composed of flowers, ferns and other natural objects, all in the best of taste and design, and in perfect proportion. This man had never been taught sculpture, engraving or any of the kindred arts; it was simply his own natural taste and ability cropping out.'

'Yes,' remarked another one, 'I have often wondered at the skill of some Boers, as shown in the manufacture of various articles of furniture and nick-nacks generally. They seem to do it all without being taught or shown.'

'What surprises me more than all,' remarked Harrison, 'is the oratorical powers displayed by some of these uneducated Boers. I attended a sitting of the Volksraad the other day, and the speeches were simply grand. The earnestness and pointed argument, as well as the connected phrasing, was most surprising from men who had received no more education than how to read their Bible and to crudely write an ordinary letter. Then I attended a funeral a short time ago, at which a leading member of the Volksraad gave a funeral oration as well as a really good sermon; and, listening to him, I could hardly believe that I was not listening to a learned and perfectly educated minister of the Gospel.'

'You have only to read some of the letters on public questions, such as often appear in the Dutch papers, written by them, to get some idea of the natural abilities of the unlearned Boer,' remarked Steve, rising and leaving the room, as he was tired and wanted to go to bed.

CHAPTER II

A GREENHORN

TWELVE months passed after this—uneventfully, so far as Steve's private life was concerned. But at this time he had an attack of malarial fever, which left him weak and pale. He decided to take a week's holiday, and spend it at the farm of an old farmer who had often asked him to pay him a visit.

After a couple of days' stay at this farm, he found his health and strength coming back to him. On the third day of his stay, he went for a walk, accompanied by Fritz, the son of his host, and a Hollander who had only just arrived the day before to take up the position of tutor in the family of the old farmer.

Fritz was a merry, mischievous young fellow of eighteen; and as he was considered old enough to assist his father in looking after the farm, he was not a pupil of the new teacher, and therefore considered himself at liberty to make as much fun of the *green* Hollander as opportunity offered. During the walk above mentioned, Fritz had taken the opportunity to begin *Mijnheer van der Tromp's education*, as he termed it.

'How is he going to educate the children while *his* education is being neglected?' was his question, in answer to his father's remonstrances.

He began the Hollander's education by marching him through the orchard, in Steve's company, and giving him the names of the different kinds of fruit and vegetables —all wrong, of course.

'Do you see this tree, mijnheer? It is the sweet potato tree,'—it was a peach.

'Oh, you don't say so! Do sweet potatoes grow on such a tall tree? I should like to taste some of them when they are ripe.'

'And this is a pine apple tree,' remarked Fritz, pointing out a fine banana bush.

'How wonderful Nature is,' soliloquised the poor city bred Hollander. 'Everything in Nature has its peculiar wonders, and is made by God with its own peculiar habits.'

'And this tree, teacher, which you see is full of beautiful yellow ripe fruit, is our South African fig?'

continued Fritz, now drawing the attention of the teacher to a fine specimen of the prickly pear. (Turkish *fig* is the Dutch name for it literally translated.)

'What, are these figs? and are they fit for eating now?' asked Mijnheer van der Tromp.

'Oh, yes, teacher, and I can assure you they are delicious eating too,' replied Fritz, turning away and walking on. Of course Fritz knew what was going to happen. Steve had walked on a few paces, as he was afraid he would be unable to contain his laughter if he listened any longer to Fritz's fooling; so the poor Hollander was perfectly at the mercy of Fritz, as Steve did not overhear the information just given about the prickly pear.

The first intimation Steve had of what was going on was when he heard suppressed laughter behind him. He looked round, and at what he saw he thought that both his companions must have taken leave of their senses. Fritz was red in the face from laughing, as he lay on the grass, throwing his hands and feet about in the air like the four arms of a windmill. He seemed to be absolutely mad.

As to the poor Hollander, his actions were almost indescribable. He was standing, holding his arms out full length, fingers extended, while his head was held out forward, with his capacious mouth open to its full extent, and an expression of agony was depicted upon his countenance, while he was uttering such inarticulate sounds as a man could utter while holding his mouth open without moving tongue or lips. What had happened was this. The Hollander, as soon as Fritz's back was turned, had seized one of the most tempting looking prickly pears, and had taken a hasty bite out of it. The result was that the inside of his mouth was covered with hundreds of the minute needle-pointed thorns. Only those who have felt the irritating pain of a prickly pear thorn in the mouth can understand the torture poor Van der Tromp had to endure. Steve led him home, where he was seated on a low stool for hours following, while the members of the family took turns to hunt the thorns out of his mouth.

But prickly pear thorns are not picked out of a man's mouth in one day, especially after they have been planted there in such a wholesale manner, as was the case with Van der Tromp. For days after those thorns *would* intrude themselves upon the attention of the teacher. Every time he would make sure that not a single thorn was left in his mouth. But suddenly, every half hour or so, while Van der Tromp was eating, singing, or speaking, an expression of agony would pass over his countenance as another of those little demon thorns would make itself felt. And then every other occupation would be suspended while that little thorn was being hunted for.

Of course, Fritz did not think, or expect, his little joke to turn out such a serious matter for the poor teacher. The most he hoped for was that the teacher would pluck the prickly pear, and thus feel the thorns. He never thought that Van der Tromp would *bite* the fruit. When he saw the agony of Van der Tromp, he was genuinely sorry, and apologised most humbly, but I am afraid he was never forgiven.

CHAPTER III

GOLD BEYOND THE DREAM OF AVARICE—DESPISED

THE following day Steve and Fritz went for another walk, farther this time, but alone. Van der Tromp was still occupied in digging out prickly pear thorns.

During the night a heavy thunder storm had raged; the air was pure and fresh, so that the young men walked far out into the veld, as they enjoyed the bright face Nature had put on after the storm.

When they had walked some distance, they met a herder herding some sheep belonging to Fritz's father. He came up to them, and showed Fritz a bar of metal two feet long and about one inch in diameter, more or less, as it was of irregular thickness.

'See, baas, what a nice piece of brass I found. The rain of last night had washed it clean, so that I saw it shining amongst the rocks.'

Steve took it from him and examined it closely, and felt the weight of it.

'Where did you get this, boy?' he asked.

'I found it sticking to two rocks, baas. Each end of it was fast on to a rock, so that it was a sort of little bridge between the two pieces of rock.'

'Come and show me and Baas Fritz the place.'

The boy went on ahead to show the place as requested.

'Do you think it is gold, Steve?' asked Fritz.

'I am sure of its being gold. There must be lots of it, too, if it can be picked up in this way,' was the answer.

The boy stopped and pointed to some rocks which were lying in the cleft of a low hill. The cleft was a little rivulet when it rained, as the sides of the hill sloped down to it, thus causing all the water to run towards it, and so form a temporary stream.

The boy pointed to two masses of quartz forming the two banks of the cleft or ravine. He showed them the marks where he had broken off the bar of gold.

The young men examined the masses of rock or quartz closely. Steve took a large stone and knocked two small pieces off the quartz, and looked at the freshly-broken surface. It was interlaced with gold! They examined an outcrop of quartz further on, and found it to be as rich as the other. Fully twenty-five per cent. of the quartz seemed to be gold.

Fritz had whispered to Steve not to let the boy know what it was. He had to put forth great self-control to restrain his excitement.

They turned quietly back and walked home.

'I say, Fritz, this means that you are going to be one of the richest men in the country. There is not another such mine of gold in the world as this one is going to be.'

'Wait and hear what the old man says about it first,' said Fritz.

'What do you mean?' asked Steve.

'Wait,' was the laconic reply.

They arrived home and found the old man superintending the planting of some *shade* trees near the house. They went up to him, and showed him the bar of gold discovered by the boy.

'See, father, what April found,' said Fritz.

'What is it?'

'Gold,' said Steve.

The old man stood looking at them for fully a minute, then asked for an explanation. He was told all that had taken place.

He did not say a word, but Steve could see that he was by no means pleased. In the evening, when the herds were all safely in the kraal, Steve, Fritz and the old farmer were sitting on the stvep smoking. In front of the stvep half-a-dozen cows and heifers were standing. The old man had ordered them to be driven out of the herd, and to await his further orders.

April the herder, and discoverer of gold, was sent for. He came.

'April,' said the farmer, 'I believe your time is up at the end of the week?'

'Yes, baas.'

'Do you intend going home then?

'Yes, baas!'

'I owe you three heifers for your time of service, do I not?'

'Yes, baas!'

'Well, there are six. Three in payment for your service, and three if you will leave to-morrow morning early without saying a word to anyone, and I want you never to come on my farm again. You must also promise me never to tell anybody about the copper you found on the stone to-day. Do you promise?'

The Kaffir was amazed. To receive double his salary, and to go before his time was up, with an order never to return again, was incomprehensible to him. However, he gave the promise required, and left.

Steve could hardly make out the drift of the old man. He simply stared in surprise at his host.

'Now, Stephaans, I want you also to promise me never to tell anyone of the gold on my farm, unless I give you permission to do so.'

'Of course, Oom Hans, if it will spoil your chance of getting a good price for the mineral rights, I will say nothing about it. But what is the good of keeping it secret? You ought to make it known as much as possible, then you will be able to get the highest offer.'

'Stephaans, you do not seem to understand. I do not want to sell the mineral rights of my farm, nor the farm itself. I only wish to live quietly and at peace on my farm.'

'But why so, Oom Hans? Consider the price you could get for a farm with quartz on it like this?' said Steve, taking out a piece of the quartz he had put in his pocket in the morning. 'You could buy a dozen other farms for the money, and have still enough left to live on to the end of your days.'

'I do not want any more riches than I have. I have enough to live on, and enough to leave my children when the Lord should take me away. Why should I sell my farm? My father and mother lived and died here. They are buried here, and here I wish to be buried when I die. It is not good for us to have too much of the riches of the world.'

'But, Oom Hans, God has placed the gold there to be used, and it would be sinful to leave it there, buried under ground, or the Lord might say to you when the time of reckoning comes, "I have given you so many talents of gold to work with, and to do good with, and to win other talents with; but ye buried it under ground and used it not as I directed ye, ye bad and unfaithful servant, go forth into the outer darkness." Consider, Oom Hans?'

The old man shook his head.

'No, Stephaans, we do not see the matter in the same light. When I feel that the Lord wishes me to leave my farm, and let the gold be dug, I will tear from my heart the love I have for my home and my birthplace, and leave it. But I do not feel so yet. No one will lose by it; I shall be the only loser; but the loss I consider gain, so long as I can keep my home unpolluted by the drunken, the profane, the blasphemer, the canteen-keeper. These you know are always to be found where gold is being dug.'

And no amount of arguing or talking on the part of Steve could induce the conservative old farmer to change his views. He again made Steve promise not to tell of the gold, lest the Government should take the bit in its own mouth and proclaim his farm as public gold diggings.

CHAPTER IV

THE JEW

THE following day Steve's host had decided to go to Johannesburg to arrange about the sale of some slaughter bullocks. He invited Steve to go with him and act as interpreter. Steve said he should enjoy the drive, and went.

After business was concluded, Steve and Oom Hans were seated at a table in a *café*, partaking of some refreshments. On the opposite side of the table were seated two Jews, discussing some samples of quartz before them.

At last one of the Jews turned towards Oom Hans,

with the usual insinuating familiar manner of the Jew and said,—

'Mijnheer, don't you tink dis quartz is goot? Dere ought to pe lots of gold in it?'

Oom Hans indulged in his usual quiet, good-natured laugh, and, turning to Steve, said,—

'Let us make the hearts of these Jews ache a little. Show them a piece of the quartz you put in your pocket, but (aside) mind you don't tell them our names or where we live?'

Steve smilingly took out a piece of quartz—it was by no means the best, and handed it to the Jews, and asked,—

'What do you think of that?'

The Jews took the quartz, looked at it, and nearly jumped out of their boots from excitement when they saw the richness of the quartz.

They laughed, they shouted, they danced They called for coffee, tea, lemonade, and a dish full of the nicest cake in the establishment, and placed it before the strangers, who carried *such* samples of quartz about them.

'*Eet, mijnheer, drink, mijnheer, ons zal betaal*'—'eat and drink master, we will pay.'

When they had quieted down, the Jews came and seated themselves near to Steve and Oom Hans, and started pumping operations.

'Is dis quartz from your farram, mijnheer?'

'Yes,' was the uncompromising reply.

'Where do you lif, mijnheer?'

'In the Transvaal?'

'Yes; put where? What district?'

'Oh, in one of the districts?' was the laughing rejoinder.

'Near what town, mijnheer?'

'Oh, within a thousand miles of Johannesburg?'

The Jews laughed as if this was a very good joke. They were confident of getting round this stupid old Boer.

'Will mijnheer not have a drink—whisky, prandy, or gin, whatever you like?'

'No, thank you. We do not drink strong drink,' interfered Steve. They had not touched the refreshments supplied by the Jews.

'What is mijnheer's name?' continued Jew No. 2.

'Hans?'

'Yes; put Hans what?—your family name, I mean?'

'Oh, just Hans; that is enough for you,' said Oom Hans, laughing. The eagerness of the Jews amused him.

'Well, look here, Mijnheer Hans, what will you take for your farm?'

'Nothing?'

'What!'

'Nothing?'

'What do you mean?'

'I don't want to sell it!'

'Not at any price? I will give you a big price for it.'

'No; I do not want to sell at any price.'

'Not for a hundred tousand pound? two hundred tousand pound? five hundred tousand pound? Come, if you show me a reef like that quartz on your farm, I shall give you one million pounds. Don't say no, mijnheer—*Ten hundred tousand pounds?*'

'No, I don't want your money.'

'You tink I have no money! Come to the bank, I will show you. You tink you get more from annuder man. I tell you one million pound very much monies. Ask the young man!' pointing to Steve.

'No, I don't want your money. Come, Stephaans, let us go.'

The Jew ran towards the door and said,—

'Don't go yet, Mijnheer Hans. I give you what you ask; you make your own price. Or I tell you what, you keep your farm, you just tell me where it is, you show me the place that sample comes from, and I will give you five tousand pound—ten tousand pound,' eagerly added the Jew, visions of a rich prospector's mijnpacht floating before his eyes.

Oom Hans was getting tired of this, as well as annoyed at the Jew's perseverance. He must get rid of him.

'I will think of it, and let you know to-morrow,' he said.

'Where shall I see you?'

'If I want to do business with you, I will come here at ten o'clock to-morrow,' was the non-committal reply.

Steve and Oom Hans went to the boarding-house, where they had secured a room. They noticed that the Jews followed them, and after having seen them into the boarding-house, left again, apparently satisfied that they could lay their hands on the old Boer when they wanted him. But they counted without their host. The old man paid his bill before going to bed; and when the sun rose, he and Steve were far on their way home.

CHAPTER V

THE JEW AGAIN—DISCOURAGED

STEVE was once more in Pretoria. He had been for a week back in work, when one evening, as he was walking leisurely home from business, he heard an eager exclamation of joy behind him. The next moment his arm was firmly caught hold of, and he heard a Jewish voice, not quite unfamiliar, saying,—

'Oh, mine tarling poy, how I have looked for you; oh, praise pe to father Abraham, I have found you.'

Steve's hand was snatched up eagerly and joyfully shaken. It was one of the Jews they had met in Johannesburg.

'Oh, how I have looked for you, mine frint. I have

made two horses tie, so I have rode them, to find you, and your honest old frint. Come, come, let us go into this bar and have a bottle of fiz.'

'No, thank you, I do not take wine or spirits, and I have no time now to talk to you,' replied Steve, annoyed at the scene the Jew was creating in the street, causing the passing people to stand and stare at the vehement joy of the Jew.

'But, my frint, I must speak to you, I can't let you go now, after looking so long for you; I tell you I have been everywhere trying to find you, from the day I saw you in Johannesburg. Oh, no, I will not let you go; you must speak to me, I have much to tell you.'

Steve saw it was no use trying to get rid of the Jew in this way.

'Come to my room, and do not talk so loud in the street,' said he, walking rapidly on, the Jew sticking to him like a leech.

'Now, quick, what do you want from me?' said Steve, as he handed the Jew a seat in his room.

'Oh, come, you know I want to puy de gold farm of your friend—what's his name?' said the Jew, thinking to catch Steve off his guard.

'Never mind his name now. As regards buying his farm, he has already declined doing business with you. Why do you pester me now about a thing that is settled?'

'Oh, he will sell to me, I shall give lots of money, only tell me where I can find him, that is all I ask of you?'

'I certainly shall not tell you where to find him, so you might as well go home.'

'Look here, young man, you are not rich, I will make you rich if you will only bring me to the farm, so that I can speak to him myself. I will give you one tousand pounds for only telling me the man's name and address.'

The Jew mostly spoke with a fairly good accent, but whenever he got excited, he dropped into his Jewish accent.

'I shall *not* give you his name and address, not for a thousand pounds or more,' was Steve's reply. The Jew looked surprised, but he thought Steve must be *sticking* out for a better offer.

'I shall give you two thousand pounds, only for a name and address,' he bid again.

Steve shook his head.

'Young man, don't tread your fortune under feet; you will never get such an opportunity again; I shall make you a good final offer now. Give me the name and address, tell me where you got that sample of quartz from, and I shall give you *five thousand pound*, and if I secure it, I shall give you *ten thousand pound*, now is your chance, take it.'

Steve smiled at the persistance of the Jew. He sat thinking for a minute or two, while the Jew sat watching him eagerly. At last he said,—

'I will tell you what I will do. I shall go out to-morrow and see the gentleman. I will do my best with him. If I can persuade him to see you, I will tell you so the day after to-morrow; if you can succeed to buy the farm from him, I will accept your offer, if not, then I do not want your money. Good night.'

The Jew saw that he would get nothing more from Steve, but he left perfectly satisfied apparently.

Steve obtained leave of absence for the following day that same evening. The following morning he left early on horseback.

Several times while riding on he fancied he heard hoof-strokes behind him, but the country was undulating, and covered with patches of trees, so that he could see a very little of the road behind him; besides, he did not attach much importance to the fact.

When he arrived at the farm of Oom Hans, he immediately told him all the Jew had said and done. Oom Hans was annoyed that the Jew should have discovered Steve, and preached a little sermon to himself for having indulged in what he considered at the time a little harmless pleasantry. But he could not help laughing that the Jew should have been hunting for him so long and so earnestly.

'Well, Steve, if you think it hard on you that your promise to me prevents you from accepting the Jew's offer of five thousand pounds for my name and address, I will release you from your promise; tell him my name and address, but I warn you I will make it hot for him should he come here.'

'Oom Hans, I hope you do not think so badly of me as to think I would break my promise to you for five thousand pounds. No, I will never tell the Jew unless you change your mind as to the selling of the farm; besides, it would be very dishonest to take the Jew's money, if I know that he will get nothing for it.'

At this moment a knock was heard at the door.

Oom Hans looked out of the window to see who it was. He turned to Steve, with anger on his face, and said,—

'So, then, you come to me like a hypocrite, and pretend that you come to ask my permission to give the Jew my address, while all the time you had the Jew waiting for you outside.'

'What do you mean, Oom Hans?'

'Come and look for yourself.'

Steve looked, and there the Jew was standing on the stvep, waiting for an answer to his knock. Steve remembered the hoof-strokes he had heard behind him. He saw that the Jew had been watching and following him.

'Oom Hans, I give you my word of honour that what I told you was the truth, and that I know nothing of the Jew's being here, except that I think the knave has been following me without my knowledge.'

Steve's voice and manner conveyed the truth of what he was saying to Oom Hans. He was believed. This made the old man all the angrier with the Jew.

He went to the door, opened it, and looked at the

Jew. The Jew flew towards him with open arms, and an angelic smile of affection on his face.

'Oh, mine frint, how I have wished for you,' and the Jew went on in a flow of affectionate terms.

Oom Hans coldly waved him off, and said, 'Wait a moment.' He went in again, closing the door after him. He went to a shelf, took down a rusty old elephant gun, as large as a young cannon. He poured about a quarter of loose gunpowder down the capacious barrel, rammed down half a newspaper by way of a plug, and went out again, putting on as severe a face as he could.

Steve came out now and took Oom Hans by the arm, saying,—

'For God's sake, Oom, don't shoot the man!'

'Be quiet, you fool!' roared Oom Hans, and turning round, he winked at Steve, giving him a momentary smile to reassure him. Steve saw that it was only going to be a farce, and not a tragedy, as he at first feared.

Oom Hans now turned to the trembling Jew, who stood quaking with clasped hands, afraid to run, and afraid to stay.

'My God, these Boers are terrible when angry,' he muttered.

'What do you say?' roared Oom Hans.

'I say, sir, that the Boers are the best people in the world, and that the English are dogs.'

'Say that again, and I shall send a bullet through you in a moment. The English, sir, are our friends, while they live at peace with us, so be careful what you say.'

'The English are a good people, sir. Oh, yes, they will always be the best friends of the Boers.'

'Silence, you dog! You say that because you are afraid of my gun. Now, look here, is that your horse there?'

'Yes, sir, I will make you a present of him, if you want him.'

'Silence! I will count ten to give you time to get on your horse, and ten to get out of gunshot, after that I fire.'

'Oh, but, sir, I come to do pisness; I bring you lots of monies. Just listen one word.'

'One!'

'One word only, sir,' said the Jew, tears running down his eyes.

'Two!'

The Jew began to retreat, still praying for an interview.

'Three!'

The Jew was now running.

'Ten!' he heard shouted at him, as he mounted his horse. He waited no more after that, he used spur and whip to urge his horse forward. He thought that he had gone but a short distance, when he heard a report like the report of a cannon behind him.

'Oh, father Abraham, receive my soul,' he prayed, 'for I must be hit; a Boer never misses.'

He was surprised to feel no pain or wound.

'Now, I must race, before he can load again,' he muttered, applying spur and whip with fresh energy, as he lay forward on the neck of the horse.

When Steve and Oom Hans recovered from their fit of laughter, into which they had fallen at the sight of the Jew's fear of a charge of loose gunpowder, they saw the Jew disappearing on a rise about a mile away, his arm still rising and falling as he lashed his horse furiously. The Jew must have done the distance from the farm to Pretoria in record time that day, as he was seen by several people on the road, riding his horse at full speed, looking back every minute to see if he was pursued.

He was never seen on that farm again.

CHAPTER VI

HISTORY *A LA* RHODES

WE shall pass on now to more stirring times in the life of Steve, who has grown into a strong young man of twenty-seven years of age now. He has always borne in mind the dying words of his father, and has never neglected his weekly letter to his mother and sisters, or his monthly contribution towards their house-keeping at home. He had kept that part of his promise to his father to the best of his ability. As to the patriotic promise his father had obtained from him, that was hardly ever out of his thoughts. Walking in the quiet suburban walks in which he delighted, the thought of his country and his race was ever with him. If he could not sleep at night, the same thoughts occupied his mind. And many a plan did he think out—only to reject—as to how his people could be raised up to a higher level as a nation, or how they were to be united in all the states and colonies, as a free and united people.

He had watched the political events in South Africa closely. He saw that the Republics were slowly being driven into a corner by the great Imperialistic amalgamator.

He fancied that he could see how Rhodes was using the Afrikander Bond of the Cape Colony to manufacture a rope, which was intended to be used eventually to strangle their own hopes of national existence.

There was only one doubt in his mind. Was Rhodes working for Imperialism on behalf of the British Empire? or was he so flattered by being called the *South African Napoleon*, that he wanted to really earn that name, and to build up a new empire, with himself as emperor? However, whichever of the two was intended by Rhodes, both must be resisted to the death. We neither desire to be a united British colony, nor a united South African

Empire. We wish to be a united South African Republic. Such were Steve's thoughts on the matter. But everything seemed to be tending towards a crisis. He felt that the time was not far distant when it would be decided whether a great new nation would be formed in South Africa by the fusion of the races, or whether South Africa would be put down, and kept down as a vassal state, for, perhaps, another decade, or maybe two decades. He never doubted that in the end South Africa would fulfil its destiny, and become a great Free country.

Steve had watched with pain how the Republics were robbed of all just claims for northern extension, through delusive promises of eastern extension towards the sea-coast. He had seen the formation of the British South African Chartered Company; only another name, he said, for an anti-Boer company.

He had seen how this company had dispossessed Afrikander holders of concessions in Mashonaland. How this company had robbed and deprived poor Lobengula of country and life on the shallow pretence of Matabele aggression in Mashonaland. Ah, if a *Boer* republic had done what the Chartered Company did in Matabeleland, how they would have been reviled, how they would have been abused. New names would have been invented to call the Boers by, as the English language had already been exhausted on them when they defended their own country. How the Boers were called murderers, slaveholders, and God knows what more, when they subdued two rebellious chiefs in Zoutpansberg in the interest of law and order. After having treated those two chiefs with the greatest consideration and kindness, both before and after their subjection, the Boer haters invented lies and deeds of cruelty never perpetrated in order to blacken the name of Boer before the world. But Rhodes and his followers were called 'Napoleons,' 'heroes,' and all sorts of high-sounding names, for doing what no Christian man in the world ought to have countenanced—shooting down naked human beings, armed partly with comparatively harmless assegais, or in their hands harmless rifles, in hundreds and thousands, with Satanic inventions of machine guns. Ah, God! how long wilt thou permit the strong to murder the weak? All those hundreds and thousands of poor innocent human beings were murdered or driven starving from their homes, for the sole reason to make a dividendless company pay dividends—Civilisation? The sooner such civilisation is swept from off the earth the better it would be for humanity in general. It must be remembered that these Matabeles were not rebels, but were fighting in defence of their own country, which up to then had been free and independent.

Steve saw how the Chartered Company was not yet satisfied. They must have Khama's land too. Poor Khama went to England to ask the Great White Queen for protection, for he had had a terrible object lesson in Lobengula, and knew what his fate would be. Khama had a partial success. He was at least safeguarded against total extinction by the Chartered Company.

The attention of the Chartered Company was now given to the rich and free republic—the Transvaal—with whom England held treaties of peace and amnesty. But what does that matter to a Chartered Company, or to a Rhodes, a Jameson?—we shall see!

Steve saw how all the injustice done to the Afrikander race by England at Slachtersnek, in Natal, at Boomplaats, Kimberley, and during all the existence of the Transvaal as a Dutch Afrikander State, was finally capped by the English in annexing Amatongaland.

Where does the injustice come in?

We have already seen how, through Mr Hofmeyr and others, the Transvaal was promised the incorporation of Swaziland with the Transvaal, and a passage to the sea through Amatongaland, on condition that the Transvaal gave up all rights towards northern expansion.

Transvaal subjects had obtained concessions in Mashonaland previously to those obtained by the agents of Rhodes. The Transvaal kept its promise. Transvaal subjects were forced, by a proclamation issued by the President, to stop a trek towards Manacaland to take possession of country in that territory, ceded to them by its legal owners; and Rhodes and company were left in undisturbed possession. How was the agreement fulfilled by the other side? Only after long, patient and persevering waiting the Transvaal was at last reluctantly allowed to incorporate Swaziland in a half-hearted sort of way. But—

The Transvaal had obtained the cession of Amatongaland from its legal owners—the chiefs of the tribes living there. When the Transvaal asked England to ratify the annexation of Amatongaland, according to the agreement made with said chiefs, England refused, on the plea that, if it should be decided later on that Swaziland should fall to British rule, Swaziland would be inaccessible to England, as it is almost surrounded by Transvaal territory, and that Amatongaland was the only passage open to Swaziland for England in such a case. However, the Transvaal was given to understand that its claim was *legitimate;* and that, in case Swaziland was ceded to it, there would be no difficulty raised to its expansion towards the sea *via* Amatongaland.

When Swaziland was given up to the Transvaal, because England could hardly do otherwise, as Swaziland belonged to the Transvaal by all the rules of nations—Swaziland really belonged to the Transvaal, was part and parcel of its territories, lying as it does within its borders, having been kept out of it as a protection (?) for the natives by treaty with England. Well, what did England do when the Transvaal at last had possession of Swaziland? Did she say to the South African Republic, 'Now you have Swaziland, you might as well realise your *legitimate* desires for a seaport; you had better have Amatongaland too, as it means so much to you, and is really worthless to us.'

Did she say that? *One morning the Government of the South African Republic awoke to find that Amatonga-land had been annexed by England on the quiet.*

The Transvaal had received no previous notice from England of her unjust intentions in Amatonga-land, no—such a deed could hardly bear the light of day to fall upon it before it was an accomplished fact; once accomplished, possession is nine points of the law.

South Africa was shocked at such a deed. The Transvaal protested. The Orange Free State protested. Even Natal and the Cape Colonial Government were ashamed of the deed, and disowned all knowledge of it.

Steve had taken note of all this and more.

He had seen how England had unwarrantably interfered in a question which did not concern her in the least. The Transvaal had closed certain drifts between itself and the Orange Free State—mind you not between the Transvaal and British territory—it was a matter of policy to meet the machinations of the Cape Colonial Government under Rhodes, who were trying to strangle the railways of the Transvaal by ox-waggon competition. England interfered, and told the Transvaal that its Government had no right to close those drifts—why? Because England says so, of course! The Transvaal—once more to show its desire for peace—*opened those drifts.*

We have only touched some of of the main points South African history for the last few years, so that we may be understood as the story proceeds.

CHAPTER VII

THE REPTILE PRESS OF SOUTH AFRICA

THERE was one thing which Steve had long noticed, viz., that there could be no doubt of the existence of an organisation formed for the purpose of *killing* the Transvaal as a republic.

This organisation seemed to have taken for a motto,—

'If you want to kill a dog, give him a bad name, and nobody will object to your killing him.'

To achieve this dirty work, newspapers were started in Pretoria, Johannesburg, and all over South Africa. Only one line of conduct seemed to have been laid down for the editors of these newspapers, viz.,—Paint the Government of the South African Republic and Boers generally with the blackest verbal paint you can invent; the editor who can invent the most lies and write the dirtiest libels on the Transvaal and on Boers that editor shall receive the greatest reward.

This programme was well followed.

The amalgamator of mines and countries had chosen his men well.

These editors must be in the possession of dictionaries unknown to the rest of the world. Dictionaries with an alphabetical list of all the bad names ever invented, with the addition of some specially invented for the occasion. The writers for the papers belonging to the organisation for *painting Boers black* seemed to have a special mode of writing their articles. A string of bad names is selected, and manufactured into some tale of Boer cruelty, duplicity, dishonesty, or something of the sort.

This story would be published and taken up by the various papers belonging to the organisation, and any other paper in foreign lands which might be misinformed enough to believe such stories. How England and the rest of the world would be shocked with these tales. How well-meaning people in distant England would cry shame at these savage (?), cruel (?), and dishonest (?) Boers. Ah! this cowardly, strike-a-man-behind-his-back, blacken-a-dog's-name-and-then-kill-him, Boer-hating, anti-freedom, anti-republican organisation knew well that England can yet boast of millions of honest, fair-minded and well-meaning people, who would not allow a free, peace-loving and God-fearing people to be trampled under foot by a speculating, company-mongering, Matabele-exterminating organisation. For this reason, the Boer must first be blackened, his name must be made to stink in the nostrils of the English and European public. It must be made to appear a great deed of chivalry to exterminate these *women-killing* (?), slave-dealing (?), Uitlander-oppressing (?) Boers.

But the sequel has shown that there is a just Heaven above, who watches over countries, empires, republics and peoples as well as over individuals. The machinations of these plotters were made to fall back upon their own heads by a just God. They were made to fall into their own pits, dug for others. Read on and see.

Although evidently directed from Cape Town, the operations of the organisation were centred in Johannesburg, as being the place where the materials to be used for their purposes—*the Uitlanders*—were most plentiful, and, also being in the heart of the Boer Republic, they could strike more to the purpose.

Every pretext was made use of to find fault with Boers and Boer government. Let them come across a God-fearing, religious Boer, and he is described as a hypocritical, sanctimonious, double-faced knave. If, on the contrary, a Boer is met who moves with the surrounding world, speculates, goes to entertainments, or takes a drink at a bar, he again is called a drunken, cheating, parasitical, half-civilised scoundrel.

Again, should the Government take righteous umbrage at haughty and unjust demands from their particular party, and refuse them, the Government is called a tyrannical, autocratic and oppressive government. Should the Government again consider a request fair and just, or tenable in any way, and grant it, then they are jeered at, now they are beginning to be afraid and are obliged to give way. Or, again, it was granted through favouritism, or through bribery. Such was the one-sided criticism indulged in.

Familiarity brings contempt. The Government got to be so accustomed to this one-sided abuse, that they really treated it with the contempt it deserved. This gave courage to the black libellers.

Constant droppings will wear away a stone. The constant hacking and pegging away at the Government began to take effect on the Uitlander public. They began to believe it, saying, 'Where there is smoke there must surely be fire?' At least such was the effect on the least-informed portion of the Uitlander population.

The first visible and material victory obtained by the organisation was the FLAG INCIDENT.

CHAPTER VIII

THE TRANSVAAL'S PRESIDENT AND FLAG INSULTED BY THE UITLANDERS

THE President of the South African Republic is obliged by law to visit outlying districts as much as possible, in rotation, to ascertain the views, grievances and wants of the public.

The turn of Johannesburg came to receive such a visit. The President went there in order to give the public an opportunity to state to him personally what they wanted in the way of improvements generally. If they had any wants or grievances to be redressed, now was their time to say so, and obtain their desires as far as was just and fair. Was this done?

No! When the President mounted the public platform, he was received with groans and hootings. Paid roughs caused a disturbance, which was taken up by the lower element amongst the crowd, and the President had to escape as best he could from the dastardly roughs, who would not have scrupled to lay their hands upon his person. The sacred, beloved flag of the Republic was torn down and rent to shreds.

This was the way Johannesburg sought redress for their grievances.

The loyal public were righteously enraged, and had it not been for the conciliatory speeches of the President later on, the Burghers would not have rested until due revenge had been taken for the dishonour done the chief of their Republic and their flag.

But the Government refused to punish the scoundrels; they hoped to win the Uitlanders over by gentleness and forbearance.

The next grand opportunity for the organisation to revile the Government and the people came with the Malaboch war.

A petty chief rebelled, causing general disorder in the Zoutpansberg district, and setting a bad example to the thousands and tens of thousands of natives living in the district. Malaboch had to be subdued and made to obey the laws of the land or the whole native population would soon have been in rebellion. This was done.

Steve went as a volunteer on the expedition (he having privately got the field cornet to commandeer him). He saw with surprise with what consideration the rebels were treated. They were regarded as a civilised nation; and repeated offers of mercy were made them if they would submit. An invitation was sent them to send out their women and children for safety, which was done, thereby prolonging the siege of the native stronghold, as the provisions held out so much longer.

After the submission of the tribe, they were treated with all kindness. They were conducted to Pretoria and well provided for.

To prevent a repetition of the rebellion, and of their retaking possession of their former almost inaccessible stronghold, the native tribe was broken up (as per precedent established by the English administration in former years), and homes given them elsewhere.

The result of all this was that the Government was abused more than ever before. It was affirmed that the grossest cruelties had been perpetrated on the poor, innocent natives; the Boers made slaves of the natives, etc., etc.

The most ridiculous statement of all was that the Boers ravished the native women! Anybody knowing a Boer would know how impossible this is! A Boer shrinks from touching the hands of the dirty, oily, reeking native; how much more would he shrink from *embracin g*a native woman!

As we have said, Steve had been to the Malaboch war himself. He had seen for himself the treatment accorded the natives, and the lying statements published all over the world made him shiver with disgust and anger.

The following year, with the Magoeba campaign, the same thing was repeated all over. The causes were the same, the effects were the same. Sir · E. Ashmead Bartlette and others of his stamp (either deceiving, or being deceived by others here) made ridiculous and untruthful statements in the House of Commons, in public speeches, or in the daily papers. All this was the result of the wire-pulling, worked by the secret organisation for 'painting Boers black.'

Finally, another grand opportunity came for a general carnival of abuse and lies against the Government of the country—the festivities in connection with the opening of the Delagoa Railway.

Not that we mean to state that these were the only

times when the Government was abused and libelled; daily opportunities were found to distort facts; an ant-hill was made into a mountain; a good deed into one of the blackest imaginable. And when no facts could be found to distort, something was invented by some fiendish imagination. But the festivities offered a grand opportunity for exaggerations and distortions.

The Government was made to spend thousands of pounds sterling on favourites, contracts for decorations were given to favourite Hollanders, money was wasted, the Volksraad vote was greatly exceeded, and goodness knows what besides. It is too sickening to enter into all the petty lying faults that were found.

In this way the Government and people of the country had daily to tamely and quietly hear themselves belittled and besmeared with the lying libels of their foes; it was all patiently and quietly borne; they wished for peace, and were always conciliating. This was taken by the opposition as signifying fear and conscious weakness.

Matters went on in this way until December 1895 was reached. Steve was watching the approaching clouds. He could hear the distant thunder. He could see that a storm was coming, gathering force as it aproached. A crisis was at hand.

It was coming sooner than he could have wished. He knew it was coming, but he would have liked it to have come a few years later, when the Afrikander race, at the rate they were strengthening now, would be considerably stronger and more able to cope with their opponents. But let it come. We shall do our best to conquer, and if it is God's will that we should come out victorious, all praise be to Him. And if it be His will, WE SHALL be victorious! If it be His will that we should be conquered, His will be done; we can but die.

The secret organisation had lately taken more visible and definite form. First, a National Union was formed by a few in the secret. The innocent Uitlander public were led by the nose. When a meeting was convened by the self-elected leaders of the so-called Union, the public were only too glad to attend a meeting where some excitement was promised them. They went to hear the inspired spoutings of their self-elected leaders, and cheered where they were expected to do so, or listened indifferently to eloquent advocates, speculators, etc. Many of them were surprised to be told that they really had any grievances. They had always thought they were better off in this country than they had been in their own land; here they earned good wages, paid little or no taxes, and were left alone and in peace; while in their own countries, they earned very little, of which little they had to pay a large percentage in taxes and rates of one kind or another.

But these learned men say we have grievances; they ought to know! And if we really have any wrongs to be redressed, the sooner it is done the better; so hurrah for these philanthropic (?) gentlemen who are going to redress our wrongs. They say we ought to have the franchise, so the franchise we will have, and so on.

It went uphill, it is true; the agents of the organisation found great difficulty to get the public mind wound up to the right pitch, and when they did succeed for an hour or so to get an enthusiastic audience together, it only lasted for that brief hour.

But even for this want of enduring enthusiasm a remedy was found, viz., a committee was appointed who were supposed to represent the Uitlander population, who made up in themselves for all want of public enthusiasm. Gold could do a great deal; besides, the head of the organisation knew the art of *buying* enthusiasm.

For a time the National Union took a spurt, kept alive by inflaming speeches and circulars; but as soon as a little boom in shares took place, the public would have nothing to do with politics, and again and again the committee found the Union to consist of *themselves*.

This would never do; the objects of the Union would never be attained if something was not done soon.

The plans of the parent organisation were nearing completion. Soon it was rumoured that the president of the Union and other members of the secret organisation were preparing to issue a manifesto, by which means they hoped to once more wind up public opinion, and to inflame the hotter Boer haters to the fullest extent. When once the public were excited enough, a meeting would be held, where revolutionary proposals would be made by certain agents, which, it was hoped, would be taken up and supported by the public. This was December 1895.

CHAPTER IX

THE NATIONAL UNION MANIFESTO

IT is Christmas 1895.

Peace on earth, good-will to all men is supposed to prevail at this season; not so with the enemies of the country.

The President was away on one of his yearly visits to outlying districts. He would return on Boxing Day, expecting everybody to be indulging in the usual festivities of the season.

Alas! it is not so in a certain building in Johannesburg. A group of men are exulting over a document. It is a proof of the famous National Union Manifesto, issued by the chairman of the Union; issued in the name of the Uitlander population, without their consent. On their own responsibility, the chairman of the Union and a few of his fellow-conspirators issued a manifesto with the full and deliberate intention of causing a civil war in South Africa, a war of races—a war, the result of which, and the ending of which, no man could surmise.

Steve went to the station on Boxing Day to see the President arrive by train from his tour. As he was standing talking to an acquantance about the air of mystery and expectancy on the faces of most people in the crowd, he heard a newsboy crying,—

'*The Star! The Star! National Union Manifesto!*'

'Hillo! I might as well buy a copy and see what they have to say,' he remarked, calling the boy and buying a paper. He read it with the closest attention.

The manifesto was composed of several newspaper columns of close printing.

What struck Steve was that, of all the grievances detailed in the manifesto, only one was really worth complaining about, viz., the want of franchise. All the rest were open to difference of opinion, or did not exist at all. After a great deal had been said on one subject or another, a list of ten wants was given:—

Firstly.—'The establishment of *this* Republic as a true Republic.' I wonder if the compiler of the manifesto is an Irishman. He wants a republic to be made a republic; he wants a cow to be turned into a cow; a horse into a horse; a mule into a mule. Why he ought to know that if he *is* a mule, a mule he is.

Secondly.—'A Grondwet or constitution is wanted, which shall be framed by competent persons.' Who? The committee of the National Union, I suppose! No more need be said.

Thirdly.—'An equitable franchise law, and fair representation.' This is the only real grievance that the Union could complain of. But then a poor man sometimes complains because another man is rich and possessed of more than his share of this world's goods. The rich man had patiently worked for and acquired his wealth, the poor man will not work and will not wait for his time to come to make his 'pile.' Let the Uitlander bide his time patiently and earn the right to obtain the franchise, and obtain it he will in the end. We all wish for the franchise and hope to get it by proving to the Government that we wish it well and not harm. But who is going to impoverish himself to enrich his neighbour? Who, when attacked by an enemy, is going to hand over his own revolver to be shot with? That is what the National Union has proved itself to be up to now—*enemies* pure and simple of the Government. Let them show more good-will, more conciliation, more honest friendship, and they may expect more consideration from the Government.

Fourthly.—'Equality of the Dutch and English language is demanded.' This is a Dutch republic, founded by the Dutch, civilised and reclaimed by the Dutch. Dutch is the official language of the country. The English language is given all consideration in courts of law and public offices. English is spoken freely everywhere, in courts of law or other offices of administration. The law is winked at as regards enforcing the use of Dutch. More cannot be claimed at present. If the English language wins its way into further favour no one is going to grumble.

Fifthly.—'Responsibility to the legislature of the heads of the great departments.' That is going to come without the aid of the National Union!

Sixthly.—'Removal of religious disabilities.' The law of the country allows every man to worship and think as he pleases. Only, the holders of office and public officials must be Protestants. *The Transvaal Burghers are mostly descended from Huguenots!*

Seventhly.—'Independence of the courts of justice, with adequate and secured remuneration of the judges.' Even so, we all want that, and are thankful to say 'we have it.'

Eighthly.—'Liberal and comprehensive education.' The State has been striving and aiming towards this laudable object for years, and is striving for it still. Improvements in the department of education are made yearly, and, let us hope, will be continued to be made.

Ninthly.—'Improved civil service and provisions for a

pension fund' is asked. I wonder if the members of the National Union committee had an eye for their own future prospects when they asked for this. Of course they were going to be provided for in the way of offices in the improved government and civil service, and they naturally wished to make provision for their pensions.

Tenthly.—'Free trade in South African products.' Free trade is an old question, and need not be discussed here. If it suits one party it does not suit another, and the products of the State must be protected.

Something like the above were the mental comments of Steve as he read the 'Ten Wants' of the Union. He saw no harm in the ventilating of their wants by the Union, if it is done peacefully and constitutionally, but the implied threat which appears in the question 'How shall we get it?'—that is where he sees the spirit of the manifesto. There is no reason why they should not get all, or nearly all, they ask, if they ask for it in the right way. It all depends upon what they decide to do to get it whether they get it or no; under *threats* they will *not* get it.

The meeting to be held on the 6th January 1896 had to decide.

At last the train with the President on board steams into the station. A line is formed from the saloon carriage to the President's private carriage, and the Transvaal 'Grand Old Man' steps forth, hat in hand, bowing right and left. As Steve gazes upon that firm, calm and strong countenance, all doubt as to the future prospects of his race disappear. With *such* a man as their leader, victory must attend them. He gazes with exultation upon Paul Kruger; he had often seen the President before, but he looked upon him with renewed interest after reading that bouncing manifesto; and as he looked, he fancied he saw before him a stormy sea, the billows roar, the winds blow, and amidst all a strong, firm, upright rock receiving the dashing waves and howling winds against its sides, unmoved. Such was the impression Paul Kruger gave Steve that afternoon. The *simile* was not out of place; the storm was gathering. *Will Paul Kruger remain firm?*

CHAPTER X

A FISHING PARTY ON THE VAAL RIVER

FROM the time of publication of the National Union Manifesto, a cloud seemed to hang over the country. On every street corner and under every verandah where two or three were gathered together, politics were being spoken of. What is going to happen? Was Johannesburg really going to take the bit in its own teeth and go its own way, or was it all only big talk and a case of the Union playing the bogey man to frighten the Government into submission and into giving way to their demands. There *were* a few fiery-minded youths in Pretoria who talked big of the mighty things the Uitlanders were going to do. They were armed; they had twenty Maxims, cannons and small arms in plenty; they were going to remove the Boer Government and raise a government of their own, etc., etc.

But the majority of the Uitlanders living in Pretoria expressed their intention to stand by the present Government. They were not going to have either the Imperial Government again, or a government of capitalists. The former had made too many mistakes in South Africa already to be desired; besides, are we not men, cannot we work out our own salvation? As to the latter, enough of that has been seen in Europe, America and Kimberley. No, we are satisfied with the present Government, and with the improvements we know that we shall get soon. The Government received daily assurances from leading Pretoria meu of staunch support in case of need. Even in Johannesburg, the Government was not in want of many thousands of Uitlander friends.

One hardy old Scotchmen, interviewed by a countryman lately arrived, in answer to the question as to what his intentions were in case of disturbances, replied by pointing to a gun standing in a corner and saying,—

'You see that gun? Well that gun and myself are at the service of Oom Paul whenever he wants us. I am not going to see such an unrighteous thing as deposing a just and kind Government by a lot of capitalists and other knaves.'

Steve, amongst many others, never for a moment supposed that any disturbance or breach of the peace would take place before the 6th January, which was the date appointed by the National Union for their great meeting, when they would decide upon future action. How was he or the general public (mostly concerned) to know of the secret preparations (whispered of, but not believed) made by the conspirators to let the dogs of war—and that civil war—loose on or before the date appointed? How was he or they to know that preparations were far advanced for the invasion of the Transvaal by Chartered troops? The different Governments concerned did not know of it; how could private individuals know?

So Steve and his friends made preparations for a fishing party during the New Year holidays on the Vaal River.

Accordingly, Saturday night saw Steve and his friends embarked on the Cape train *en route* for the Vaal River. They were going by rail as far as Vereeniging, from which place they had made arrangements to leave by a mule waggon, which they had chartered for the week. Arrived at the border town, they loaded their tent and provisions on the mule waggon, expecting to have a quiet but enjoyable picnic on the banks of the Vaal. The site for their camp was chosen about eighteen miles west from Vereeniging, as they wished to be away from the bustle of town life for the few days of rest. Sunday afternoon saw the party comfortably settled on a pretty spot on the river's bank. A few beautiful trees supplied them with the necessary shade from the heat of the sun.

Sunday afternoon and evening were spent in quiet rest, after the necessary operations of fixing up camp were over.

Monday morning early, fishing was begun in earnest. A fairly successful day was spent on the river bank. Towards sundown the party returned to camp.

After coffee had been made and partaken of, Steve proposed that they should go to the little country store, lying about half-a-mile away.

'It will be a nice little walk before supper,' he remarked, 'and, besides, we might hear some news from the shopkeeper, as he is the post-agent here.' His proposal was accepted, and the party strolled forth. Arrived at the store, they found the proprietor to be one Nande. This Nande was an Afrikander born, but an English educated young man; handsome, stout, and well spoken, but slightly deaf. As to his character, that will be sufficiently gathered from his conversation and acts.

After a few trifling purchases had been made in the store, as a sort of introduction, Steve inquired if he had heard any news from Pretoria or Johannesburg to-day.

'Oh, yes, I have heard news, and if it is true, I shall be jolly glad; it will show these miserable Boers that the British people are not to be trifled with. I hear that Jameson has entered the Transvaal with eight hundred troopers, and is marching on to Johannesburg at full speed; it is only a rumour as yet, I heard it at the station this afternoon.'

At the first few words Steve trembled with agitation and apprehension for the Transvaal, for, if this was true, it really meant war with Great Britian, for Jameson and his men were really British troops. But a moment's reflection showed him how improbable such a thing must be. He could not believe England capable of such perfidy. The Transvaal was at peace with England, and had done absolutely nothing to provoke an invasion, or even a talk of an invasion from England. Besides, the last decade of the nineteenth century was not a time when one civilised country invades another, unprovoked and without rhyme or reason. No, the wish was only father to the thought, it was not to be believed for a moment. But what struck Steve with disgust was that this young man, who looked like an Afrikander, appeared to wish for such an invasion, and seemed to glory in the very idea of it.

'May I ask what your name is, sir?' he said, turning to the storekeeper.

'My name is Nande.'

'But that is a pure Afrikander name.'

'So it is. I was born in the Cape Colony, and have been in the Transvaal now for five years.'

'But why do you speak as if you wished for the downfall of our Afrikander Republic?'

'Because I do not think it right that we should be governed by these Boers any longer. Why, they refused to give me a situation just because I could not write Hollander-Dutch; they rather gave it to a Hollander than to an Afrikander.'

'I think that shows their good sense,' replied Steve; 'if you had learned your mother tongue as well as you did English, they would not have refused you.'

'Well, I only hope that Jameson and the Uitlanders will succeed in chucking the whole lot out, then a man who has received an English education will be able to get a Government situation too. I hope to see the British flag flying once more over the Transvaal in a week or so.'

'Hurrah for Jameson and the British flag!' cried Steve's cousin.

This young man had been in the habit of running the English down ever since he had come to the Transvaal, because he thought it good policy, but now that he believed the English were going to be victorious, he thought it was high time to put on his Anglo-Saxon coat and go with the winning party. It is all very well to be an Afrikander while Afrikanderism is popular, and while Afrikanders hold the handle of the knife. But now it seems England is going to wrest the handle out of the hands of the Boers, so 'British I will be now,' was his philosophy—ugh!

Keith and Harrison did not say a word; they seemed to be stricken dumb at what they heard.

'Oh, so you are taking a fit of Anglo-mania, too, now —you—cur, you—dog, you coward.'

'And I am a Britisher too, and I also say Hurrah for Jameson,' cried Nande.

Steve stood with clenched hands, pale as death.

'And I say that the man who turns his coat and stands away from his countrymen in their time of need is worse than a *dog*, is worse than a Kaffir, for even a Kaffir will stand by his people in time of need. You are both dogs—*curs*, and worse than curs, you mongrel Afrikanders.'

'Look here, young man, you must be careful what you say; you must remember we are four against you alone; we will soon take your gas out of you,' said Nande.

'Come on then all of you. One true Afrikander can always *down* half-a-dozen cowardly curs like you. I do not believe a hundred like you would have the pluck to tackle one single Boer. Come on, I am ready for you.'

He stood with his back against the wall, with clenched fists, fierce set face, and gleaming eyes.

Nande snatched an axe handle standing near, and crying to the other three to come on and let us silence this miserable Boer,' he walked in a threatening way to within three paces of Steve. Steve stood calmly but determinedly awaiting the attack. When Nande stopped three paces in front of him, Steve looked him full in the eyes. Nande could not stand that look; he trembled with fear, and looking away, he turned to the others and said,—

'Are you fellows not going to help me to give this Boer a good thrashing?'

Keith and Harrison looked contemptuously at him, the former remarking that,—

'If any help were required, we would certainly give it to Steve. *He* is a *man*. You are a cowardly renegade. I would be ashamed of you, if you really were an Englishman.'

'Thank God there are very few Afrikanders such as these two,' said Steve. 'It would be a bad lookout for us if there were many such.'

'You are right, Steve,' said Harrison. 'They are about the only two I have ever met. I wish I had the privilege to be a born Afrikander. I would not thus turn renegade, but would be only too happy to fight for my country; and, by God, if this is true about Jameson, I *will* fight for them. If Englishmen can act as treacherously as this, then I shall disown my own country and become a true citizen of this, my adopted country; that, at least, would not be turning renegade, for I should be fighting for the country I live in.'

'And so say I, too,' said Keith.

Nande, seeing how the land lay, and the mistake he had made when he expected to be supported by the young Englishmen, backed out, and retreated behind his counter.

The party now left, and returned to their camp with Steve's cousin slinking on behind them. He kept out of Steve's way for the rest of the evening, as he saw that he was in the minority now, and that was not a *rôle* he delighted in playing.

CHAPTER XI

NEWS OF AN UNEXPECTED INVASION AND BREAK UP OF THE FISHING PARTY

THE next day fishing was resumed. Steve did not attach much credence to Nande's story of Jameson's invasion, so he was not much disturbed about it. He thought he had plenty of time to enjoy his little holiday and to be back home by the 6th January, when he would be able to watch events and be at hand in case his services were needed to defend his country.

What a surprise awaited him!

As the party returned about midday to camp for lunch, they found a young man there who had just drawn rein for a moment to let his sweating horse breathe, and get a drink of water for himself.

'Hillo! Whither away in such a hurry?' hailed Steve in a hospitable way. 'Stay and have lunch with us.'

'I dare not. I am in a great hurry. Have you heard the news?'

'No; what is it?'

'Jameson has invaded Transvaal territory, and is marching on to Johannesburg.'

'My God! is it true after all?'

'Only too true. I am postmaster and telegraphist at H——, and I have just received a wire from headquarters to let the field cornet know at once, with orders for him to *commandeer* every available Burgher without a moment's delay. They are to guard the borders against any further invasion from any other direction. The Burghers from Potchefstroom, Rustenburg and Krugersdorp are ordered to intercept Jameson and to capture him before he enters Johannesburg.'

'May I know your name, sir?' asked Steve.

'Certainly; my name is A——n.'

'But that is a British name, is it not?'

'It is; but I am colonial born, and I consider myself an Afrikander, and I am going to stand by the Afrikanders to the bitter end. My God! do you think I will stand by and see our Republic invaded in such a treacherous manner, and not do all in my power to resist it? I am not obliged to bear dispatches in this way, but for such a cause I would do a great deal more.'

'I am proud to shake hands with you, sir,' said Steve,

suiting the action to the word. 'With such men as you to stand by us, our future is assured.'

'I am glad to see you're one of us, sir, and hope to meet you again in more peaceful times; in the meanwhile, now my horse has had a breathing spell, I must hurry on.'

'One moment, sir,' said Steve. 'I want to leave at once for the scene of action. Which is the best way, do you think, to reach it?'

'I suppose, to take train as far as you can, and where you find yourself stopped, to get a horse (the best way you can), and go on horseback until you reach the place where fighting is going on.'

'Thank you, sir. Good-bye, and God speed the Republican cause.'

'Amen, good-bye, and good luck.'

Steve was intensely excited, his breath came in short, quick gasps. He turned to Keith and Harrison, saying,—

'Look here, you chaps, I do not know what you intend doing, but I can't stay here another hour, I must get away without a moment's unnecessary delay.'

'But, Steve, what could you do if you did go? One man more or less will make no difference. Stay and let us finish our fishing. Time enough to go fighting when we have to go back and our holiday is over.'

Steve shook his head, saying,—

'No, old man, if everybody were to say that, and want to enjoy their New Year festivities before responding to their country's call, then Jameson would have an easy march to Johannesburg. No, I must go. The only question is, How? Will you fellows go too, or will you stay and let me have the mule waggon to the station, then I can send it back to you, and you can stay here and have the full benefit of your holiday.'

'No, Steve, if go you must, I go too,' said Keith.

'And I will go too. If there is going to be excitement on, we might as well be at hand and see what is going on?' said Harrison. 'As to fighting, I do not yet know what I shall do personally, but one thing I am sure of, I am not going to fight against the Boers. If they have to be suppressed, I will take no hand in it, while I may yet decide to fight with them; for if they are really invaded in this back-handed, treacherous way, the sympathy of all right-minded people ought to go with them.'

'Well, if we are to go, the sooner the better,' said Keith, responding kindly to Steve's wishes.

The driver was called, and told to get the mules and inspan at once, while the rest of the party busied themselves in getting everything packed and ready for their departure.

Steve's cousin was not consulted as to his willingness to leave or not; he was in the minority and had to accept the decision arrived at; he was sulking on one side, refusing to render assistance in the preparations for leaving. He was undecided what to do; he was not quite sure yet whether the Boers were going to lose or not, so he thought he would keep quiet a little longer, and see in which way matters tended. No notice was taken of him by the others.

In a short time the driver's assistant arrived with a message to the effect that the mules were lost and must have strayed away. The driver had gone farther to search for them. Steve was in despair.

'My God!' he cried, 'what have I done that this should come to me? Would that I had never left Pretoria, then I might at least have been able to do something.'

'Keith, come with me like a good fellow and help me to bribe Nande into selling or hiring me a horse. I *must* get away.'

'I will go with pleasure, Steve; but I am afraid that after last night's scene, Nande will by no means be eager to render you a favour.'

They went, but in vain. Nande was still feeling very sore at the straightforward words of Steve, and refused absolutely to let him have a horse on any terms whatever. Steve offered to pay any price, but in vain. He attempted threats, but Nande was strong in the knowledge that in this case, law was on his side, and that Steve could not force him to give up his horse.

'Well, Keith, old man, I am going to walk. Good-bye, and thank you for your kindness.'

Keith remonstrated in vain, telling him to wait until the mules were found, and that he could never arrive in time to catch the train if he walked, but Steve was mad with excitement. He felt that inaction was impossible; he must do something, and with one handshake he started on his way on foot. He walked fast and long. It soon began to rain, but he walked blindly on, on and on. 'I must get on. If my people must fight for liberty I must be with them.' He did not heed the water running into his shoes or streaming down his clothing. The road was very indistinct; the water was running over it, so that he was not sure always whether he was on the road or not. It was getting dark. Surely he ought to have reached the station by this time. He had walked six long hours, and he must have covered more than eighteen miles now. Where can the town be? He could barely walk now, he was so tired and so wet, but on and on he struggled. The strongest human passion possessed him: the passion of outraged patriotism. At last he saw a small building in front of him; it was only a small place, but he hoped to find somebody from whom he might inquire his whereabouts. He did find a man there.

'Will you please tell me where I am, sir. I am afraid I have lost my way. I want to go to Vereeniging.'

'Why, sir, you are walking away from Vereeniging. You are about twenty-five miles from the station now. Where are you coming from?'

'I left about one o'clock from Nande's Store on the Vaal River. I am afraid I must have taken the wrong road.'

'Yes, you must have taken the left instead of the right hand road, a few miles after you left Nande.'

'My God! what shall I do now?'

'Where do you wish to go to?'

'I want to reach Johannesburg or Krugersdorp as soon as possible.'

'Well, you are at least twenty miles nearer your destination now than when you left Nande, so your time is not altogether lost.'

'Sir, will you not do me a great favour by selling or hiring me a horse, or tell me where I can get one near by; it is most important that I should lose no time.'

'I am very sorry, but I have no horse; you might get one three miles away, where there is a Boer farm. They have several horses; but come in and have a cup of coffee first. You are wet and cold. I will give you some of my dry clothing to put on in exchange for your wet ones. It would be death for you to keep those wet clothes on.'

Steve accepted with pleasure. He was wet, tired and hungry. He had had nothing to eat since breakfast, as the news received at lunch time had taken away all idea of eating. He entered, had a cup of coffee with a dry biscuit, changed his clothes, and, in spite of his host's invitation to spend the night there, departed.

'No thank you, sir. I thank you for your kindness to me, a stranger. If at any time you come to Pretoria, here is my card. If I can return your kindness, please let me know.'

He proceeded in the direction pointed out to him and soon arrived at the Boer farm. It was a well-appointed substantial building, and it was evident that well-to-do people lived there, so no doubt he would be able to get a horse.

CHAPTER XII

OFF TO THE WAR—A NIGHT'S RIDE—TERRIBLE NEWS

When about two hundred yards away from the house, Steve came across an old bushman with a pail of milk in his hands, evidently coming from the cattle kraals.

'Naand, baas.' (Good evening, baas).

'Good evening, my boy. Who lives here?'

'Baas Meyer lives here, baas.'

'Is your baas in?' Steve asked.

'No, my baas left with his two sons this afternoon, on commando. They say the English are coming to take the country again, and my baas left to fight the English.'

'Who is at home now?'

'Only the *novi* (mistress) and her daughter.'

'What is your name?'

'Jankie, baas.'

'Well, Jankie, here are two shillings for you.'

Steve thought it best to make friends where he could.

'Thank you, thank you, baas,' said the bushman, receiving the coin and slipping it into his mouth.

'Look here, Jankie, is there a good riding horse in the stable?'

'Only young Baas Willim's horse, on which he goes courting.'

'Is it a good horse, Jankie?'

'I have never seen a better one, baas; it is a black stallion. He never gets *flamed* (never gives in).'

'That is just the horse I want, Jankie. Do you think your mistress will lend him to me to go and fight the English?'

'I am afraid not, baas. Young Baas Willim never allows anyone besides himself to ride that horse; but come in and ask the *novi*.'

Steve went up to the house and knocked. The door was opened by a pretty, fair-haired girl, evidently the daughter of the house. He was shown into the sitting-room, the good and well-appointed furniture of which again indicated the wealth of the owners.

Steve asked to see Mijf Meyer. She soon appeared, and without much beating about the bush, Steve stated what he required.

'Madam, I was on a picnic on the Vaal River. There I heard that the English were again invading the country. I want to go and fight against our enemies, but I have no horse to go from here. Will you lend me one?'

'No, sir; you look too much like an Englishman yourself to go and fight against the English. Why do you shame your face, just like the *rooi nekke.* No, sir, I know your people's tricks too well to be caught by you. If a real Afrikander wants a horse to fight the English, he can have all we have, but you look like one who is more likely to help our enemies than to fight for us. I don't know you.'

Steve explained and expostulated, begged and threatened, in vain. The old lady believed him to be a spy and enemy. His looks were against him; and in any case he was a stranger to her; and an Afrikander has never been known to tramp about in city clothes like his looking for a horse; she would neither sell nor lend.

Steve saw that he was distrusted, and that further pleading was in vain. He turned to leave, when the girl came up to him, saying,—

'Sir, you must excuse my mother, but we cannot risk giving an enemy a horse to fight against our own people. Perhaps you know how the Uitlanders have been threatening us lately; my father and brothers are even now on their way to fight against the English, who want to take our country from us again. But if you want food, or anything else, you are welcome.'

Steve thanked her, and told her he could not blame them for distrusting a stranger. 'But,' with tears in his eyes, 'I do so long to be in the fight. I would dearly like to strike a blow for our liberty against our enemies, and now I am so tired I can't walk much farther, and time is passing by. Oh, that I could find a horse.'

He walked out; he was in despair. The tears were running fast down his face, and he was ashamed to let the girl see him weep.

Steve did not walk more than a hundred yards away from the house when he sank down on the ground in a passion of tears and despair.

'Oh, what have I done that I should be caged like this? My countrymen are perhaps even now struggling for life and liberty, and here I am in the open veld, without a horse or means of reaching the commando in time. Oh, my God, send me aid, help me to get away. Oh, God, I would give all I have for a horse to-night. Jesus, thou hast so often answered my prayers before, answer me now, when I ask for a horse to go and fight against our enemy.' He shook with a passion of tears and intense earnestness as he prayed in his despair. Steve had great faith in prayer, and when all else failed, he believed that God would not fail him. As he prayed thus, a feeling of comfort and relief came over him; he fancied he heard a voice say, 'Fear not, my son, thy prayer is heard.' The next moment he felt a touch on his arm; a pale face looked into his eyes. Steve saw that it was the girl he had just left. She was weeping now, too; a great faith in him was shining in her face.

'Oh, forgive us for mistrusting you; I see now that you are one of us. I stood looking after you, I saw you were in trouble, and when I saw you drop down here, I came to see what was the matter with you, and I heard all you said in your grief and despair. Come with me, God has heard your prayer.'

Steve was surprised at this turn of affairs. He followed the girl. She led him to the stable and lighted a lantern. In the lantern-light Steve saw a beautiful black stallion standing. He thought to himself that Jankie had not said too much for young Baas Willim's courting horse.

The girl showed him a saddle and bridle hanging on a peg against the wall, and bid him put on the saddle.

'But what will your mother say?' he asked.

'I will answer for everything. It is for our dear country and liberty you want the horse. If mother believed in you as I do now, she would never have refused you. Be quick now.'

Steve looked at her for a moment, but he reflected it was for a great and noble cause, moreover it was urgent, so he hesitated no longer. The horse was soon saddled and led out of the stable. He took the girl by the hand and said,—

'God bless you for your goodness. I hope I may earn your good opinion in the struggle we are going to have. I will try not to disgrace your brother's horse. Good-bye, and God bless you,' and with a hearty handshake he jumped on the horse.

'Wait a moment,' the girl called. 'Which way are you going?'

'I don't know.'

'I would advise you to go in the same direction our Burghers went to-day. Take that road,' pointing in a northerly direction, 'keep to the main road, and you are sure to meet with some of the Burghers going to the commando. They all expect the fighting to take place somewhere between Johannesburg and Krugersdorp, so you had better inquire your way to Krugersdorp first.'

'Thank you. Good-bye.'

'Good-bye, and good luck.'

Steve let go the rein, and the stallion, nothing loth, shot forward like an arrow. But Steve was a good horseman, he knew he had far to go, and a horse, however good, is yet not a machine, therefore the strength of the horse must be economised. He soon got the stallion to settle down to a good, easy, comfortable pace at the rate of six miles an hour.

As Steve sat on his pleasant, comfortable seat, with his horse going as easy as a spring carriage, he had much time for thought. It was a beautiful but weird moonlight night. Thin, long streaks of mare's-tail clouds stretched across the sky, and Steve fancied he saw all sorts of fantastical shapes in those clouds. He remembered the old superstition that, when such clouds filled the sky, somebody was dying? Who was dying? Was it, perhaps, his countrymen, who, surprised by the sneaking enemy, had been overcome and murdered? Who knows? Perhaps a few score Burghers only had met the enemy, and had been overcome. The postmaster of H—— had told them that Jameson had Maxims and field-pieces; and what could a hundred or two hundred Burghers do, armed only with rifles, if they were to meet Jameson and his eight hundred freebooters?

When such thoughts came to Steve, he would unconsciously urge on his horse. 'On—forward—who knows, every man may mean the straw which might break the camel's back. Even I may do something which might turn the tide of battle.'

With such and other thoughts Steve rode on. He saddled off three different times for an hour before day broke, to give his horse a rest and to allow him to crop the grass along the road. Even this he grudged; he wanted to go on, always on, but prudence taught him to go slowly if he wanted to keep on going. Steve saw that he really rode an exceptional horse. When day broke, with the little rest he had had, the horse seemed almost quite fresh.

When day came, Steve began to come up with straggling parties of Burghers, who were moving forward as rapidly as their different modes of travelling permitted. He questioned some of them.

'Your horse does not seem to be going very good, uncle.'

'No, he is not of the best; he can keep on, but he can't go very fast. If he could go as fast as the rest, I should not be so far behind. All the best horses are in front. The order of our field cornet is for every man to go as fast as he can; never mind those who stay behind. You see there is no time to wait. Those who can ride fast must go ahead and keep the enemy busy until we come up.'

He next came to a party of six young men, dressed in holiday attire, but on foot.

'Hillo, *neefs* (cousins), are you off to the war too?'

'You bet we are; you won't catch us staying behind.'

'But how is it that you have no horses; you do not seem too poor to possess horses.'

'No, but we were too far from home to go for our horses. We had come by ox-waggon to spend New Year's Day at Oom Paulus Stichling's, and when we heard that the English had invaded our country again we just set off on foot, and let Jameson just wait till we come there we will show him, *waar David de wortels gegramved het.*'

Steve met many more such parties who had been spending their New Year's holiday from home, and who had left just as they were to go and meet the enemy. All the mounted Burghers he met were mostly of the very poorest, who could not afford horses of the best speed, and were consequently left behind. As Steve saw that the order of the day was for every man to go as fast as he could, and never mind those who stayed behind, he thought he could do no better than follow suit; consequently, he did not stand on any ceremony, but rode on as fast as he thought prudent, leaving one party after the other behind him.

About midday, he came to a small copse of trees, which he thought just the place to saddle off for a good rest for his horse and himself, as he felt a little tired by this time, and as he was somewhat more reassured now, and the excitement he had felt was a little worn off; he also began to feel a little sleepy. He decided to knee-halter his horse and sleep for an hour, after which he would again proceed. As he was taking the saddle off, he thought he heard voices a little deeper in the copse. He knee-haltered his horse and went to see who was there. He saw two boys of about twelve years of age, gun in hand, sitting eating slices of bread and butter.

'Well, sonnies, and where are you off to?'

'Going to fight Jameson.'

'*What?*'

'Are you deaf, uncle? We are going to fight Jameson.'

'Does your pa know that you are going to the war?

'Oh, no, our parents are all away; my father and his (nodding towards his companion) are both gone to the war. They left us to look after the house, but as soon as they were gone, we each took a gun and followed; *we* are not going to stay at home while the old people fight, ha! ha!'

'Well you are the right kind of Afrikanders, you are no cowards; the English will never take our country while our young men have such patriotism,' and Steve felt proud to shake hands with these youngsters; he saw that in such a spirit lay the strength of his nation.

The boys, with the usual spirit of Afrikander hospitality, offered to share their bread and butter with Steve. He gladly accepted a slice, as he had eaten nothing since the evening before, when he had had a biscuit and a cup of coffee with the stranger.

After the boys had finished their dinner, they shouldered their guns and resumed their journey, while Steve laid himself down on the grass and fell asleep. When he woke, he saw that he had slept an hour and a half. He hastily saddled his horse and rode on. The horse seemed to have taken full advantage of Steve's long sleep, as he seemed quite refreshed again. Steve could not but congratulate himself again and again as he saw what great enduring powers the horse possessed.

At dusk our hero arrived at a wayside hotel. His horse was now thoroughly tired. He saw that he would have to stay here several hours, unless he wanted his horse to give in. His first inquiry was for forage, which luckily was to be had in any quantity at a big price.

After having seen his horse well fed and rubbed down, Steve went into the house and asked for some supper. Some cold meat, bread, butter and coffee was placed before him, and he made as good a meal of it as could be expected.

After supper, he asked for a room to lie down for a few hours. He was shown a room not very clean and neat; still a tired man could at least rest in it; besides, beggars could not be choosers.

But before lying down, Steve went out to once more see his horse supplied with forage. As he was superintending the cutting up of the oat sheaves, the proprietor—whom he had not yet seen—came up to him. After a few introductory remarks between them, his host asked him in English where he was going.

He replied in the same language, with as pure an accent as the Englishman's own, that he was going to Krugersdorp.

'Have you heard the glorious news?' asked the host.

'No; what is it?'

'The Boers and Jameson have met, and Jameson has defeated the Boers, killing three hundred of them.'

Steve turned pale in the dark. He could hardly speak at first. At last he managed to say,—

'How do you know this?'

'I have just come back from our post-office, where I had been to get some news. I there met a man who had left the battlefield at noon; it was near Krugersdorp; he had been riding post-haste to carry despatches somewhere. He says it was an awful sight to see it. Jameson's troops were simply mowing the Boers down with Maxims and Nordenfelds. The Boers had no Maxims or field-pieces, and could simply do nothing with their rifles against the troopers.'

'But who is this despatch rider? Can his story be believed?'

'Oh, as to that, there can be no doubt of it, he is one of Jameson's own officers; his name is Captain Thatcher, so it must be true. It is a glorious day for Englishmen. Amajuba has been wiped out at last, and the English flag shall now once more fly over the Transvaal.' He thought he was speaking to an Englishman. Steve answered not a word. He walked away. He felt he could not restrain himself much longer in this man's presence. He walked blindly away towards the open veld. It was moonlight, but he saw nothing about him. He could only see in his mind's eye, on an open plain, a battlefield, and on this battlefield he could see hundreds of his beloved countrymen lying —dead—murdered—by the freebooters. Oh, what a fearful sight. What homes are rendered desolate to-night in this country? Can it be true? Alas, I am afraid it is only too true. Jameson's troops are well prepared and armed. Those terrible Maxims *mowed* down thousands of Matabeles in the same way, and our poor Burghers were unprepared. There was no time for them to wait for cannon and Maxims to come up; they had to try and stop Jameson's advance as best they could, before he entered Johannesburg; and, unprepared as they were, they fell into the terrible death-trap laid for them.

'Oh, my God, why hast Thou permitted this? What hast Thy people done that Thou should desert them now in their hour of need? Oh, God of Mercy, have mercy on Thy people. Jesus, it can surely not be Thy will that these murdering, grasping, gold-worshipping, godless freebooters should slay Thy people in this way. Oh, Father in Heaven, it is surely Thy will —nay, it *is* Thy will, that we should become a people, a nation, FREE and UNITED. God, Thou hast shown it in the past; Thou hast led them on step by step, day by day, year by year, and Thou hast always given them glorious victory in their greatest time of peril. Thou hast ever been their salvation; wilt Thou desert them now? Nay, Thou art not a God who does anything by half; Thou wilt not leave Thy work incomplete. Oh, God of Battles, show Thine wondrous power once more, and save Thy people yet.'

With what earnestness did Steve pray. He prayed and wrestled with God as he had never prayed or wrestled before. When he left his landlord he was faint with grief; great sobs of woe welled up from his very heart; but now his faith in God once more brought comfort and hope. He believed that God would not desert his people.

He went to a stream which he heard rippling near by, pulled off his clothes and had a moonlight bath, after which he felt so much refreshed that he thought he could sleep now. Going to his room, he once more uttered a prayer for help and guidance, and fell peacefully asleep, trusting all to his God.

He was awake at earliest daybreak, and, after rousing his landlord to pay his bill, he resumed his journey.

CHAPTER XIII

THE BATTLE OF DOORNKOP

STEVE'S horse went bravely on, but with slackened speed. We will not follow his further journey too closely; he met many people, all telling different tales as to the fortunes of war. One confirmed Captain Thatcher's tale, while others totally denied it.

Steve now found himself in the vicinity of Krugersdorp. It was Thursday, the third day since he had left his friends on the banks of the Vaal. He had travelled about one hundred and fifty miles or more during the forty-eight hours since he had left them.

He was riding along as fast as his horse would go; for he knew he was reaching his journey's end, and he could restrain his impatience no longer. He saw a man galloping towards him in a slanting direction, which would take him towards Krugersdorp. As the man approached near enough, he recognised him to be a newspaper reporter whom he had known in Pretoria.

He stopped the reporter and inquired eagerly for news.

'Oh! the Burghers are holding their own bravely. Since yesterday they have kept Jameson dancing about, trying to force his way through to Johannesburg, but in vain; Jameson can't get any nearer Johannesburg. The Burghers are gradually enclosing him, and soon they will have him and his freebooters at their mercy.'

'Thank God! but how many Burghers have been killed?'

'Up to now, two or three at the most, and as many wounded, while Jameson has lost heavily all along.'

'What? You are fooling me!'

'Why?'

'Last night I heard a report, spread by one Captain Thatcher, a despatch rider of Jameson's, that three hundred Boers were killed, and that Jameson had beaten the Boers.'

'It is a d——d lie!' was the impolite but emphatic denial. 'You can take my word for it that not more than two or three Boers are killed, and one was killed by accident in the dark by his own people, while the Boers have never been beaten yet by Jameson; on the contrary, the Boers have held Jameson in check all along, and have only been waiting for reinforcements and their artillery to carry Jameson and his troopers by storm.'

The reporter here stopped, and sat looking at Steve open-mouthed. The antics of this young man were really amusing, to say the least of it. He had rolled off his horse, and was now lying on his back, kicking his feet in the air, and now he was capering about on the grass, throwing summersault upon summersault, all the while shouting and laughing like one possessed.

'I say, Joubert, stop that; are you mad? Get on your horse and go on; I have no time to look after a lunatic now, or to take you to the lunatic asylum.'

'I beg your pardon, old man; I had to do it, or I should really have gone mad from joy, but I am better now,' said Steve, remounting his horse. 'Where are you going to?' he asked of the reporter.

'Oh, I am off to town to send news to the *Pretoria Press*, which I represent here. And what do you intend doing?'

'I wish to join one of our commandos; where shall I find one?'

'If you will go to the top of that rise there, you will see the whole position. When I came over it, the Burghers were retreating from the railway cutting (which they had occupied during the night) towards that very ridge. I think they intend taking possession of it and the drift, so as to finally stop the progress of the Chartered troops. Good-bye; I must be off to send particulars of our position to our paper. Take care of yourself and keep out of the way of the Maxims.'

What gratitude filled the heart of Steve now when he knew that Captain Thatcher's story was all lies and invention.

It went beyond Steve's comprehension what object any man could have in telling such deliberate lies. This Captain Thatcher ought to have known that what he was saying was all lies, and that ultimately his want of veracity was bound to be discovered. Steve could find only one explanation, and that was that such a person tells lies simply for the love of the thing, and for the temporary notoriety that such sensational tales may bring. Some people have a way of manufacturing their news according to the demand of their audiences. If the audience were composed of Government haters and Jameson sympathisers the news was made to suit their wishes, while if it were friends of the Government, the contrary rule was observed.

When Steve came to the top of the height he saw a party of Burghers coming directly towards him. At a distance he perceived a large troop of men coming in apparent pursuit of the Burghers. These latter he correctly took to be Jameson's filibusters.

'Thank God! I have arrived in time to fight with my countrymen for life or—death. And if it is to lose, I would a thousand times rather die than live!' thought Steve to himself.

Where he was standing on the rise or ridge, a reef was cropping out, throwing out projections of rocks, which formed splendid natural fortifications, giving good protection against the fire of an enemy coming in the direction from which Jameson was coming.

The Burghers seemed to be retiring from the enemy—*so were* they. The fire from Jameson's Maxims and long-range field-pieces could not be resisted on the open veld, for which reason they were retiring towards the aforesaid out-croppings, where Steve was standing. When they arrived on the spot, Steve discovered the field cornet in command of the Burghers to be an old acquaintance and friend of his. It did not take Steve more than a minute to explain matters, and to be provided with a spare rifle and a belt of ammunition.

The Burghers now took up their position amongst the rocks (which were situated exactly on the sky line of the ridge mostly, thus giving them the command of the approaches to the drift through which Jameson must pass if he passed the Burghers at all) and prepared to oppose the passage of the enemy. Jameson came on now—Maxims, field-pieces and all; his force was variously estimated from five hundred to eight hundred men. His troops were forcing onwards towards the drift.

Opposing his passage to the drift were eighty-seven Burghers (this is correct, as near as possible; there may have been a difference of one or two, more or less—but rather less) disposed in the following manner:—

In the first patch of rocks, two hundred yards from

the road, twenty-five men occupied a position; farther on fifteen men were disposed a little nearer to the drift, but in a line with the aforesaid twenty-five men; still nearer to the drift seven men were lying in wait. Beyond the drift, about seven hundred yards away, forty Burghers occupied a small kopje. These forty men could only fire at long range on the enemy, as the long range field-pieces of the enemy prevented their leaving their shelter. The seven and fifteen men mentioned had to do most of the fighting, and had to stand the hottest fire, as the Maxims were playing almost continually on their position, but they were nobly supported by the twenty-five men stationed a little higher up. Jameson's passage to the drift was soon stopped by the heavy fire of the Burghers, ; his men were dropping continually. He was obliged to give up all idea of crossing, and took possession of a farmhouse, a cattle kraal and stone-walled land. His Maxims and field-pieces were protected partially by the stone wall of the land. The majority of troops took possession of the kraal and the house. The men in possession of the kraal and house found themselves directly opposed to the twenty-five men on the ridge. The Maxims directed their fire mostly on the parties of fifteen and seven, who were directly opposite them. The field-pieces directed the full force of their fire on the forty Burghers occupying the kopje beyond the drift, who were seven hundred yards away, while the party of twenty-five was about two hundred yards from the kraal and house occupied by the enemy, and the parties of fifteen and seven, who were near to each other, were about one hundred yards from the troopers, and four hundred yards from the Maxims. More Burghers, amounting to over one thousand, were certainly in the neighbourhood of the battlefield, but were too far away to take part in the fight, and those occupying the positions above described were the only Burghers fighting—actually fighting, I mean—against Jameson at the battle of Doornkop. Steve found himself amongst the party of fifteen described as being opposed to the Maxims.

It was a terrible ordeal for those twenty-two men lying flat behind the rocks. The Maxim bullets literally rained on them, and, unprotected by the rocks, every soul of that little band would have been wiped out in a few moments.

Steve heard (in fact, felt) a continuous patter against the rock in front of him. It seemed to him as if a whole battery of Maxims were firing at that particular rock. The chips of rock and sand were raining upon him, thrown up by the bullets. Luckily his rock was just large enough to protect him against the heavy and continuous fire. Once he just peeped ever a little dent in the rock, took aim and fired, when *whew* came a bullet right through his hat. Next moment his body must have moved slightly outside the line protected by the rock, when he felt a stinging sensation at his hip, a bullet had just grazed him. He got several more through his clothing in this way, as he moved and wormed himself about to take aim to fire. Luckily the Maxims could not fire all over at once, and while they fired at one party the other party would take advantage of the diversion in their favour to rain well-aimed shots on the enemy, and when a Burgher fired he reckoned upon one enemy being the less, either wounded or killed. For a Transvaal Boer never wastes ammunition; he never fires unless he is sure of his aim. A pang of pity went through Steve's heart as he saw the poor troopers of Jameson dropping down one after the other; he felt that, although they were guilty of a great wrong to his country, still they were human, and to be hurled into eternity while participating in such a cowardly, back-handed blow against a people who had looked upon them as friends, and not as foes, was awful. And while aiming his rifle as accurately as he could, he murmured a prayer for the souls of those that he was helping to send to the judgment seat of God, but

—in self-defence, in defence of country and national existence.

When first the fight began, Steve had felt the trembling, half fear, half suspense and excitement, usually experienced by the soldier on first facing the fire of battle. But soon he felt as calm and cool as if he were taking part in a target practice.

'By Heaven, but these English can fight better than I thought,' remarked a Burgher on the left of Steve. 'I have never known them to fight so bravely before; I will give them credit for that.'

'Yes, they do fight bravely,' replied an old man next to him. 'I never saw a brave fight such as this in 1881; but you must remember they have had their training in South Africa.'

'True,' was the reply.

At this moment Steve heard a groan on his right. Turning round, he saw a young fellow lying in such a position, that he perceived at once he must be wounded. He rolled himself towards the wounded man, took his head upon his knees and spoke to him, but received no answer. On examination he saw that he had been shot through the head. It was poor M'Donald, who, although shot through the brain, lived ten days longer, and then died, when he received an honoured funeral.

Steve helped to carry the wounded man down the opposite side of the ridge into safety, where he was left with one more wounded Burgher, in a small deserted house, in the care of two men. Steve then returned to his place, and resumed his share in the fierce fight.

The battle was raging fierce and hot. The cannon of the Chartered troops roared hoarsely above the rattle of small arms; while the continuous rat-a-tat-tat-tat of the Maxims was also to be distinguished from the more irregular and less incessant cracking of the rifles. A heavy cloud of smoke was floating above, concealing the sun as if it wished to hide the murderous work from the sight of Heaven. The slaughter amongst the Chartered troops was terrible. One detachment after another bravely charged the position of the Burghers, under the protection of their Maxims; but it was in vain, the heavy and accurate fire of the Burghers forced them to retire with great loss every time; and the Chartered troopers were only too glad to regain their shelter.

In spite of his pity for them, Steve's heart throbbed with a joy almost savage in its intensity when he saw the troopers giving way all along the line. They seemed to look for some point of safety towards which they might fly. But 'tis a vain hope. Look towards whatever side they will, they could see Burghers in the distance awaiting them. *They were thoroughly hemmed in.*

Steve saw all this and realised the position in which Jameson must find himself. He tried to place himself in Jameson's position in imagination.

'What should I do if I were to find myself in such a hole of my own making? Should I surrender and take my chance of getting out alive? Could I expect to get out alive in case I surrendered? No! A filibustering murderer can expect nothing but death. Death would be my sentence, by *Human Laws*, by *Moral Law*, by God's Law. I could not even expect a word of mercy from England. She has disowned me and my expedition, and I have disobeyed her. *No*, rather than give in now, after having ventured so much and risked so much to obtain my aim (whatever that may be), I would rather fight to the end and obtain that sympathy and that martyrdom that the grave always brings. That would be something, at least, while to surrender *now* would mean eternal disgrace, trouble unending, and perhaps death on the scaffold.

But Jameson must have thought otherwise, as we shall see. He was either too cowardly to die such a death, or he must have known beforehand that external aid (of which Steve did not know then) would be rendered him. He must have known (maybe it was promised him in case of failure) that the full weight of Chartered influences and Chartered capital would be exerted in his favour.

While Steve was thus meditating, as he surveyed the field of battle and Jameson's hopeless condition, the battle was still proceeding as fiercely as ever. Turn and twist as they would, the Chartered troops found that the Boer bullets followed them everywhere.

Suddenly a cheer was raised by the Burghers. Steve looked to see the reason for this, and saw, directed by the joyful looks of the Burghers, the State artillery taking up a position on a distant rise.

The artillery had arrived at last, but too late. At this moment a white flag was hoisted by the Chartered troops. It had been asserted by some that the Burghers fired a volley after the white flag was hoisted. It is partly true. The flag was hoisted by the troopers directly facing Steve's party of Burghers. The white flag was out of sight of the twenty-five Burghers stationed higher up, as the rocks hid the lower end of Jameson's line from their view. Therefore a few shots were fired by them the moment after the flag was hoisted. But the shouts of their companions who saw the flag apprised them of the fact, when, of course, they immediately ceased firing.

The Burghers now left their shelter and came out, walking and riding towards Jameson's position. Jameson's troopers deployed, so as to place themselves between the Burghers and their own Maxims and cannon.

The field cornet now ordered a Burgher named P. Nagel to go and see 'what the English wanted.' He went, and returned with a request from Jameson to be allowed to return over the border. He (Jameson) was informed that his request was impossible, as he had had the opportunity given him to return before any fighting took place, and he failed to take advantage of it, but that a meeting of officers would be called together at once to further consider his request.

In the meanwhile Commandant Cronje, who was with the Burghers beyond the drift, sent to Jameson to know whether he surrendered, being unaware of the messenger sent by the field cornet, and whose report had been submitted to Commandant Polgicter of Krugersdorp. Jameson replied to Commandant Cronje's message with an offer to surrender if the lives of himself and men were guaranteed, whereupon Commandant Cronje informed Jameson that if he laid down his arms and would promise to pay the expenses of the Government of the South African Republic, that he would guarantee the lives of himself and men *until handed over to the Commandant-General, when the Krijgsraad would further decide upon his case*. More, he had no authority to promise. He gave Jameson thirty minutes to consider and accept. *Jameson accepted.*

CHAPTER XIV

PROBABLE DANGERS AVERTED BY DOORNKOP'S FIGHT

A SHORT time later, Commandant Malar arriving on the scene, inquired as to what the terms of surrender were. After being informed as to the promise given Jameson to safely deliver him into the hands of the Commandant-General, he made a member of the Burgher party, who spoke English well, to distinctly make Jameson understand that the lives of himself and men were guaranteed only while on the field of battle and while on their passage to Pretoria, when the proper authorities would further decide as to their ultimate fate.

Of course these conditions could hardly be called conditions, except the conditions extracted from Jameson, that they would lay down their arms and pay all expenses; and even that followed as a natural result on defeat. While the promise given by the commandant, that his life would be safe-guarded while in transit to Pretoria was also but a natural result of civilised warfare (if fighting a filibustering murdering foe could be called civilised warfare), and would have followed in any case, promise or no promise. But the promise was given, as Jameson and his officers seemed to fear the anger of the justly incensed Burghers.

When the white flag was hoisted by the Chartered troopers, the Burghers were distrustful. They reasoned thus: 'These people are not to be trusted. They came into our country in a treacherous manner. They slunk in when they thought we were off our guard. Now, having acted once in a treacherous manner, are they not capable of acting so again? Is it not their object to draw us out of our position and shelter, and then to cut us down with their Maxims and cannon. No, before we expose ourselves, we must be assured of their honest surrender; and someone must first go and see what they want. Who will go?' Without a moment's hesitation Steve jumped on the nearest horse, and rode full speed towards the Chartered troopers. On looking round, he saw he was followed by half-a-dozen more young fellows of the Burgher force. So he was one of the first to speak to the invaders after the white flag was hoisted.

Another incident, tragic in its result, took place after the surrender of the Chartered arms. A young, inexperienced Burgher was curiously handling and examining one of the magazine rifles, forming part of the spoils of war, when, somehow or other, the *thing* went off, and wounded a fellow-Burgher, standing in front of him. The poor fellow died from the wound.

That careless young man got the severest reprimand from his commandant that ever he had in his life before; but being able to satisfactorily prove that it was an accident, he was not punished. But he seemed sufficiently punished by the thought that he had caused the death of a companion. He seemed to take the disgrace, and the death of the victim much to heart, and hardly spoke for days after. He wept when he left the commandant's tent.

Jameson's men received the best attention possible, even on the field of battle. Those who had provisions shared with them; and afterwards they were taken to Krugersdorp, where they were treated more like guests than prisoners. Of course any attempt at escape was guarded against.

Jameson and officers were forwarded to Pretoria without unnecessary delay. Jameson seemed especially sad and broken-hearted. Who knows what hopes were dashed to the ground? Who knows his thoughts when he entered the territory of a State at peace with his own country, into which he was carrying the torch of civil war, murder and famine? It was like taking a lighted torch into a powder magazine. He knew that his advent meant 'war to the knife'—to the bitter end; and the more success he had at first, the more disastrous must the end be. Had he reached Johannesburg, who could foresee where the bloodshed would have ended? And the thousands of innocent, peaceable citizens of Johannesburg must have suffered, and did suffer, with the guilty. All to satisfy the love of power, glory, and lust of gold of a few unscrupulous men. But be assured, O reader, that, if man does not punish them, a higher power *will*.

Whatever Jameson's reward for success was to have been, president (?), governor (?), administrator (?), or prime minister to the modern Emperor Napoleon, I do not know This I do know, he seemed to recognise that all was lost, that all the grand dreams of power and gold dreamt by him and his fellow-conspirators had vanished into mist; for he never spoke a word but—wept. Would that he had wept tears of repentance at the bloodshed, the distress and heartburnings he had caused, instead of weeping for failure. Or would that he had wept tears of joy that he had failed to set the Powers of the world fighting a terrible war; a war such as Napoleon even never saw. A war that would have changed the destinies of many a nation on earth. A war that would have changed the map of the world, to what extent no one can say. *What an escape.*

Small things have world-wide effects. The battle of Doornkop saved the world many a battle. Why? Because if Jameson had not been defeated, and had not surrendered, and had reached Johannesburg, Johannesburg would have taken courage. The strong would have been stronger, the wavering would have wavered no more, even the peacefully inclined would have been peaceful no more. The rebellion would have been an accomplished fact. The proclamation, proclaiming the provisional government, instead of being secretly destroyed, and put out of type, would have been proclaimed. Civil war would have raged. England would have stepped in and interfered. And although the South African Republic did NOT ask for European aid, Europe *would have* interfered. France, Germany, Russia and (believe it if you will or not)—the sister Republic—the United States. The chance would have been too good for these powers to lose the opportunity to give effect to their growing jealousy of the increasing colonial wealth and power of England. The whispered coalition between France, Germany and Russia (which only died out because *the fuel on which it was fed gave up*, viz., the fear or hope that England would take up the part of the rebels and go against the Boer Government) would have been proclaimed and given effect to. What would have been the result? We can only surmise.

However, one of two things would have happened. England would have been raised to a higher pinnacle of power than she ever occupied before; or—the breaking up of the British Empire.

Well, analyse England's position.

England was *gloriously isolated*, as a certain Canadian politician termed it.

Germany was against her.

Germany of course meant *the* Triple Alliance.

France and Russia could not be depended upon.

The United States of America had set her foot down against English pretensions in Venezuela.

Europe was against England! Turkey? No need to say anything about Turkey? Everybody knows the situation there at the time America was against England. Upon whom could England reckon in her time of need? Her colonies? Her colonies will need to be protected by her, instead of rendering any aid! Herself? Could Great Britain and Ireland reckon upon HERSELF? How about Ireland? Has England any right to depend upon Irish aid in time of need? The contrary rather! No, Great Britain could reckon upon Great Britain, but not upon Great Britain *and Ireland;* nor Greater Britain either!

And as to South Africa (remember we are considering the extreme case). England thus situated could not bring much force to bear upon South Africa. And how would South Africa stand in such a case? Of course, with such a provocation, the Transvaal and Free State would stand together, that is taken for granted without argument—that has been proved. But what about the Cape Colony? Nine tenths of the population of the Cape Colony and Natal are Afrikanders. Those Afrikanders would have seen that THEIR TIME HAD ARRIVED. No more need be said, except that a united South Africa would have been realized at last, *and a Republican united South Africa.* Of course, there are those who will call this reasoning *all moonshine.* There are those who call England's isolation *glorious.* There are those who consider England capable of fighting the united world, and still being victorious. Well, let them think so. Let them put their head in the sand, like the ostrich, and refuse to read the signs of the times. It is good for *such* British subjects that they are not at the head of the British Government. It is fortunate for the British Empire that they have men in their ministry like Chamberlain. *He* saw the breakers ahead; and like a good steersman, kept clear of the rocks. *He* saw that it was better to make friends of a quiet, peace-loving nation rather than foes. It is true he has made a mistake now and then; but he is only human, and almost unhuman like, he acknowledged his mistakes, more credit to him. Let him continue to maintain peace, by being just and fair, and he may reckon upon making friends, instead of foes, of the great Afrikander nation that is being built up in South Africa.

CHAPTER XV

THE FIGHTING PREVIOUS TO DOORNKOP'S BATTLE

STEVE inquired from his friend the field cornet for particulars of the fight previous to his arrival. We give the words of the field cornet *verbatim*:—

'Fighting began yesterday. We were only a small party of Burghers at first, and could hardly expect to defeat Jameson on the open veld, so we harassed him as much as possible, to delay him until reinforcements arrived. But we had to remain at a distance most of the time, as we had only rifles to fight with, and they had Maxims, which carried much farther than our Martinis, not to speak of their field-pieces. But later on in the day we reached a strong position. We were directly in Jameson's road. He had to conquer us before he could pass on towards Johannesburg *via* Krugersdorp. But we were quite confident that our position was inaccessible to the enemy. We had selected a *rise*, crested with rocks, offering good shelter against the enemy's fire. Below the rise, and between us and the enemy, was a spruit, spreading out into a marsh. Through this marshy spruit the enemy had to pass before reaching our position. Beyond the marsh the enemy took up a position with their cannon and Maxims, sending out three detachments to charge us. One party of about eighty troopers charged our centre, through the usual drift of the spruit, while the other two detachments charged our left and right wings respectively. At this moment our ammunition was giving in. We had anxiously been awaiting an ammunition train, which we had been informed had been despatched from Pretoria for our use. Half-an-hour before the enemy prepared to charge, a messenger had arrived from Krugersdorp to inform us of the arrival of the ammunition train there, with a promise that a trolley loaded with the required ammunition would soon follow. Now, just at the moment when the enemy were leaving their own position to charge us, and when we most needed it, the much-longed-for ammunition trolley arrived upon the scene. An old man, with several others, was standing on the trolley handing packets of cartridges down, when a shell from the enemy fell right on top of the ammunition trolley between the group handing the cartridges down, and burst. Marvellous to relate, the shell did no injury to the ammunition, nor was anyone hurt.

'"A miracle! a miracle, brothers!" cried the old man. "God is with us, let us fight and conquer; God has given them into our hands." The face of the old patriarch glowed with faith as he spoke.

'This seemed to give us all fresh courage and enthusiasm, and as the enemy came charging in their three divisions we repelled them with great loss to themselves. The right and left divisions of the enemy were simply forced to retire in disorder, leaving several of their comrades on the veld. The centre detachment of the enemy succeeded in reaching the drift of the spruit, but the Burgher fire was too hot for them; a part of them fled back and succeeded in rejoining their main force, but seven of them were left wounded on the road, and, as we afterwards ascertained, nineteen of them took cover amongst the tall grass of the marsh, and lay in the mud and water until their main force retired from the scene towards evening, when we took the above-mentioned nineteen troopers prisoners. Poor fellows, they were in a sorry plight; they had been lying under water and mud all the time, with only their noses and mouths out of water for breathing.

'As I said, the main force saw that they could not force our position, and retired, cutting across the veld with the hope of avoiding us; but while the majority of us remained to guard the road at the drift, about one hundred of us kept abreast of Jameson's force, so as to prevent them from slipping through.

'We saw Jameson was heading towards the railway cutting, so we raced on ahead and took possession of the cutting, using the embankment as a breastwork, and again brought the invaders to a full stop. As it was getting dark now, Jameson encamped for the night, out of rifle shot from the embankment; but he was near enough to keep on shelling our position, off and on, during the night. But as we were well protected by our embankment, no harm was done.

'During the night, a sad accident happened.

'The son of Commandant Cronje, who was rather too venturesome, had crossed the railway cutting and was riding about on the other side. We could not recognise him in the dark. We thought it was a spy from the enemy. We called out three times, "Who goes there?" but received no reply. Whether he did not hear us, I cannot say; some of our men fired and he fell, severely wounded. It is a sad thing that, out of five of our Burghers who have been killed, two have been killed by our own men, besides the one wounded just now by that careless young man. And another, I hear, has been killed to-day by our own men. He was near to the enemy, and as his dress was somewhat similar to Jameson's troopers, he was fired at and killed; and our men only found out their mistake when too late.

Well, to resume, when day broke, Jameson once more earnestly set to work, trying to beat us back from the embankment, but in vain. We drove him along the line, always keeping him back and preventing him from crossing. But while he kept us busy, he sent some of his heavy field-pieces on ahead, which crossed over before we saw their dodge, as we were busy repelling charge after charge from Jameson's troopers. As he was able to sweep our side of the embankment now, we had to leave Jameson in possession of the line. We now resolved once more to retire, and go on ahead to cut Jameson off at some other convenient place. Jameson was now on the road to Doornkop, and in possession of the road. It was vain for us to attempt stopping him on the open road, as he had the advantage of numbers, as well as having cannon and Maxims against our rifles. We resolved to cut across the veld towards the drift at Brinks' farm, which Jameson must cross to reach Krugersdorp, unless he took the other road, on which our commando was waiting for him. We raced across the veld and arrived here, finding you in possession already. The rest you know yourself.'

'Yes, but you say one hundred of you left the main commando to watch Jameson as he was dodging about; what has become of those hundred men? There are only eighty-seven here on the battlefield, besides those who came after the battle was over. What has become of the rest?'

'Well, you see, as we raced across the veld to cut Jameson off here, those who had the weakest horses were left behind, and they, in their turn, were again cut off by Jameson's men, and they had to go a roundabout way to reach us. I see they have arrived now, but too late to take part in the fight.'

Steve thanked his friend for the information, and resumed his investigations elsewhere.

Steve was detailed to assist in guarding the prisoners, and as he spoke English well, he questioned them and got much information from them.

One of them told him that he had been lying in a

slight depression of the ground during the fight. He said,—

'I thought that, if I lay flat, the Boers could never hit me, as a slight hollow seemed to afford me all the protection I needed. But the bullets kept striking right in front of my eyes, and the ground seemed to be wearing down more and more in front of me, so that the bullets, instead of passing over me, threatened to soon pass through me. I had a hatchet, which I used to deepen my little hollow as fast as my protection was being shot away. Thus, by hugging the ground closely, I managed to escape safe and sound to the end.'

Many of them told tales of marvellous escapes from the unerring aim of the Burghers, as well as unheard-of hiding-places used by them during the battle.

They told of how they had to leave dead and wounded, the day before; Jameson seeming to think that the dead might bury its own dead!—he only cared for the living.

I may here state that the Government sent parties on the route travelled to bury the dead and succour the deserted wounded. Some of these last had undergone terrible sufferings—wounded, unprotected, unsheltered, deserted by their friends, they lay on the veld; but Jameson has enough to answer for already—over this we shall draw a veil and say no more.

Another told how he was one of several who had been sent from Johannesburg to join Jameson beyond the border. They had been engaged to fight Kaffirs. When they were told that they were going to march to Johannesburg, many deserted. These latter were Afrikanders of the right sort, and declined to fight their own countrymen.

'Even I would have deserted if I had had the chance, but I was too closely watched,' remarked his informant.

'But could these Afrikanders, who meant the Transvaal well, not send a telegram to warn the Government of their danger and of Jameson's intentions?'

'No; why we could not even write a letter to our

relatives unless it was submitted to the officers to first read it.'

'When did you first learn your true destination?'

'When Jameson and other officers addressed us, and told us that we were going to assist men, women and children at the Rand, who were in danger of their lives. He told us that we were going to assist in upholding British supremacy in South Africa, and that he was sure not a shot would be fired; also, that the Boers would not be molested.

'He asked for volunteers, but no one moved until ordered to do so. Great promises were made to us. We were promised £1000 and a farm each if successful, besides other considerations. I am afraid we have lost that farm and £1000,' he concluded smilingly.

Another one informed Steve how Jameson had been preparing for months back for his raid into the Transvaal.

'We were not supposed to know what the great preparations were made for; it was stated by our leaders that we were going to fight some native chief, but many of us had our suspicions. There was too much mystery and private conference amongst the officers. I for one had my suspicions, and it has exactly turned out as I expected. I am only surprised that your Government did not suspect what was going on. Why, all along our route we found buildings erected, containing stores, forage and food for ourselves, and even fresh horses. All this must have taken time to prepare. Always in due time we found one of these stores, containing food and forage.'

'But how is it that I hear your leader wrote, in reply to the protest of the Commandant of Marico against his entry into the country, that he came in reply to a request for help from leading men in Johannesburg to protect life and property, and to help them to obtain certain political rights, for which they had asked a week ago. He also gave you and others to understand that he was going to Johannesburg to protect women and children against goodness knows what. Now the only danger that Johannesburg and its inhabitants may be in might be because they have been in a revolutionary state for the last few days. How could Jameson have known months ago that this would be the case, if he has been preparing himself for months?'

'Oh, you must be innocent! Do you believe, or do you think we ever believed this story about protecting women and children. Look here! I am a man of the world, and I know when two and two make four. I have kept my eyes and ears open, and I have found out a thing or two, and you may believe me when I say that the whole thing is a deep laid plot to dispossess your Government of all responsibility of the government of the Transvaal. You must know that Johannesburg is altogether too rich to be left in the possession of the Boers, and certain wealthy and avaricious persons in England, Cape Town and Johannesburg have formed a great plot to get possession of your country. You may thank your stars that you have defeated us; if you had allowed us to once enter Johannesburg, I think Paul Kruger and his people would have been lost, and instead of Paul Kruger, Cecil Rhodes would have been your chief, and I pity your people if Cecil Rhodes had them in his power; he would rule them with a rod of iron.'

'Thank God, Cecil Rhodes is not all-powerful,' said Steve; 'even the power of a millionaire and diamond king is limited, and I hope that after this, the eyes of the Colonial Afrikander Bond will be opened, and that his power will be more limited still?'

'Do your people then know that he is at the head of all this plot and revolution?'

'We do not know yet positively, but we suspect a great deal, and will know all soon, I expect.'

Steve was very tired that evening, but he saw that many Burghers had had a very hard struggle to arrive in time, and that most of them had slept even less than he had done the last few days, and not one of them complained, or tried to shirk duty, therefore he volunteered for guard duty or anything else that he might be required for. He was then appointed to be one of the guards escorting the officers to Pretoria.

CHAPTER XVI

JOHANNESBURG DURING THE CRISIS

LET us take a look at what Johannesburg and Pretoria has been doing during the time Steve had been away from home.

Ever since the publication of the famous National Union Manifesto, Johannesburg had been in a state of turmoil and excitement. At first everything was said in whispers, and all revolutionary acts and preparations were done in stealth; only the Press belonging to the anti-Boer organisation kept up its usual vituperations of the Government, in addition to revolutionary articles well calculated to incite the population to a rebellious state. There seemed to be some electric depression in the atmosphere. Everybody seemed to distrust his neighbour, especially the guilty plotters seemed to dread detection. But soon speech and action became bolder, as it was seen the Government was disinclined to take any strong measures. The policy of the Government seemed to have been one of gentleness and conciliation. All the Government officials had received orders to avoid giving offence, or to do aught to incite the populace, or cause a disturbance of the peace; particular stress was laid on the order to avoid making a show of armed force, either of police or armed Burghers.

This was taken as a confession of weakness on the part of the Government by the revolutionists, and it was resolved to follow up the apparent advantage gained. Open enlistment now went on. Every scamp, ex-prisoner, burglar or vagabond who was willing to take up arms, was enlisted.

But now the weakness of the revolutionists became apparent. When it came to fighting nobody wanted to fight. The thousands of English miners upon whom the capitalistic schemers had reckoned, failed them. These miners were sensible men, and wise in their generation. They argued in this way:

'Why should we fight? We have nothing to fight for; we have everything we can wish for; we are living in a labourers' paradise; we are as free as we have never been in our own country; we are prosperous, and pay only 18s. 6d. a year in taxes—that is when we choose to do so. What do we care about the franchise, we are in this country to make money, and we are making it hand over fist. We did not come here to engage in political strife, or to fight the battles of scheming and plotting capitalists who would reward us when once they are in power, by combining against us, and bringing us down to the low level in which our brethren in Europe and America have been brought by capitalists. No, Messrs Cecil Rhodes, Phillips, Leonard, Farrar and company will have to fight their own battles, *we* are not going to pull the chestnuts out of the fire for them, and then be kicked for our pains—*dead off!*' Thus the honest Cornishmen and other miners argued. But all the same these miners were patriotic enough, or maybe they did not feel interest in the subject enough to take any active part in the strife at all; be the reason what it may, they refused to take the part of either side, and many of them left the country altogether for the time being. We think, if any were required, this was argument enough, that the real working men, *the people* (who are generally the first to revolutionise, where revolution is wanted), refused absolutely to have anything to do with this so-called revolution. Not only did they refuse to fight gratuitously, but when the option was given them, either to take up arms or to clear, they chose the latter alternative. This, we say, was argument enough to show that the revolution — so-called — was simply a capitalistic plot, created with mercenary motives.

The leaders—self-elected—of the National Union had assumed another name by this time; they now called themselves the 'Reform Committee'—a name which was to become notorious indeed all the world over a little later on. To gain as much influence as possible both with the outside world as with the local populace, they added to themselves the names of most of the leading men of the Rand. Many of the latter, although members of the Reform Committee, and advertised as such, were innocent of any evil intentions. Some refused absolutely to figure as members, while others consented to their names being used when assured by the original conspirators that nothing unconstitutional would be done, and that they would only agitate for certain concessions from the Government. These deluded persons of course had to suffer for their weakness later on.

What to do now? The populace refuses to fight. The Reform Committee resolved to carry on the revolution by the means of GOLD. This is the golden city. We are all gold kings, we will let our gold fight our battles, and when everything is gained, we shall get our gold back a thousandfold. Thus they argued, and the result was, *one pound sterling a day* was offered to any and everybody who would take up arms and fight against the Government.

It is true a few corps—small corps, too—were raised without pay, but with the avowed object only to protect life and property and not to fight against the Government. It seems the conspirators had foreseen this apathy or want of interest on the part of the populace in their artificial revolution, for which reason they had arranged the Jameson Raid. Whoever had first thought of this arrangement, viz., Jameson's Raid? Was it the Reform Committee, or was it the arch conspirator himself? Certain it is, it was a short-sighted policy, for Jameson's failure, as we shall see, ruined all their hopes. But we are inclined towards the belief that, although the Reform Committee sent the invitation to Jameson, it was done by the suggestion of the arch conspirator himself—Rhodes. Of course the chief conspirators on the Rand, the originators of the so-called revolution, were nothing but the agents of their chief in Cape Town, and all they did and suggested (it must be taken for granted) emanated from their leader. And we can understand his policy. If he had left the whole conduct of the affair to the Johannesburg Committee, they might take the bit in their mouth, and strike out for themselves, and leave him out in the cold, once success was assured. They might disown him, and take all the fruits of success for themselves, and possession being ten points of the law in such a case, he would be nicely sold. To guard against this, he must have decided to have a force of his own on the spot at any cost, by which means he hoped to hold the trump cards, in case his friends tried to play him false. And his fears were not unfounded by any means, as the majority of the conspirators who joined later, and especially those who were not in all the secrets of the organisation, were in favour of retaining the republican form of government in the event of success. This was evidenced by the fact that the Committee felt themselves compelled to confess to only wishing for a reformed Republic, and not for any other form of government. This was even carried so far that (whether in good faith or not we cannot say) the Transvaal flag was hoisted on the Gold Fields Office, the headquarters of the Reform Committee. This must have caused gnashing of teeth in the private cabinet of a certain prime minister in the Cape Colony when he received the news, and even his faithful agents on the Rand must have felt terrified and troubled when they saw the prize slipping through their fingers. What account will they be able to give to their lord and master of their stewardship in case of failure? One only hope was left them—Jameson. If Jameson came they would work together harmoniously, and together subdue and conquer the Boer, after which it would be time enough, and opportunity enough, with the aid of Jameson and his victorious troopers, to enforce *their* views and objects on the people of the Rand.

The eyes of all the conspirators were now fixed on Jameson.

It seems Jameson had started a little too 'previous.' Something had gone wrong. What that something was has not as yet been revealed. However, Jameson's premature advance precipitated matters. Everything was hurried forward. Guns and ammunition were dragged forth to the light of day from the places of concealment, where they had lain since being smuggled into the country during full six months. Enlistment at one pound sterling a day went merrily on. Twenty shillings a day for being drilled and carrying guns about in a martial way was not to be refused by the riff-raff, and even those who did not care to fight at first accepted the pay and enlisted for the sake of the pay. Drilling and enlisting went on openly in the streets of Johannesburg, and the Government, who still hoped for better counsels to prevail, and was anxious to avoid needless bloodshed, instructed the officials to withdraw the police altogether, to avoid a collision with the newly-enlisted soldiers.

The public of Johannesburg, who were indifferent and apathetic before, on the news of Jameson's advance became enthusiastic. Here was a *hero;* and who does not delight in worshipping a hero? Those who were neutral and indifferent before, were neutral no longer. Those who were enthusiastic before became more so now. *Here was a hero to worship.* The few women who had not fled the pestilence of war, took up the cry, 'A hero! A hero!' Poor women, they could not afford to pay their passage from Johannesburg to fly the horrors to come, but they could still manage to find a gay bonnet and a showy dress to wear to welcome their new hero. Every garden was robbed to obtain flowers to strew the path of Jameson and his brave troopers with blossoms. 'Jameson is coming! Jameson is coming! and will soon be here; out and meet him!' The balconies were covered with spectators; the streets were crowded with enthusiastic men and women, all to welcome their hero. 'He is coming. Did not our self-elected leaders declare that he had forced his way through the Boers against tremendous odds, and that he would soon be here? Nay, have not our own brave pound-a-day troops gone out to meet him and bring him in in triumph. Ladies, hold your bouquets ready to cast before his feet as he passes; men, keep your throats clear to cheer.'

'Ah, here he comes! here he comes! Hurrah! No, it is our men leading; he is sure to be behind them. But see how their horses sweat; they must have ridden hard. Where is Jameson? Where is Jameson? Alas! their hero was but clay. They had failed him. He had tried not to fail them, but fate was stronger; justice and right were against him; while they were waiting to give him a glorious and triumphal welcome, he was a prisoner. On inquiry, it was found that the brave (?) Johannesburg troops, who had gone forth to aid Jameson, had seen a few Burghers in the distance, and thinking prudence the better part of valour, had retired.

Amidst all this revolutionary turmoil, the friends of the Government in the city of gold kept calm and cool. For the Government had yet many thousands of friends in this city. But they were quiet and calm. They had offered their full assistance to the representatives of the Government, but had been requested to keep quiet and cool—they would be called upon only when it became necessary, not before. It is believed that the Government possessed friends and strength sufficient in Johannesburg alone (without calling in the aid of any outside Burghers) to crush the rebellion. But the Government wished to avoid a collision and the consequent bloodshed as long as peace was possible, and if a stronger force was displayed around Johannesburg and Pretoria than was necessary, it was only to guard against outside interference, as well as to show Johannesburg the folly of its ways of seeking reform by force. This display of force was one of the chief factors which brought about a peaceful ending to the revolution.

CHAPTER XVII

THE FOLLY OF C. LEONARD AND HIS CLIQUE

JOHANNESBURG, or rather the Reform Committee pretending to represent Johannesburg, did many inexplicable things during these few days of excitement.

The Reform Committee had sent a letter to Jameson (as per agreement?) requesting his aid to obtain their demands, as is proved by the letter Jameson had received, signed by five of the leading members of the Reform Committee. The Reform Committee had promised Jameson (so he declared) to send two thousand men to aid him in pushing his way through to Johannesburg. But what did these brave reformers do—these followers of Mirabeau, Rousseau, and who knows, perhaps, Marat? When Jameson was on his way, as per agreement with them, to fight with them, and for them, these reformers (?) sent a deputation to Pretoria and concluded an armistice with the Government, by which they bound themselves not to do anything to break the peace, or to give the Government cause to send a force against them for a stipulated time. A very laudable thing, and tending towards a peaceful solution, you would think. Quite so; only why did they not do so before? Why did they first entice Jameson to place himself in peril, and in danger of life on their behalf, and then utterly desert him. This much can be said on behalf of Jameson, and is freely acknowledged by the Boers, that he at least was no coward, and kept his part of the agreement, even though it was in an ignoble cause; but it only proves that there *is* sometimes honour among thieves, even though the honour was all on one side here.

How can the action of the Reform Committee be explained? I am afraid it can be explained no more than the action of C. Leonard (the leader and president of the conspirators on the Rand) can be explained. His cowardly action seemed to have given a very bad example to his fellow-conspiritors, and utterly demoralised them. What did he do? He threw the fat into the fire by the issue of his famous manifesto, and when he had succeeded in thoroughly rousing the public and the Government, and when Jameson was on his way, in answer to his invitation to come and aid him and his gang in their nefarious work—in short, when he saw the moment of danger had come, like a cur, he put his tail between his legs and fled the country, leaving his friends to get out of their position of danger, where he had helped to place them, as best they may. When Leonard had fled, the rest of the conspirators seemed to realise the danger of their little game of bluff. They had hoped, as one of their members had said months before, that the Boer Government would *funk* it (excuse the slang), and give them all they demanded.

Fools!

They had been living amongst the Boers for so long, and ought to have known that, while there was life, no Boer would give up the much-treasured and dearly-bought liberty of the nation.

Strange that these reformers (?) should have run their noses against a wall, without first making sure that the wall would give way without hurting their precious noses. But now, when the mischief was done, they seemed to realise *their* danger, and began to stop and consider. Now, when Jameson was fighting for life or death in their cause. Now, when thousands of poor women and children had fled from the scene in destitution and want. Now, when the veld along the Vaal and beyond was covered with these destitute, unprotected, unsheltered, barely-clothed and starving women and children, and were depending for daily bread on the very Boers whom the Reform Committee were trying to destroy. Now, when many a home was in mourning and woe for loved ones lost at that terrible railway accident at Glencoe, when a train, loaded with fugitives from the Rand, was wrecked, causing the death of many a mother, a father, a child, or some other loved one, while many a one lived to bear some terrible mark of the accident for life. Now, when the whole country was in commotion and disorder by their action. Now, when the powers of Europe were glaring in distrust at each other, ready to spring at each other's throat, and cause endless war and bloodshed. Now, when (worst of all for South Africa) a bitter and insatiable race hatred has been started anew in the whole of South Africa. Now only, I say, the few scheming, plotting and unscrupulous persons who had caused all this, began to bethink themselves, and now only, because they began to see that their own precious hides were beginning to be in danger, and followed in the footsteps of their leader, C. Leonard. They may plead that they stopped to avoid further bloodshed; but why have started shedding blood at all? Why first invite a foreign force to invade the country on their behalf, and then desert their accomplices?

No, all excuse is vain, they knew exactly what they were doing when they began their guilty plots to rob a nation of freedom and country; and they knew (unless they were idiots, and fit inmates for the lunatic asylum) what to expect. The only sensible thing the Reform Committee ever did was, when Jameson was a prisoner and the whole mess was spoiled, to accept defeat and lay down their arms. (I am not referring to the time when they concluded the armistice, while Jameson's fate was undecided, but the following week, when they laid down their arms, as we shall see farther on).

But the great guilt of the Reform Committee lay in their ever having taken up arms, and in ever having plotted to light the torch of civil war, with no other object than to throw the South African Republic into the arms of Rhodes. As to the professed object of the revolution and the demands contained in the manifesto, we shall take occasion a little farther on to show how much—or how little—cause there was for the taking up of arms.

CHAPTER XVIII

PRETORIA DURING THE CRISIS

PRETORIA, as became the capital of the State, followed in the footsteps of the Government, and kept calm and cool during all this bustle and uproar in Johannesburg. It is true there were a few hot-headed, ignorant young men (late arrivals mostly) who talked big amongst themselves, and said that the time had come for England to step in and again take possession of the Transvaal; but it was noticed that these young men either kept out of the way of, or were very quiet in the presence of, the Burghers or Afrikanders generally. But the majority of, in fact nearly all, the inhabitants of Pretoria were very orderly and quiet. There were those who in their inmost hearts wished for Jameson's and Johannesburg's success, and even said so at first; but as soon as information of Jameson's defeat was received, even these became Government supporters and sympathisers—at least so they said (?). But from the first the leading inhabitants and public men gave the Government to understand that all their influence would be given to support law and order; and on the arrival of the news that the country was being invaded by Chartered troops, the inhabitants held a meeting, at the suggestion of a leading citizen, and resolved to form themselves into a vigilant corps, to protect life and keep order. This was done. Every man of whatsoever nationality became a member of the corps, and did duty night and day, patrolling the streets and vicinity of the town. All this was done under the orders and with the assistance of the authorities, thus showing the good understanding between the Government and the inhabitants of Pretoria.

The Jingo papers, or rather those belonging to the association mentioned before, waxed bolder and bolder, as they saw the evident danger of the State. The Johannesburg papers, antagonistic to the Government, seemed to think that the Government would be unable to punish them now or hereafter, and preached almost open sedition; and a certain Pretoria paper was by no means far behind in this respect.

The rebels were encouraged to persevere, and those who refused to join the malcontents, were incited to join. The Government was abused and reviled more than before. According to these papers, the chances of the Boers to defend themselves were *nil;* while the success of the invaders and rebels was assured. With what courage these papers spoke up *now*, for they rightly considered that the Government had no time to waste looking after them, or punishing sedition preached in their columns.

But what a change came over these papers when Jameson was in prison with his officers and men and the Reform Committee had surrendered unconditionally? Now there was no abuse. Now the *dirty* Boers were heard of no more. But everything was '*our* Government,' '*our* Burghers,' the '*powerholders*,' all said and written in a most respectful manner; while in the place of the threats uttered a few days before, now nothing was heard but a plea for *mercy*. The papers were filled with articles pointing out to the Government what grand and unprecedented opportunities of displaying their wonted mercy presented itself. Truly it was a sudden and even ludicrous change of face, causing many a smile of amusement on the face of the impartial observer. But this amiability did not last long. As soon as things quieted down, and the anger of the Burghers had subsided, these cowardly libellers resumed their dirty work, as we shall have occasion to observe farther on. Those who happened to be in Pretoria when the news arrived on the Monday that Jameson was invading the country at the head of eight hundred Chartered troopers, will remember how unexpected and hardly credited the news was. It was so unexpected, and even improbable, that few could be found to believe the news—even the Government, it is said, would not believe the news wired to them from their own officials at Mirico—that 'Jameson was marching on to Johannesburg, and that he refused to turn back.' The Government wired for confirmation of the news; and it was so definitely confirmed that the authorities were forced to believe it and take the necessary action.

And now the grand military system of the country was displayed to full advantage. On the Monday afternoon information was received of the invasion. Every Burgher was living peacefully and unsuspectingly on his farm, without the least idea that his country was in danger, or that a foreign foe had already invaded the country. And yet, forty hours after the information was received at Pretoria, a commando had already intercepted Jameson's force, and had forced him to turn from his contemplated course, and in three days he was surrounded and compelled to surrender ignominiously.

Even this was eclipsed by the further mobilisation of the Burghers, for, before the week was ended, eight thousand Burghers were in the neighbourhood of Johannesburg awaiting the orders of the Commandant-General to attack, in case the rebellion was pushed, while in and around Pretoria a like number or more were encamped.

The excitement for the next few days was intense; every moment seemed fraught with the gravest results.

News from the seat of war was anxiously awaited. The office of *The Press*, which seemed to be the best informed of what was going on, was besieged day and night for news. The wildest reports were flying around, and when reliable news did come, one hardly knew whether to believe it or not.

An amusing incident was noticed during the day when news from Krugersdorp was most intensely desired

Some boys, who seemed to have grasped the situation with juvenile sagacity, got hold of a pile of blank sheets of paper of the size and shape generally used by newspapers on which to issue special and extraordinary telegrams during the day These special telegrams were eagerly awaited, and even fought for, by the public during these days of excitement. These youngsters had noticed this, and with their blank sheets of paper in their hand, walked about *à la* newspaper boys, shouting, 'News from the war. One hundred people killed. Great slaughter amongst the enemy,' or anything else they could think of to excite the people.

To give a single instance of the result. A dignified, portly and very conscious young man was strolling down Church Street. But, in spite of his dignity, black suit, shining boots, and bell topper hat, even he forgot himself sufficiently for a moment to eagerly run after one of these boys and snatch one of these supposed special telegrams from him. Several bystanders, who had already been caught themselves by the youngsters, were watching the scene with amusement. The dignified young man, after having secured the much-desired telegram (?), walked composedly to one side of the sidewalk, settled his eyeglasses carefully on his nose, and prepared to read the startling news, as declared by the amateur newspaper boys. Those who were watching the party in question saw a look of astonishment upon the expressive countenance of the Pretoria dude, followed by an expression of intense disgust and anger, as, on looking after the laughing youngsters, he saw them put their hands in front of their noses in a most impressive manner. Of course everybody laughed, while the young man looked as if he would like to punish the boys with his walking-stick. But, on second thoughts, he seemed to think that it would be too undignified, and instead, walked away, expressing his disgust at the laughter of the bystanders by the haughty erectness of his head.

While everbody was anxious and excited, the Government seemed never to lose the calm even tenor of its ways. Amidst the greatest danger and anxiety, the President and Commandant-General never for a single moment lost confidence in their ability to uphold their position, or to defend their country against the threatening danger.

Even when the Middleburg commando asked the President to proclaim martial law, the President remained calm and moderate, and told his Burghers that there was no necessity for such extreme measures, and that all that was necessary could be done without unduly inconveniencing the public.

After all the excitement and anxiety on the part of the public, the reader can imagine what a relief it was to hear of the surrender of Jameson and his band of *Freebooters*. It was as if a heavy burden had rolled off the minds of the public. Those few who did not wish it, would not believe in Jameson's surrender, and would only acknowledge the fact when they saw the invaders brought into Pretoria as prisoners. But these were only a few—enemies to the country, to liberty and justice. They were of the class of humanity (?) who would sacrifice everything to attain their own selfish wishes, or to satisfy their unjust prejudice.

CHAPTER XIX

POSSIBILITIES AND PROBABILITIES

STEVE and the rest of the guard hurried their prisoners forward towards Pretoria, as they feared a rescue. Rumours of such a rescue were not wanting. During the night the guard received information that a party of rebels had left Johannesburg, presumably to rescue Jameson. Proper precautions were taken, but it proved unnecessary. Johannesburg had evidently had enough of fighting (?).

Many stories have been circulated of the bravery (?) of the Johannesburg soldiers. It is told how bands of volunteers left the golden city with the avowed object of teaching the Boers a lesson, and of relieving or rescuing Jameson. But it is also told how these martial bands did not proceed far beyond the suburbs of the town, having seen what to their terror-stricken eyes appeared to be parties of Boers, but what proved later on to have been either troops of their own cattle or parties from their own city.

However, the prisoners were all safely brought into Pretoria, without any attempt at rescue. The men were encamped on the racecourse about a quarter-of-a-mile out of town, under guard, while the officers were kept in safer quarters in what is locally known as *The Government Hotel*, and there they were kept until the authorities had decided what should be done with them, and until they were ultimately sent by rail to the Natal border and handed over to the Imperial Authorities.

Steve was now once more at home. He was surprised, even though he expected something of the sort, to see the squares and outskirts of Pretoria covered with the tents and waggons of the various commandos, and his heart swelled with pride and joy as he viewed the brave men, who at a moment's notice had left all and hurried in answer to the call of duty to defend country and liberty.

He took frequent walks out amongst the various commandos, and made many friends amongst the Burghers, unknown to him up to now. He found them, unless excited by remarks of recent events, in a happy and frolicsome mood. 'Just like a troop of happy children out for a holiday,' as he remarked to a friend. The Burgher out on commando is always full of fun and frolic when off duty or guard. Various games of skill and strength are indulged in during the day, while the evenings are spent in reminiscences of the past; stories of Kaffir campaigns, of the war against England, and of the hunting field, passes round. The younger men would sit and listen attentively and respectfully as their elders related adventures, dangers and difficulties experienced during the early years of the *voortrekkers*. The old men would feel young again as they told of the dangers of the chase; of how they hunted the elephant, the lion, the buffalo, the rhinoceros, in the days when such game roamed the country in plenty, and could be found almost without searching for. How the young men regretted their ill-fortune, which caused them to be born too late to participate in such stirring times. How they wished that they might have lived fifty years ago instead of in these tame, prosaic days, when one had to take a three months' journey to see a rhinoceros or a lion, and when an elephant could only be seen in a circus show.

It is Monday night, 6th of January 1896. It is the night when the great National Union meeting should have been held under the chairmanship of Charles Leonard. The meeting is being held, but only a committee meeting; but alas and alack Charles Leonard is not here to take the chair. Charles Leonard is in Cape Town. Poor Charles Leonard. The body may have been willing, but the heart was *too* faint. Such is ever the fate of braggarts. While danger is yet far away, great deeds are talked of—then the braggart is a hero; and, alas for human credulity, the braggart will always find those who will believe in him. It is not everybody who can read the heart of man in his face, or from his tongue, and, least of all, the *public*. How easily the PUBLIC—the *people*—as a whole, will allow a boasting, a glib-tongued, plausible braggart to lead them by the nose. How disgusting it is for a student of human nature to see a man thus lead a crowd of credulous people to believe in him, to make a hero of him, to accept his statements for gospel, and all because the man has a plausible appearance and can TALK.

Johannesburg for a time believed in Charles Leonard!

Now the National Union Committee, self-styled *Reform Committee*, by others called the *deformed* Committee, was holding a meeting—to do what? To decide upon what they should do in reply to President Kruger's ultimatum, in which they were given twenty-four hours to lay down their arms and surrender unconditionally.

But the meeting is strictly private; it is not for the public to hear the bitter recriminations amongst the Committee because of blunders and mistakes of the few leaders, nor the regrets of those who had allowed themselves to be flattered into joining a movement which, in their hearts, they knew to be wrong and condemnable; therefore we shall not report the proceedings, but content ourselves that we shall know the result of their deliberations soon, within twenty-four hours.

After Steve had safely conducted the prisoners into their place of confinement, his first act was to report himself as ready for duty, in case of need, to his own field cornet, after which he went home, had a bath, and a good sleep before tea-time.

The members of the amateur debating society are gathered together once more The debate goes on every night now. The burning questions of the day are eagerly discussed, and everyone present airs his views of what *ought* to be done, what *he* would do if he had the control of affairs. Truly the amount of wisdom (?) wasted in this manner is really alarming. It is a pity that the wisdom, knowledge and statescraft exhausted in this private and useless manner could not be bottled up and labelled, to be used as occasion requires. Such bottled-up knowledge may even become a marketable commodity, if some great inventor would only find out how it is to be preserved. Edison might take the hint one of these days.

How easy it would make it for public men and statesmen to buy a little wisdom on certain subjects, especially when in a dilemma. How easy it would be, say, for Mr Chamberlain to buy a bottle of wisdom on 'Home Rule for the Rand,' or for President Cleveland on 'Venezuela Affairs,' or for President Kruger on 'How to deal with the Uitlanders,' or for Charles Leonard on 'The safest way to play the game of doubling on the hounds,' or for Rhodes on 'How to make the Afrikander Bond an Imperial bond (to make him Emperor?),' or even on 'How to make Rhodesia pay.' So many uses could be found for such bottled wisdom and knowledge.

Of course, I know that books and papers generally serve as bottles to contain and preserve much of this same wisdom and knowledge, but so much of it goes to waste, so few have the opportunity or means to so preserve their own knowledge.

We will at least preserve a little of the knowledge and statescraft exuded at this evening's conversation in the sitting-room of Steve's boarding-house. It will, at least, serve to show the tendency of public feeling during this time, when public feeling ran high.

'Hillo, Steve! Well, I am hanged! is it yourself or your spirit I see? Well, at least, your hand feels mortal enough.' It was Harrison who spoke, shaking Steve heartily by the hand.

'Well, I *am* glad to see you chaps again,' said Steve, as he shook hands all round, 'and you too, Keith, old fellow? When did you return, I did not expect to see you here before to-morrow.'

'Oh, when you were gone, we did not seem to enjoy ourselves, so we returned; we have been here since Friday.'

'You are very flattering to pretend that you value my company so much. Of course, you were curious to know what was going on here, and therefore you returned,' said Steve, laughing.

'Well, I suppose you are partly right; we could hardly stay there quietly in the veld without news, while we knew that history was being made at the rate of a hundred miles an hour, and as you had *skedaddled*, we soon followed suit, only we came in an orderly and comfortable way, and did not start on *shank's* pony as you did,' replied Keith.

'I suppose you returned by the way you went. Well, I think every man to his taste. I wanted to be in at the death; you preferred a more quiet, neutral position. I don't blame you; every man must do as his conscience tells him.'

'And how did you fare, Steve? You might give us a relation of your adventures,' begged Harrison.

Steve gave a rough outline of his adventures since he left the party on the Vaal River, and when he told them that he was present at, and participated in, the Battle of Doornkop, he was plied with questions from all sides, to which he replied as best and as modestly as he could.

'How many Boers were there against Jameson, Joubert?' queried a late arrival (who was also a professed Boer hater), named Hastings. Steve had noticed his antagonism towards the Government of the country, and was not at all well disposed towards him.

'Well, if you wish to know how many Boers were or are against Jameson, I could not tell you exactly; but if I had a copy of the last census papers I might be able to give you some idea of the number. If it will help you, however, I may tell you that *every* Boer or Afrikander (as we call them) in South Africa is against Jameson.'

The others present laughed at this little sally of Steve's.

'Of course, you know, I don't mean who is against him in principle, I mean how many Boers (or Afrikanders as you prefer to call them) *fought* against Jameson.'

'Oh, why did you not say so then? Well, I will draw it as mild as possible,' said Steve, with some sarcasm, which he could hardly conceal, 'so as to save your feelings; for if I were to give you the exact number, you would not believe me and would think I was trying to bluff you. Well, there were no more than one hundred Boers actually fighting against Jameson and his band at the Battle of Doornkop.'

'Bah! you must think I am a green 'un. Do you think I will believe that one hundred Boers could defeat eight hundred drilled English troops, and armed with artillery too? Tell it to the marines.'

'Oh, so you *do* call them English troops?' asked Steve.

'Well, of course, they are not Imperial troops actually, but they are mostly Englishmen, and have been drilled and disciplined by English officers, and on the English principle, but are not British troops.'

'Oh, I see, that means, of course, that if they had succeeded, and had subjugated the Transvaal with the assistance of Johannesburg, they would have been English or even Imperial troops, and would have been honoured and owned by England; now that they have been defeated, of course, they are only an irresponsible band of British subjects, for whom and whose deeds nobody is responsible. I have even heard that some Englishmen assert that Jameson's men are really mostly Afrikanders, that is because they have been defeated.'

'But, Steve,' said Harrison, 'do you really mean to say that one hundred Boers actually defeated Jameson?'

'I will swear that no *more* than one hundred Boers took part in the Battle of Doornkop; that would be on the safe side, for I *know* that there were less,' said Steve. 'Of course, there were nearly or fully a thousand Burghers in the vicinity of Krugersdorp, but they were all too far away to take part in the fight. Some parties of them were guarding the various roads, so that if Jameson did escape at Doornkop he would have been pulled up at some other spot. Others again were watching the road to Johannesburg, so that if Johannesburg *did* send any help to Jameson, *they* would have had somebody to look after them before they could join forces with the invaders. And lastly, as a matter of fact, a party of Burghers was preparing to take Jameson by storm, and was only prevented from doing so by Jameson's hoisting the white flag and surrendering.'

'Very interesting and spicy indeed,' remarked Hastings in an ironical, unbelieving way.

'Yes, indeed, and in spite of the spice, hardly to the taste of some people,' retorted Steve.

'Well, your Government has managed to overcome Jameson, as I believe, by force of numbers, and because Jameson's men were starved, fatigued and out of ammunition; but it remains to be seen whether the same game can be played with Johannesburg, which is prepared and well armed and provisioned. That will be a nut too hard for your Government's knuckles to crack.'

'To answer your first assertion first. I have already stated that Jameson really had the force of numbers at Doornkop. As to being starved, they had, as I happen to know from their own men, plenty of provisions, and found at regular intervals buildings placed there for the purpose, in which provisions in plenty for man and horse were found. In fact, one man told me they found tables laid ready and laden with food; they had only to sit down and eat. As to fatigue, the majority of the Burghers travelled as far in half the time as Jameson's troopers did, and that without preparation and without much provision. The assertion that the Chartered troops were out of ammunition when they surrendered is the most foolish of all; for I can tell you that the Government took a rich booty in ammunition alone. In fact, more ammunition was taken from Jameson, than the Boers possessed when they began the war against England in 1880.'

'I don't believe it,' asserted Hastings.

'Well, I can say this much, if Steve says it is so, and that he saw it himself, I will believe it, for I have never known him to tell a lie,' said Keith.

'I don't believe Steve *can* tell a lie,' approved Harrison.

Steve went on, as if he was unconscious of the interruption. He never lost his temper.

'As to Johannesburg, I am not a betting man, but I am willing to go a little bet that Johannesburg won't fight. If Johannesburg cared to face the Burgher forces, she would hardly have allowed Jameson to be defeated and captured without at least an effort to rescue and assist him. No, my boy, Johannesburg has no fighting men. It is all bluff. Of course, there are a few brave men in Johannesburg, who, for a righteous cause, would certainly be able to give a good account of themselves. But brave men would hardly consent to be lead by a Leonard or such as he. No. I will tell you the position in a few words.

'The great amalgamator wanted to amalgamate the Transvaal and Rhodesia for the sake of the Rand goldfields. The plan of campaign was to send a few men to the Rand to preach rebellion and revolution.

'The next thing would be to strengthen the Rand people by sending outside help, for the Rand by itself could do but little, and, besides, would not always be willing to do exactly as ordered by their would-be leaders The best outside help at hand was obtainable from Rhodesia; by sending troops from Rhodesia, which really is British territory, would embroil England in the matter, and thus England would be forced to take a hand in the game. It was hoped that if England once took a hand in the game, she would play to suit the cards of her only great privy councillor in South Africa. Now the outside help has been nipped in the bud and England is disowning the whole plot (of course it having failed so far). Thus Johannesburg is isolated and divided amongst themselves, one party being for revolution, one party being for the present Government. Do you see any chance for the Reform Committee to continue their foolish plot? Say, now, for instance, they did persist in trying their strength against the Government. In a week the Government would lay Johannesburg in ruins, or if the Government wanted to be merciful and spare the innocents in the town, in three months they would be starved out if they were not driven to surrender by thirst long before then. No, Johannesburg could stand neither a siege nor an attack from the Burghers. Their only hope for success (England) has failed them.'

'How do you know that England may not even yet take a hand in the game on her own account? The Transvaal is a blot on the face of the South African map as far as England is concerned, and it has been believed all along that England has only been waiting for an excuse to step in and once more take possession of the country.'

'Well, I do not believe England will try such a trick. Firstly, because I believe England as a power and Englishmen as a nation have yet some honour left. Secondly, even if England did wish to forget honour and treaty obligations, not to speak of right, justice and the right of nations. I say, even if England did wish to do so, I believe she *dare* not do so. She dares not, because the glaring injustice would arouse the world against her. It would be an injustice more glaring than the Armenian atrocities even, for from the Turks everybody expects injustice, oppression and cruelty, while from England one would expect at least common justice. From England one would expect that she would recognise her own treaties, for England is supposed to be, and has always been believed to be, a highly civilised power. England is a Christian country, and England is governed on Christian principles. Should England forget her old traditions of fairplay, justice and honour, the rest of the world would pull her up much sharper than they would Turkey.

'Then leaving out the rest of the world, England would have her hands fairly full in South Africa alone, should she enter upon such an unjust war. If she fights the Transvaal under present circumstances, she would have to fight the Free State, which has already called out a portion of her Burghers to be ready in case of emergency. She would have to fight the entire Afrikander nation in South Africa, including many Uitlanders, or people of foreign birth, and even many Englishman of long residence in South Africa who have learned to value self-government and deprecate Downing Street Government.'

'Why, *do* you believe for a moment that the whole Afrikander nation could beat England?'

'I believe that if England were FREE, and willing to put out her full strength against the Afrikander nation, that she would conquer in the end, for every Afrikander Burgher killed would leave a vacancy in their ranks; while, if one British soldier is killed, two could always be found to take his place. But even if England is able to put out her full might against us, it would be a long and bloody struggle. For every Burgher killed three or four British soldiers would bite the dust. In his native land, and amongst his native hills and mountains, the Boer can take long odds against himself. Then the fight will be on land and not on the sea, where England is supreme. Then again the Boers will always choose their own battlefield, and you ought to know by this time that a Boer knows how to choose a battlefield to his own advantage. The British forces would only be attacked where their superior numbers and arms would be of no advantage. In short, it would be a warfare on the guerrilla system, in which the Boers excel all other nations, and by the time England had conquered the Afrikanders (if she did conquer them), which will only be when at least half of them have been killed; by the time she had conquered them, I say, thousands, if not tens of thousands, of English soldiers will have perished in the South African veld by the bullet or by starvation. Now, I come to the chief reason why England does not *dare* to undertake such an unjust war, or rather I should say, why the English *Government* does not dare to do so: And that is because the British people, being a free people, with a voice in their own Government, would never allow their Government to undertake such a cruel —to both sides—and unjust war, and have thousands of their soldiers and relatives killed, all to please a few grasping millionaires such as Rhodes and Beit, or a few conspiring, speculating attorneys, etc., who wish to obtain power as well as riches.'

Steve became quite eloquent in his earnestness.

'Do you think, then, that England will leave everything to the Boers to do as they think fit? Will she, do you think, allow your Government to shoot down her subjects in Johannesburg, without giving them aid? or if Johannesburg surrenders to the ultimatum, unconditionally, would England allow the Boers to shoot the Reform Committee as rebels, which would probably be done if nothing was done to prevent it?'

'If it were done, it would only be what they deserve. But it will *not* be done, at least, not without a fair trial. You may be sure the Government is not going to do anything rash, and sacrifice all the advantages they have obtained. Everything will be done legally and according to the laws of the country.'

'It remains to be seen,' said Hastings, walking out whistling, giving Steve to understand that he had had enough argument for once.

CHAPTER XX

JOHANNESBURG SURRENDERS UNCONDITIONALLY—HOME RULE FOR THE RAND

THE following day being Tuesday and the day during which the Johannesburg malcontents would decide whether they would surrender or fight, everybody was on the tenter hooks of expectation and anxiety to know what would be decided.

The High Commissioner, who had been in Pretoria since Saturday the 4th January, had recommended the Reform Committee to surrender to the Government, as it was useless for them to attempt a struggle. Sir Jacobus de Wet, the British agent, had advised the British subjects to return to ways of peace and order.

The Reform Committee might have wished to proceed to extremes, but they saw that they had not a leg to stand upon. No more outside help could be hoped for. The High Commissioner had acted honourably and in good faith to the Government of the South African Republic, and in the only way he could act without sacrificing British honour. He had assured the malcontents that they could not expect British aid if they went beyond the pale of the law.

Being unable to obtain outside help, and as even the majority of Johannesburg refused to fight except those who received one pound sterling a day, the Reform Committee did the only thing left them to do, and surrendered unconditionally to the Government.

Of course they did not acknowledge that they surrendered because they could not do anything else, and because they knew that with Jameson's defeat their whole plot had failed. No, they only surrendered to please the High Commissioner, and as they would not fight (to please the High Commissioner), they declared that they expected the High Commissioner to fight for them and obtain for them their demands. In fact, they shifted the whole responsibility of past, present and future on to the High Commissioner, and consequently on to the Imperial Government. When Steve heard of the surrender he threw up his hat and shouted hurrah, and ran to the telegraph office and sent the following telegram to his mother :—

'DEAR MOTHER,—Johannesburg has surrendered unconditionally. South Africa may reckon on some years of peace again ; no fear of further disturbances.'

Foolish Steve. He did not think that England *would* interfere after all and keep the country in a state of unrest and uncertainty for months after, through holding out hopes to the discontented that she would force the Government to accede to their demands.

This uncertainty was kept up for months, and this uncertainty obtains to this very day when I write this (15th April 1896). England took it upon herself, after everybody thought that all was settled, and after the President had already promised certain privileges to the discontented, to dictate to the South African Republic what she should do and what she should not do, and this in contradiction to the London Convention, which she had only just declared she would uphold in its entirety.

It is true that Mr Chamberlain sent what he called friendly advice only, but everybody knew that it was intended to be taken as a demand. And how was this advice sent?

Mr Chamberlain, Secretary of State for the Colonies, drew up a long despatch in which he raked up long forgotten incidents of South African history. He reminded President Kruger of past friendliness shown by England to the Transvaal and Afrikanders. But he forgot to mention one incident of the overwhelming number of times that England had acted in an unfriendly and even unjust manner. He reminded the Government of the South African Republic that England had shown mercy in Bechuanaland to certain Afrikanders who had resisted English pretensions there. But Mr Chamberlain forgot to mention Slachtersnek, where Boers were hung like felons on a gallows for resisting England. He forgot to mention Boomplaats, where Boers again were shot—murdered—for fighting for their own country and for hard-earned freedom.

Mr Chamberlain did not remind President Kruger that the Government of the South African Republic was in possession of a certain document (for which Piet Relief and forty of his comrades gave their lives) by which they could prove that Natal belongs to the Boers by every just claim and by every law of nations.

Mr Chamberlain did not remind President Kruger that England took from the Free State Boers the richest diamond mine in the world, and, out of a remnant of shame, forced the Free State to take £90,000 for the Kimberley diamond mines—£90,000 for what is worth £90,000,000. But if it was worth 90 pence, every country has the right to keep what it has, without being forced to sell it. Alas no, Mr Chamberlain was not shamed into telling President Kruger that England had persecuted and oppressed the Boers for the last ninety years; he did not ask the President to heap coals of fire on the heads of the British nation by showing the magnanimity to the British subjects that Britain refused the Boers.

Mr Chamberlain capped his despatch by *advising* (?) President Kruger to give Johannesburg a variety of *Home Rule.* Alas, the inconsistency of man. Mr Chamberlain, who is a Unionist, and opponent of Home Rule for Ireland, advises the South African Republic to give Home Rule to Johannesburg.

Johannesburg is a town in the heart of the South African Republic, inhabited by a mining community of all nationalities in the world, a large proportion of whom are

British subjects. And for the sake of the British subjects in Johannesburg the district is to be isolated and Home Rule given to it, while Ireland is a country inhabited by a great nation, who are living in their own native land, and who are kept down by force of arms. To this nation, unjustly conquered by England long ago, and kept under ever after only by England's military strength, to this nation Home Rule is refused by Mr Chamberlain and his party. By what moral right can Mr Chamberlain demand, or even advise, the South African Republic to grant Home Rule to Johannesburg? I have heard somewhere a very useful adage, 'Sweep in front of your own door before you sweep in front of your neighbour's door.' Very homely, but to the point, and really I would recommend it to Mr Chamberlain's study.

This interference in our internal affairs by Mr Chamberlain, or rather this advice as to our internal affairs by Mr Chamberlain, would have been received with gratitude and thanks, if it had been given, as advice *ought* to be given, viz., privately and confidentially, but Mr Chamberlain was playing to the Jingo gallery. In truth, it was not meant for honest advice, it was done to please the friends of the Chartered Company, and to do this more effectually Mr Chamberlain, in contradiction to all diplomatic usages and etiquette, published his *advice* (?) to President Kruger in London before despatching the same to its destination.

We shall show farther on how this *advice* (?) was received in Pretoria.

CHAPTER XXI

THE CHARTERED PRESS AGAIN—JONAH!

AND who were the people for whom Mr Chamberlain was asking Home Rule? For people who ever since they entered the country have openly abused the Government, have tried in every way to abuse the freedom and liberty they enjoy in this country, by libelling and traducing the people and Government of the country. People who stood up in open rebellion against the Government, people who did not scruple to call in a band of foreign freebooters to help them to raise an unjust revolution. A people whose leaders openly declared that they had thirty thousand rifles to carry on the rebellion, and when they had solemnly promised to give up all arms gave up two thousand five hundred. Who did those leaders deceive? Did they deceive their followers when they declared they possessed thirty thousand rifles? or did they deceive the Government when they declared they possessed only two thousand five hundred?

These people had come to the Transvaal to make money. They had made fabulous fortunes out of Transvaal soil. And to show their gratitude to the Government of the country, who had fostered them and protected their industry, and had done everything possible to please them and prosper them, they evinced their gratitude by maturing the vilest plot known to history to overthrow this Government. This much for the rebels. On the other hand, the people for whom Mr Chamberlain asked Home Rule, ridiculed his proposal and would have no more of his home rule than they wanted of Downing Street rule. Those who were not satisfied with the Boer rule simply wanted to rule themselves, not only in Johannesburg, but the whole country. If they could not get the franchise, by which they could get to rule the whole country, then they would not have any rule at all other than they have now.

Then what would Mr Chamberlain do with the large proportion, if not the majority, of the inhabitants of Johannesburg, who are, and have always been satisfied with the present Government. *They* would have no other Government than their own legitimate Government.

But the whole proposal is so ridiculous that it would be foolish to discuss it further here. We shall proceed with our story. The utter ridiculousness of giving Home Rule to Johannesburg must be apparent to everyone who knows the state of affairs, and those who do not know have only to read this story to the end and they will see for themselves what the Jingo element in Johannesburg is composed of.

Now as regards the reception of Mr Chamberlain's Home Rule Despatch. We have already stated that the *people* of Johannesburg ridiculed it. But the Jingoes received it with joy.

'Now at last,' thought they, 'England is committed; and either the South African Republic must knuckle under and do as the Secretary of State demands, or—fight Great Britain; once more "Rule Britannia" is sung with gusto. Mr Chamberlain has restarted, or very nearly so, the gassing and warlike talk of Jingoism. It will not be his fault if the peace is not broken once more.'

Now what will the Government of the South African Republic do? Will it brave the anger of the British Lion? or will it knuckle down and beg?

No! Once more the calm, manly and firm old man, the President of the Transvaal, stands to his guns, and fearlessly sends the Secretary of State for the Colonies of Great Britain a dignified, friendly, but *firm* reply, in which the assertions of Mr Chamberlain are fairly refuted, and the right of England to interfere in the internal affairs of the South African Republic totally and distinctly denied.

At last the Jingoes rejoice, and many a firm friend of the Republic holds his breath in anticipation of disaster to its liberties. The President has thrown down the gauntlet, and England cannot but take it up and force the Transvaal at the point of the bayonet to accede to its unjust demands, or maybe to take away its freedom from the Transvaal altogether. Many began to make their preparations anew for the great struggle they thought they saw inevitable. But what was the surprise to many, disappointment to some, and joy to others, when the cables brought the news that England had quietly and tamely received President Kruger's lesson in etiquette to Mr Chamberlain, and calm request to 'mind your own business.' Such was indeed the case, for Mr Chamberlain declared, in the House of Commons, that he had no intention to press the acceptance of his *suggestion* on President Kruger. Once more PEACE seemed possible and probable. Once more the rival factions argued their various contentions with a calmer and more dignified spirit. Only the Chartered Press in South Africa and in England raged louder and louder as peace became probable. It seemed as if Mr Rhodes was aware that the only hope he had for his actions to be passed over or condoned was in war—war at any price, was consequently the cry of the Chartered Press. For if war with Great Britain brought to a successful issue Mr Rhodes' scheme, viz., the suppression of the Transvaal Republic, then Mr Rhodes might reasonably hope that no inquiry would he held as to what part he had in the plot. Such an inquiry must be averted at any price if possible; for such an inquiry meant that light will be thrown on many a dark deed and conspiracy in the past life of the arch conspirator and his partners and subordinates. Such an inquiry would show that the trusted high official, Privy Councillor to the Queen, and Prime Minister of an important British colony, managing director of a large territory (ruled under a British Charter), had betrayed his trust in every case, and had brought dishonour upon his Queen and country; and would bring to the light of day the names of partners in the plot, never suspected, or, if suspected, only whispered as yet.

To avert such an inquiry then, all the influence of *gold*, power, position and birth, of Rhodes and his friends were brought to bear on newspapers, great and small; on

Government officials, and even the ministry in power in England, to avert the dreaded inquiry—honour and truth even were sacrificed. Mr Rhodes totally denied all complicity in the plot—at first. But in spite of his denial, all his actions proved his guilt. His consciousness of guilt forced him to at once resign his premiership of the Cape Colony. Then he slunk off to England to avoid the reproachful looks of his betrayed fellow-ministers, and trusting friends, and also to set in motion his hireling Press in England, to defend or to justify, by hook or crook, his actions, and patch up his wrecked reputation. But even in England his guilty conscience would not let him rest; again he slunk off to the wilderness of Rhodesia that time. But to avoid meeting his duped friends in Cape Town again, he went *via* the Red Sea this time. But the steamer that bore him refused to carry such political guilt, and cast him like a Jonah forth to proceed as best he might. Arrived in Rhodesia again, his advent seemed to be the signal for a native rebellion; a rebellion which is raging to this day (30th June 1896), and the consequences of which no one can foresee, except that there seems to be a probability of many more innocents being lost, in addition to the hundreds already lost, in the struggle against the natives by the inhabitants —a struggle that was caused solely through Mr Rhodes allowing the police forces, which ought to have protected the country, to be sent on a filibustering expedition against a friendly neighbour—a neighbour who, after being attacked in a cowardly and dastardly way by the Chartered Company, offered to fight the company's battles against the Matabele out of sheer generosity and pity for the innocent inhabitants; but more of this anon.

Mr Rhodes' absence in Rhodesia did not prevent his agents from continuing the newspaper fight against the Transvaal Government and people. Mr Rhodes' actions were excused in a hundred different ways. Some denied his complicity in the plot altogether; while others, forced to admit his guilt, said he did it to lay bare some fancied plot between the Transvaal and Germany. In short, so many contradictory excuses emanated from the Rhodesian Press and party that one excuse confounded the other; but every impartial observer could see that these excuses, one and all, were rotten to the core. There being no defence that would stand the light of day, the Chartered combination of hireling newspapers, headed by the *Times* of London, saw that all they could do was to abuse the other side, viz., the enemies of Mr Rhodes and his company, and thus find an excuse in the bad (?) administration of the South African Republic Government, giving forth that Mr Rhodes sought to bring a better (?) government into existence in the Transvaal.

To obtain their object, viz., the old one of blackening the people of the Transvaal and its Government, no expense of either money or truth was spared. But they overreached themselves. The more they *lied* the more their lies were exposed and proved to be untrue. To-day the *Times* would publish some telegram from Johannesburg, telling of some imaginary wrong perpetrated by the Transvaal Government, but the next day the assertion would be disproved by some authority not to be denied. In short, so apparent was the untruth of their statements, that the public soon learned to discredit all statements coming from newspapers known to be Chartered. Even Mr Chamberlain felt constrained to warn the public to accept with caution these interested wires from Johannesburg.

We shall see farther on how the Transvaal Government triumphed against all these truth-ignoring libellers.

CHAPTER XXII

OUT OF EVIL CAME GREAT GOOD TO THE TRANSVAAL

VERILY, never was the saying realised to a fuller extent, that 'out of evil cometh good,' than was the case with the Transvaal after the events of January 1896. On New Year's Day Stephen Joubert thought that never was his country and people in greater peril than they then were. And even though he hoped and trusted that they would at least escape the extreme peril of national suppression and total loss of freedom, yet he dared hardly hope that this great evil would bring forth great good. He hardly hoped for the Transvaal to retain the full prestige and strength that she possessed before the crisis. How great must his joy now be, in common with his fellow-countrymen, to find his country's power, prestige and good name doubled and trebled since New Year's Day. First of all, he read with joy the cables announcing that his country possessed the sympathy and goodwill of all the nations of the civilised world. He saw that Germany, France and Russia, especially the former, were determined to see the Transvaal's independence maintained. He saw that the German Emperor sent a cable of congratulation to President Kruger that left no doubt of his opinion. Indeed, his opinion was expressed so plainly that England feared German interference, and sent a flying squadron to Delagoa Bay, to prevent Germany from landing troops at that port to aid the Transvaal—*a fool's errand.*

Transvaal never asked for German or any European aid !

After the Transvaal Government had foregone its just right of punishing Jameson and his men, and had most magnanimously given them up to the British Government to be punished according to British law, the Transvaal acquired a new (?) virtue in the opinion of the world. The enemies of the Boers had always described them to be of a savage and cruel nature. Now the world saw a practical demonstration of the fact that the Boers were Christians ! Christians as well in deed as in name. For they had shown mercy to those who had refused mercy to them and theirs. But even this act of mercy was not recognised by the enemies of the Republic. Motives of policy were ascribed to this act by the Chartered Press. Not even all those who were the recipients of this mercy were grateful for the mercy received. One of them wrote to the papers that the President had no alternative but to spare their lives, as they had not surrendered unconditionally, but that their lives had been promised on the field of battle. We have already shown that their lives were only safeguarded until handed over to the Government in Pretoria, and that the Government would then decide as to their ultimate fate. But even if it were granted that their lives had been promised in full, their liberties were still in the hands of the Transvaal Government, and for that liberty, which they had forfeited, they might at least have shown some gratitude. But gratitude does not seem to be part of the constitution of filibusters, even when the filibusters are of good birth and position.

However, if all the prisoners were not grateful, and did not recognise the mercy shown, the world did. Even the Queen of England gave her subjects a lesson in gratitude by thanking President Kruger for the mercy shown to the prisoners. The South African Republic had taken another step higher in the estimation of the world.

Steve now saw his countrymen holding the happy reputation of being patriotic, brave, fearless and merciful. Soon he saw his Government slowly acquiring a greater reputation still—that of possessing great diplomatic skill. Mr Chamberlain is supposed to be one of the most skilful of statesmen and diplomatists, and yet it soon became apparent to the world that he had found his match in President Kruger. It was like a skilful game of cards. It is true that President Kruger possessed the better hand, but it is also true that he played his cards with marvellous skill and precision, while it cannot be denied that Mr Chamberlain weakened his hand considerably by several false moves.

Mr Chamberlain has one grand excuse for his want of

success so far to outwit President Kruger, and that is that President Kruger is working in a just and holy cause, while Mr Chamberlain is trying to uphold an unjust cause. He is trying to paint the rotten sepulchre of a chartered company white, and to prevent the rottenness within from being exposed. He is trying to save from the storm a house built upon the sand; while the house President Kruger is shielding is built upon a rock, the Rock of Ages.

When the Governor of Natal congratulated the President upon the mercy he had shown his foes, the President replied that the South African Republic was governed upon Christian principles—and so it is, thank God.

We have shown that the world gave the Transvaal its due when it recognised the mercy shown to Jameson and his men. How much more did the world applaud the President when the territories of the Chartered Company, being ravished by a native rebellion, he offered to allow his Burghers to go and help Rhodesia in its moment of danger; verily that was heaping coals of living fire upon the heads of Rhodes and company, especially as many Burghers were eager and willing to go and assist, and did not go only because their offer was not accepted. We can hardly blame the High Commissioner for not accepting the President's offer, for it would hardly tend to uphold England's vaunted supremacy in South Africa if the Boers had to succour British territory from the Matabele; but the people of Rhodesia suffered for the refusal, and is suffering still.

But even though his offer was refused, President Kruger moved his country a step higher in the world's estimation. One would almost have thought that the Transvaal could have afforded to rest upon the laurels gained during the first few months of the year, but the greatest of all was yet to come. After Johannesburg's surrender, the Reform Committee were arrested and arraigned for trial. The Government possessed such overwhelming evidences of guilt that the prisoners considered that there was nothing left for them but to plead *guilty*—the four leaders to '*High Treason*,' and the rest to minor offences. The four leaders were sentenced to death by an impartial judge, specially sworn in, to ensure having a non-political and disinterested man upon the bench, and the rest were sentenced to two years' imprisonment, £2000 fine, and three years' banishment.

It is needless to enter into the world-wide interest taken in the trial and its results. It is needless to enter farther into the justice of the sentences. It is sufficient to state that all fair-minded men had to acknowledge that the sentence was deserved, and yet the day after sentence was pronounced, the Executive Council commuted the death sentences, followed later by giving all the prisoners their liberties after the various fines had been paid. Was ever such clemency shown by human government? Would such mercy have been shown by any other government for such offences? We doubt it.

We regret to say that even after this, the enemies of the Transvaal did not cease even yet to attempt doing it harm. But the Transvaal can afford to treat these—as a mastiff treats the barkings of curs—with contempt. It is sufficient that the Transvaal has seized its opportunity, and by the blessing of God has turned the evil intended her, into good.

The world has heard President Kruger's reply to the deputation of mayors from all South Africa. When the deputation came to thank the President for the magnanimity shown to the prisoners, he replied by laying his hand on a Bible and saying,—

'I recognise no rule or law for my deeds and works but what is contained in this book.'

The world now knows the policy of the Transvaal—England knows it, let her respect it.

It is no wonder that Mr Stead, the bitter enemy of

the Transvaal, and the friend of Rhodes and his company, has to acknowledge that President Kruger had diplomatically scored against his enemies every time. It could not be otherwise. For not only, as we have shown, was the cause of the Transvaal just, but President Kruger had received his first lessons in diplomacy from English statesmen, and had learned to be careful how he exposed his policy when dealing with English diplomats. It must be remembered that Mr Kruger was already vice-president of the Transvaal when English statesmen unjustly annexed the country. Mr Kruger was also a member of the triumvirate who allowed themselves to be duped into a peace in 1881 (after having been victorious in every battle), by which England retained the suzerainty of the Transvaal, which was only got rid of in the London Convention of 1884. No wonder if President Kruger refused to accept an unconditional invitation to visit England to confer with Mr Chamberlain on matters which only concerned the internal government of the Transvaal. Once caught, twice shy! President Kruger already saw the cloven foot of the 1881 Convention reappear, when Mr Chamberlain advised him to weaken his Government by giving Home Rule to Johannesburg; and when this failed, to offer to safeguard the South African Republic from all attacks against its independence from British or foreign territory on certain conditions, viz., on the franchise being given to all Uitlanders. We have already seen the President's reply to the Home Rule scheme. To the offer of England's promised safeguard on condition that the Uitlanders were given the franchise, the President replied that 'the Transvaal was already safeguarded against attack from British territory by international law. And as regards safeguarding the Republic against other foreign powers, the Transvaal had never asked to be thus safeguarded'—Scored again! It would require volumes to detail all the events of the invasion of the Republic, or the results of the crisis of

1896, or the various good results of the Government's wise policy of firmness, combined with gentleness and mercy. Yet we cannot end this chapter without referring to the greatest good of all that came to South Africa out of the intended evil. We refer to the great *Spirit of Unity* that came to the Afrikander nation of South Africa. Never was such glorious unity of purpose, of opinion and feeling, seen in South Africa. From the Cape to the Zambesi the holy spirit of patriotism and unity was awakened and displayed in beautiful colours of fellow feeling and love of country and people. Never was truer word spoken than when a man of position exclaimed in Pretoria, on receipt of the news of Jameson's defeat: 'To-day the nation of South Africa is reborn.' Afrikander national feeling was reborn indeed, never to die again. The most bitter political opponents of President Kruger in the country became his most staunch supporters. All party feelings were forgotten and forgiven. All territorial or trade jealousies between states and colonies were cast aside. One cry of shame went up against the plotters from town to town, from state to state, from colony to colony. And the people of South Africa became as one man.

It cannot be denied that there were certain Imperial Jingoes who belonged to the same faction as the plotters, and who sided with the filibusters and rebels. But these were in the small minority, and are hardly to be recognised, except where they showed forth in their true colours, as when they hooted their own governor in Maritzburg for having upheld his country's honour when in Pretoria, and expressed his regret to President Kruger that Englishmen should have acted in such a dishonourable way. Or again, when a party of young roughs in the Cape Colony seized upon a single unarmed young Burgher, because he defended his adopted country, and tarred and feathered him. Such methods of expressing their feelings and opinions only served to prove the badness of their cause. But on the other hand, we have the great proof of sympathy and goodwill expressed to the Transvaal by all its most peaceful and honourable men. Even in Johannesburg most men of South African birth, of Dutch or English parentage, supported the Government. And in Pretoria and other towns, the Government received the unqualified support and sympathy of nearly every citizen of respectability, Burgher or not.

Then again we have the practical proof of sympathy shown by the Free State! Without a moment's delay the Free State called up her Burghers, and marched them up to the Transvaal borders, ready to assist her sister Republic in case of need. Every Free Stater was as ready as any Transvaaler to risk his life to uphold Republicanism in South Africa. Then again we have the warm sympathy expressed for the Transvaal at public meetings at such places as Graaff Reinet, and the Paarl in the Cape Colony. Sympathy which was ready to take practical form at any moment if needed. Then we must not forget to mention that Steve was agreeably disappointed in Mr Hofmeyr, the leader of the Afrikander party in the Cape Colony. He, with many others, had seen with regret Mr Hofmeyr assisting Mr Rhodes to undermine the aspirations of the Republic towards northern and western expansion. But now it was seen that Mr Hofmeyr, in common with many others, had only been deceived and infatuated by Rhodes. Therefore Steve, in common with all Afrikanders, was pleased when Mr Hofmeyr expressed such warm sympathy with the Transvaal, both before and after the crisis was decided. Truly times of adversity bring to light who are friends and who are foes. The trouble of the Transvaal during the first half of the year not only showed the world her true strength, the true feelings of the Burghers, the patriotism, love of liberty, the bravery and magnaminity of the Afrikander race, but it also exploded a long existing idea, viz., that the Boers are a half-savage, bloodthirsty, and cruel race. For it was seen that when sentence of death was impartially, legally, and rightfully passed on the enemies of the country and liberties of its people, they, the Burghers, were the first to petition their Government to be merciful.

CHAPTER XXIII

MIJNHEER MEYER CLAIMS HIS HORSE, ONLY TO GIVE IT UP AGAIN—THE SONG OF THE BOER

DURING the last few chapters we have almost lost sight of our hero's daily life. But it must not be forgotten that we are not writing a mere romance, but are recording a narrative of real life, earnest and real. Nor must it be forgotten or lost sight of, that the real object of the work is to tell of the hopes of future national existence, of the patriotism and love of people and country of a young Afrikander brought up from his youth with the idea that his race is struggling for a place amongst the nations of the world, and that he must do all in his power to further that object. Therefore, we have during the last few chapters told of the struggles of his countrymen towards that object, in which he so greatly sympathised, and of his thoughts and opinions on those struggles. We have been simply recording his thoughts, his joys for victories won and troubles overcome and avoided by his race. The story of his country is his own story. We shall resume the thread of his own life where we left it off, having brought the political question of the day that so much interested him up to date. After Steve had sent off the telegram to his mother informing her that Johannesburg had surrendered, he thought he could do no better than to take his horse (or rather Mijnheer Meyer's horse) out for a little exercise, especially as the horse had been having a good rest, and had been well fed since his arrival at Pretoria. While Steve was riding proudly along the streets of Pretoria on the beautiful stallion, the thought which had troubled him before re-occurred to him again. How was he going to return the horse to its owner? He had made inquiries as to the whereabouts of Mijnheer Meyer, but owing to his speedy departure from Krugersdrop with the prisoners of war, he had been unable to find the gentleman in question, as the commando with which Mijnheer Meyer served remained in that neighbourhood.

Suddenly Steve heard an exclamation of surprise.

'*Alle magty Kerd*, where did you get that horse?'

Steve saw that this question was addressed to him, and he also felt that it was a most awkward question to be asked. He could not answer the question, so he asked another.

'Why do you ask, sir?'

'Because it seems to me I know the horse,' was the reply of the man, who was a fine-looking, good-natured, elderly man. At his side walked a stalwart, broad-shouldered young man, who seemed strong enough to fell any ox with a blow of his hard fist. This young man seemed to gaze on the horse with great interest.

'Sir, if you know the horse, you can perhaps tell me where I can find its owner, as I wish to return him his property,' said Steve.

'Well, you won't have far to go to find his owner, for here is the owner himself,' said the old man, pointing to his companion, who it was apparent at first sight must be his son.

'Perhaps you will allow me to ask your name, sir?' said Steve, suspiciously.

'I am Meyer,' was the reply.

Steve did not answer until he had dismounted, when he walked up to the young man with the reins on his arm, and said,—

'Mijnheer Meyer, I hope you will forgive me, but I came in possession of your horse under most peculiar circumstances; I trust you will accept my explanation and allow me to pay for the use of your horse, and any other reasonable expense incurred, or to be incurred.' And Steve told in a few words how he had come in possession of the horse.

The old man and his son did not say much, but asked Steve if he had been in time to see any of the fighting; to which Steve replied by telling them that he had taken part in the fight at Doornkop.

'Can you prove this?'

'Yes, sir, easily; as it happens that the field-cornet under whom I served is near by, if you will take a short walk with me I will take you to him.' This was done in silence. Steve introduced Mijnheer Meyer to the field-cornet, and at the request of the former left them together.

After ten minutes' talk to the field-cornet and a short conference between the old man and his son, they walked up to Steve, when the old man took Steve by the hand, and warmly shaking it, said,—

'Mijnheer Joubert, my son feels happy that his horse should have served to bring such a brave young fellow to the assistance of his country. Your field-cornet has told me how bravely you fought at Doornkop, and we have had a letter from my daughter in which she told me how, and why, she had lent you the horse. You have done well, and my son thinks you have taken such good care of the horse, judging by appearances, and that you ride him so well, that he wishes you to keep him as a remembrance of Doornkop.'

'But, sir, that would be too much kindness on his part, much as I have learnt to love the noble animal. I cannot consent to rob him of the best horse in Pretoria.'

'Never mind, he shall not lose by it; I shall see to that; I have one as good as this, which he shall have,' replied the old man, in a way which showed Steve that to refuse would be taken as an insult.

'I accept your kind offer on one condition,' replied Steve, turning to the smiling young man, 'and that is, that you will accept this little offer in token of my gratitude,' and he took off his only extravagance—his gold watch and chain—and handed it to the young man, who received it as graciously as he had given his horse.

Steve was indeed glad to be the owner of the beautiful horse, all the more so as he had learned to love the animal that had borne him so enduringly and so swiftly, and had given him his heart's desire—the opportunity to strike a blow for his country.

Mijnheer Meyer and his son stayed for a week in Pretoria, during which they and Steve were almost inseparable, as a great friendship had arisen between the young men, and the old man had learned to love Steve as a son.

But soon the order came for all Burghers to return home: amongst others, Mijnheer Meyer and his son—as only a guard of a few score Burghers was to be retained for a little while longer; and a temporary parting came for the new-found friends.

I can conclude this chapter in no more fitting way than by quoting here—

THE SONG OF THE BOER

O'er hill and o'er dale,
O'er mountain and vale
Went a cry:
'For our dear country's right,
Ye must arm for the fight,
To do or to die!'

And ev'ry man heard,
And straight booted and spurred
To war 'gainst the 'Queen of the Sea';
'For our children and wives
We will lay down our lives,
Or live to be FREE—to be Free!'

CHORUS.—Then ride! ride! ride!
The Asvogel screams o'er the lea,
And to-night I may rest,
With his beak in my breast,
While my children may orphans be.

With cannon and drum,
The invader hath come
In his might;
But our courage ne'er fails,
Nor no heart ever quails
At the perilous sight.

Now the roar of the battle
And musketry's rattle
Goes up to the vault of the sky;
While the plain gleameth red
With the blood of the dead,
And the blood of those doomed to die.

CHORUS—

But the God of Battles had fought on our side,
And our country so loved is free;
For the strength of His arm doth with us abide,
And we thank Him on bended knee.

He hath scattered our foes in the pride of their ways,
And shielded the lowly Boer;
To Him be the glory, to Him be the praise
For ever and ever more.

CHORUS.—Then ride! ride! ride!
For my loved ones are waiting for me,
And to-night I shall bide
With my vrouw by my side,
And my little ones round my knee.*

* The above is a composition of Mr Luscombe Searelle's, which was published in *The Press* of Pretoria some time ago, and is taken over from that paper.

CHAPTER XXIV

IN THE MIDST OF LIFE WE ARE IN DEATH

AFTER peace was once more partially restored, our hero resolved to pay Johannesburg a visit and see how the *City of Gold* looked after its effort to amuse itself, *à la*

South America, with an abortive revolution. It was not until Tuesday, the 18th February, that he was able to carry out his resolve—the evening of which day found him comfortably dining at a leading Rand hotel.

Steve found excitement, although cooled to a great extent, still running high. Arguments, pro and con, on late events were still the chief, if not the only, conversation indulged in during leisure moments.

It was after dinner, in the smoking-room, that our hero found himself in the midst of a party of men hotly discussing politics. The conversation was led by a colonial, who was taking the part of the Government, and a Jingo of the first water, who was as hotly defending the freebooters and rebels.

'It is no use talking,' said the latter, who was burdened with the name of Bock; 'the Boers will ultimately have to go under. They are in the minority; they are illiterate; they are only half civilised! They are *Boors*, and it is presumptuous to hold that they will continue to rule this country—still less that they will ever rule South Africa! Englishmen are bound to *chuck* them out in the end.'

'Anyone can see that you are using the hackneyed arguments of the Jingoistic enemies of the Government, and that you are not speaking from your own knowledge or experience, but from what you have read in Jingo papers. It is true the Boers are illiterate, or the majority of them are; but it is also true that those few who have had the benefit of education have proved that the Afrikander is as capable to learn, and as susceptible to education, as any race in the world. As to civilisation —they are more civilised, as civilisation is taught in the Christian code, than many of their European contemporaries.'

'If you call Bible reading and psalm singing, civilisation, I won't argue the matter with you; in any case, they are bound to bend before the English race, sooner or later.'

'By your faith shall ye be saved!' interposed Steve.

'By which you mean, sir?' inquired Bock.

'I mean that the Boers do not believe that salvation lies in superior learning, in high civilisation, or in superiority of numbers or arms, but in right and justice and the blessing of God?'

'Cant!' was the sneering reply of Bock.

'You may call it *cant* if you like. But it was such *cant* that gave Dingaan and his twelve thousand warriors into the hands of five hundred Boers. It was such cant that enabled the Boers to carry on the war of independence against mighty England to a successful issue. It was such *cant* that brought the elaborate plots of Rhodes, Jameson and the Johannesburg revolutionists to utter failure. It will be such cant that will make South Africa a free and united Republic, in which all the races of the world shall live free and united! The Boers believe in the efficacy of prayer: they believe that by prayer and through faith they can move mountains, and—England itself.'

'Bah! do you believe in such nonsense? Do you really believe that you have only to ask God, if God there be, for anything you want, from a needle to an anchor, to receive it?'

'I certainly believe that God *is*, and that if we ask we shall receive, if it be good for us, and if we ask in faith. I also believe that blasphemy and unbelief shall be punished,' said Steve, reprovingly.

'Rot!' was the irreverent reply of Bock. 'I do not believe that there is such a thing as God, beyond the godliness there is in Nature. There is no such thing as a God that answers prayer, or punishes blasphemy.'

'I am sorry for you,' was Steve's gentle reply; 'for the day shall come when you shall *know* that there is a God of Wrath, who punishes blasphemy as well as a God of Love, who answers prayer.'

Bock answered with a roaring and mocking laugh, and said, 'Well, I shall prove to you that there is no such

God as you worship. *If there be a God, Who punishes blasphemy, I call upon Him to strike me dead, now or within forty-eight hours.* There, I have thrown the gauntlet down, let your God pick it up. I have given Him time enough to do it in.'

Steve answered by jumping up from his seat and running towards the door, where he stood looking at Bock with terror in his face.

'What is the matter with you now?' inquired Bock, laughing.

'I fear me that God may take you at your word, and in your doom include me, for being in such evil company. For your soul's sake speak not thus, but at least treat your Maker with reverence.'

Even the others present were shocked at Bock's blasphemy, and seemed to share the fear of Steve to be punished for being in the same room with such a tempter of God; for they now rose and strolled out of the room, leaving Bock alone.

The following day Steve went for a long and extended stroll. He was surprised to see—all considered—the bustle and life still to be seen in the streets of Johannesburg; and he could hardly believe that he was walking in a city whose revolutionary state, a few weeks previously, was the talk of the world. He had no doubt that business men and the mining interest were still feeling the effects of the crisis severely; but the crowds in the streets seemed to hurry and bustle, with the usual intentness in their own missions in life incident to a large and busy city.

Steve had lunch at some restaurant, and then journeyed towards Aukland Park; and after a lengthy stroll about, was thinking of returning, and hailed a passing cab to do so, when he felt the earth tremble under him, and the glass of a house opposite fell crashing to the ground, and a noise as of distant thunder or artillery was heard.

'Is it an earthquake, or Johannesburg fighting in

earnest at last?' Steve asked himself. He jumped into the cab, and told the driver to drive his best. A cloud of smoke was now seen ascending the sky; and after a few minutes a party in a cab was hailed and asked for information, as they seemed to be coming from the direction of the smoke. The driver replied that he 'expected some magazine had blown up, as a stone had fallen from the sky a few yards from his cab.

On reaching town, Steve was informed that a tremendous explosion of dynamite had taken place at Vrededorp. Evidence of the severity of the explosion was not wanting, as everywhere smashed windows were seen, and on nearing the scene of the explosion, the signs of damage done increased at every pace. All along the road our hero's heart bled to see the number of wounded being conveyed to the hospital. But, on approaching the scene of the catastrophe itself, Steve felt sick and faint at the signs of death about him. He got out of the cab, and told the driver to put the cab at the service of the wounded, and look to him for payment when done. He himself assisted to place two of the wounded on his cab, and forgetting his natural repulsion at the sight of human blood and gaping wounds, set to work assisting in the labour of rescue.

'My God! it is too horrible,' he murmured, as he saw a severed head lying alone and ghastly here, with set and staring eyes. It reminded him of his thoughts, in times past, of what the day of doom must be like. It seemed to him, as he found a human arm here, a leg, a hand, a head, or some portion of a body, there, that these portions of human bodies were waiting to be re-united to their other parts. He ran about, as if in a fever, and as if he would avoid seeing these terrible emblems of death lying about. Spade in hand, he would now assist in following a limb protruding from the mass of debris, lying on the brink of the vast hole that had been made by the explosion, after which task had been done, he would rush down to the bottom of the hole itself, and there again work and dig till the sweat poured from his face. After he could find no more rescue work here to be done, (so many others being busy in the same task that there was hardly room for all), he rushed towards the many fallen houses, fallen upon the inmates, where there was work enough for all. Oh, what a sight! A sight, once seen, never to be forgotten, if you live for a thousand years! Here is lying a dead mother, clasping her dead child to her cold breast. Here are a mother and three children, all found dead in one room. Here is a father, mad because of his grief, holding his dead child in his arms while moaning over his dead wife—dead, all dead—*death* here, *death* there, DEATH everywhere! How the men worked! Affliction makes us all of a kin. Not one skulked. Everyone was doing his best to rescue the wounded from the wrecks of once happy homes. No thought of politics here; no racial distinctions thought of. Here, in this great affliction all were of one race—the human race. Dutch and English work together like brothers. An Englishman rescues and handles a child of Dutch parents as tenderly as if it were his own. A Dutchman pulls out of the ruins a 'rooinek,' and supports his head as tenderly as if it was his own father, while he holds the restoring cup to his lips. When God wishes our hearts to be softened towards each other, he sends us affliction.

While the work of rescue is still going on, others, moved with pity at the sight of homeless and friendless ones not killed or wounded, begin to subscribe of their plenty, so that these may be provided for—a movement that was responded to most liberally from all South Africa, so that, at least, those who were left behind were provided for. Steve worked hard as long as he could, but at midnight he gave place to fresh ones who came up, as he was now thoroughly knocked up, and went to his hotel to get a few hours rest.

CHAPTER XXV

THERE IS MERCY, EVEN AT THE ELEVENTH HOUR, IF YE REPENT

EARLY next morning, at five o'clock, Steve was again at the scene of disaster. Gangs of men were still busy looking for dead and wounded.

Steve was told that the hospital was full to overflowing, and that the Wanderers' Hall had also been formed into a temporary hospital, and was also nearly full of wounded. As Steve was walking from one ruin to another, seeking for likely places where aid may be required, he came to a mass of ruins. As he stood, looking thoughtfully and sadly at a home, only one day before tenanted by, perhaps, a happy family, now lying in a heap of debris, its inmates no one knows where—perhaps sick and wounded to death—perhaps *dead!* he heard a moan of despair.

'Who is there?'

Only another mournful moan for a reply.

Steve walked towards the sound, and came to a dog—a mongrel, wounded and crippled.

He was moved to pity to see the look of entreaty, almost human, in the eyes of the dog. It seemed to ask his aid. Steve lifted the dog tenderly, and carried it to a pool of water near by. But the dog would not drink, it only whined, and, wagging its tail, crawled back to the spot where found, looking still, with its entreating eyes, towards Steve. Steve was puzzled at its action, and followed it back to the spot. The dog gave a few feeble scratches at the debris on which it lay. A beam of mental light seemed almost to dazzle Steve, as it occurred to him that the dog wanted him to search for some loved master or mistress. He lost not a moment to begin, and further aid soon coming up, ere long they succeeded in laying open what seemed to be the ruins of a dining-room. Under a heavy beam they found a dead woman with a spoon in her hand, having, apparently, been occupied in feeding a child of about six months, who was lying, apparently unhurt, under an arch formed by the falling timbers. The child was sleeping, and, from the signs of tears on its cheeks, Steve judged that it had cried itself to sleep. Poor child ! it had escaped by a miracle. Who knows what work this child was born to accomplish? When scores of strong men and women perished, this weak babe of six months lived. God, apparently, has work for it to do before it may die. Perhaps, when Steve is old and trembling, this child, saved so miraculously, may be accomplishing its destined work, and doing something that shall benefit the whole human race, and causing its name to be inscribed on the list of imperishable names.

The joy of the dog seemed almost human when it saw the wakened child, crowing as if nothing had happened. Steve waited to see that the child was safely handed to the care of a kind and motherly-looking woman, and then returned to his hotel for breakfast. At breakfast Steve learned, with pleasure, that the President and other members of the Government were on their way to Johannesburg to visit the scene of disaster. He resolved to go to the station to see the arrival of the Presidential party.

A great crowd was waiting at the station to welcome the man, who, a little more than a month ago, would have been hooted and jeered at, if not murdered, if he had ventured to visit Johannesburg unattended, as he was doing now. But the generous and humane actions of the President, during the last month, had prepared the way for the conciliation which was now to take place; drawn towards each other, as both parties were, by common sympathy at this moment of mutual loss and suffering. Here, across the dead and wounded of Burgher and Uitlander, the representatives of both parties shook hands, and forgot for the time, if not for ever, their political differences.

The President and many of the most prominent men of Pretoria, who were of the party, were driven through the destroyed township. They then drove to the improvised hospital at the Wanderers. The President showed visible emotion as he viewed the many wounded. The tears were seen to force their way down the face of the man, who, in times of greatest danger, showed no fear or emotion. But such is ever the way with great and noble men. When danger threatens themselves, they know no fear or pain; but when others suffer, they know how to sympathise and feel for them.

With deep emotion, His Honour thanked the people of Johannesburg for the sympathy and practical aid they had given to the wounded, and promised that the Government should not forget to do their share in succouring the needy ones who had suffered loss of parents or friends.

His Honour then reminded the suffering wounded that there was a Great Physician on high, Who would heal all their wounds, bodily and spiritually, if they would only ask Him.

His Honour was presented by an address from the Relief Committee, thanking him for the practical sympathy shown to Johannesburg in this visit, to which the President replied in suitable terms.

After a visit to the room upstairs, where some fifteen orphaned children were housed, and some kindly words of consolation and advice to the children, His Honour visited the permanent hospital, which was also crowded with wounded.

As Steve was following in the rear of the Presidential party, his sleeve was pulled by one of the attendants, who informed him that one of the wounded patients, who had seen him passing, earnestly requested to speak to him.

Steve readily consented, wondering who of the wounded could know him.

Following the attendant, Steve found himself before a mattress, on which a man was lying, whose face was so mutilated that he could not decide whether he knew the man or not. He knelt down, and taking the hand of the wounded man in his own, gently asked him what he could do for him.

'Do you not know me, Joubert?' the man faintly asked.

As Steve looked at him inquiringly, without seeming to remember him, he said,—

'Do you not remember Tuesday evening?'

The voice of the man, faint as it was, seemed now to recall to Steve the scene of two evenings before, when a mortal man denied the existence of his Maker, and dared God to strike him dead, if indeed God there was.

'My God, hast thou indeed taken this man at his word, and shown sinful man Thy might? Bock, Bock, why did you ever deny your God, and bring yourself to this?'

'Why, indeed? Joubert, for God's sake, for the sake of the God you worship, tell me what I must do to escape from the wrath to come? You said truly there is a God of Wrath as well as a God of love. Teach me to escape the God of Wrath and find the God of Love, before it is too late! for now I know that there is a God of Wrath! He has found me indeed. Oh, God, it is terrible—terrible! The darkness surrounds me. Give me light? Give me light?'

Steve was shocked and grieved inexpressibly at this scene. He murmured a prayer for guidance how to aid this erring soul.

'Bock, old man, your sin was terrible. But God has already shown you some of His great love; for it can only be out of love and mercy that you were not killed outright, and were given the opportunity to still live and repent. If you truly repent, there is still mercy for you, even now!

'Oh, is there, is there? Oh, God, how can I know that there is still grace for me?'

Steve motioned for the attendant to come to him, and asked him if there was a Bible to be had. He was handed a copy of the New Testament, which he opened, and asked Bock if he might read him a chapter out of it, to prove to him that there was still grace for him. The poor wounded man gratefully accepted, and Steve read to him the beautiful story of the repentant sinner on the Cross, at the side of Jesus. Greedily the dying man listened to this true story of the Cross, which he had often heard and read in his youth, without appreciating the wealth of mercy and hope there was in it. When he heard the answer Jesus gave to the repentant sinner: 'Soon shall ye enter with me into the kingdom of Heaven,' hope once more came to him, and a faint beam of joy seemed to light up his wounded face.

When Steve had finished, he said gently to Bock,—

'Do you believe now that there is hope?'

'Yes, oh, yes. Won't you pray for me? God will hear your prayer; you are so good to me.'

'God loves to hear the sinner pray. We are all sinners; I as well as you. I will pray; but you must also pray.'

And Steve, kneeling as he was before the dying man, lifted up his voice and prayed. His prayer began in supplication, but, as he prayed, he seemed to feel that God had already answered, for he ended his prayer in thanksgiving, thanking God that another sinner had been gathered to His fold.

When Steve opened his eyes he saw that a great change had come over the face of the dying man. A beautiful smile dwelt on the mutilated countenance of the repented sinner, while a far-away look shone in his eyes, as if he already saw beyond this world.

'Thank you, Joubert, thank you. God will reward you. I thank thee, O Lord, that Thou hast heard me, even now, and hast pardoned me my great sin. Hark!

how beautifully they sing; surely 'tis angel voices sounding so sweet. Ah! that is music indeed. What are they singing? "Glory be to God and the Lamb, for a sinner saved! Amen, Amen."'

As he uttered the last word he seemed to fall gently asleep—it was the last long sleep, from which he shall only wake at the sound of the trumpet, calling him to the judgment seat of the God he had denied in life, but found in death.

Steve knelt long before the dead man in prayer, in earnest thought. He could not help thinking how many of those killed in this terrible disaster were as unprepared to die as was this man; and how few of them had the opportunity given them to repent before they died.

After a while, the nurse, finding a spare moment, came to see how her patient was progressing. When she saw that he was dead, she remarked to Steve that she was not surprised, for the doctor had said that he could not live; his injuries being too severe.

Steve asked if she knew anything of how Bock happened to be in the accident. She replied that she only knew what Bock himself had told her a few hours previously, viz., that he had gone to the scene of the accident on business. That it was the first time he had ever gone in that direction. That he was standing at the door of a tall building, inquiring his way, when suddenly it seemed to him as if the earth was turning upside down, and as if the house in front of him was tumbling over on to him. That was all he remembered until he came back to consciousness in the hospital.

After the funeral of the dead man was over, Steve took the first train back to Pretoria, sad at heart at the scenes of suffering and death he had witnessed.

CHAPTER XXVI

STEVE MEETS A SYMPATHETIC BRITISHER—A RETROSPECT

Another month went by. The political turmoil still went on. Every day seemed to bring new probabilities forth. One day peace seemed assured; the following day some despatch, or public speech of the British minister's, seemed to threaten the Transvaal with war. Meanwhile, the Government, with President Kruger at its head, went steadily on, pursuing its policy of conciliation and mercy, combined with great firmness where its rights were concerned. But, in spite of the many diplomatic victories gained by the Government, and the sympathy shown towards it by all the world, including many prominent British statesmen, yet the attitude of the Imperial Government seemed to be as if seeking a quarrel with the Transvaal. Consequently, it is not to be wondered at that the Transvaal Government was quietly preparing to defend itself. Whispers went about of large quantities of arms and ammunition being imported. Every field-cornet had orders to see that his men were all properly armed and ready to be called up, in case of need.

In the Free State the Government was giving full attention to the question of fully arming every Burgher. Even here President Kruger had won a great victory without lifting a finger, for a new President had been elected—a President heart and soul for the Afrikander cause; a President working for a closer union of the two Republics, which meant almost doubling the strength of the Afrikander nation. What is more, everyone felt that the Free State had a man for a President who was thoroughly unselfish. A man whose sole ambition seemed to be to live for land and people. A man who would not hesitate to give up his own ambition and position if it would benefit his country. May he long be spared to his people. In Cape Colony it was whispered that the Afrikanders were quietly arming and preparing for the struggle, should it come; determined, should the opportunity occur, to strike a blow for liberty.

But England seemed to realise the volcano on which she stood; the fire, which she would light, should she unjustly attack the Transvaal—and—desisted.

Steve received an invitation one day from a prominent townsman to a small dinner-party, to meet some friends.

Steve was placed at table between a Scotchman and an Englishman. After some conversation on general topics, the Scotchman, who seemed to be a kindly, genial old man, turned to Steve and said,—

'It is so strange to me that I have met no Boers yet, and here I am in the capital of the land of the Boers. I have been six hours in Pretoria now, and during all that time I have seen no one whom I could recognise as a Boer from the descriptions I have heard and read of them.'

Steve smiled and said,—

'What is your conception of a Boer? By what description would you recognise him?'

'Oh, I would easily recognise one if I were to see one. Shall I describe to you what my idea of a Boer is, from reading and hearing him described? Here you are, then. I will begin from the top. Dirty slouch hat; long, greasy, unkempt hair; tangled and untrimed beard; sly, crafty eyes; a sensual and unclean mouth; dirty and unwashed face; dirty, baggy, ragged clothing; if any shirt at all—dirty; if any shoes at all—made of untanned leather. In short, a *Boer* is a man uncivilised, untaught, untamed.'

This was said in such an innocent, inoffensive way that Steve took no offence, but only laughed heartily, as if at a good joke.

'Now, what are you laughing at? Do you mean to say my description is not true. If so, then you must blame those who have written the different descriptions from which I have gathered my ideal of a Boer.'

'Pardon me, sir; but are you the only stranger in Jerusalem? Where are you from?'

'I am from Glasgow, Scotland, at your service,' was the smiling and good-natured reply.

'But how long have you been out of Glasgow?'

'Not quite a month. I arrived here to-day, and I came straight here.'

'But surely, on your way from the coast, you must have met many a Boer?'

'No, I did not; but I suppose it is because I came straight on to Pretoria after leaving the steamer.'

'Well, sir, you have a few things to learn yet, for I am afraid you will have to journey far to meet your ideal of a Boer. He does not exist.'

'Well, I shall see. I suppose I will come across one or more during my stay.'

Steve could not suppress another hearty laugh; but as he saw that the kind-looking old man seemed hurt at his mirth, he hastened to say,—

'Excuse me, sir; it amused me to hear you say that you would recognise a Boer when you saw one, and immediately after express a hope that you would see one or more during your stay. Why, don't you know that half the guests round this table are what you call Boers, or, rather, what we call them as a nation—Afrikanders?'

'Well, I am—blessed! Do you mean they are born Boers, or are they naturalised Uitlanders?'

'No, sir; born and bred in the Transvaal or Cape Colony. That one there was born in the Cape Colony; this one to the left was born and grew up on a farm in Waterberg; this gentleman just opposite us made his living by farming, until he became a Government official; that one to his right is an attorney, whose father was a true old Boer of the old school.'

'Well, who would have thought it! One never gets too old to learn. It is lucky for me that they did not over hear me.'

'It would not matter if they did. We Afrikanders are accustomed to be misunderstood and underrated.'

'What do you mean by saying "*we Afrikanders?*" Surely *you* are an Englishman; your speech betrays you.'

'I am as true an Afrikander as Oom Paul himself; may I be as good a one as he is.'

'You an Afrikander? *You* a Boer? Surely, sir, you are trying to make fun of me?'

'No, sir; we Afrikanders know how to respect our elders. I mean what I say. I have never been out of South Africa.'

'Well, well, the world is full of deceit and lies! and when I go back to Scotland I shall tell the people of our country what a Boer really is. But this gives me just the opportunity I wished for. I wanted so much to have a talk with a Boer, but was afraid that I would not find one who could understand me. I want you to give me an idea of what the real feelings of your people are on the situation in South Africa, and of the events of the past few months. I came out to see and hear for myself what the Transvaal and its people are like; and you, I can see, are an educated man, and just the one to give me the information I want. Are you willing to speak to me on the subject?'

'With the greatest of pleasure, sir. We ask for nothing better than to be better known and better understood; therefore I am willing to give you all the information you want.'

'Well, then, if you will be so kind, give me, in a few words, the events which led up to the present situation.'

'To begin from the very beginning: you know, sir, that South Africa was first colonised by the Dutch. To the Dutch was added a sprinkling, later on, of French Huguenots, also a little seasoning of German blood.

These three nationalities readily united, and formed a sturdy race of hunters and farmers. A farmer in Dutch is a *Boer;* hence the name Boer, which really means the occupation and not the nationality of the race. Living a life of seclusion and simplicity on their farms, the one great characteristic of this people came to be their love of their Bible and their love of freedom. This was bred in them from their youth, and their faith is rather to die than to lose either. When the English came, they would or could in no wise understand or appreciate this race of simple, quiet and peace-loving people. Their love of peace was taken for cowardice. This at first led the English to feel contempt for the Boers. This naturally bred antagonism between the two races, which effectually prevented any fusion of the two nationalities. Then, also, the English wished to place the blacks on an equal footing with the whites. This led to further antagonism; for the Boers, while treating the blacks kindly and humanely, do not believe that blacks and whites were intended to be on an equal footing in this world. They contend that even the Bible teaches that the children of Ham shall be servants to the children of his brethren. In a dispute on this matter, a Boer and some of his relatives resisted the law, and were shot in the act, while several others were hanged at *Slachtersnek* for the same offence. This settled the matter. The Boers saw they were the weakest; so they determined to leave their dearly-loved country and seek for a land in the wilderness, where they would be at rest, and the English cease from troubling them.

'The first country they took possession of in the interior was what is now the Free State, and, soon after, Natal was occupied. In both of these territories they had to fight many a bloody battle with the fierce Zulus and other native tribes before they could live at peace. But no sooner were they settled, and had built homes and ploughed lands, than once more England followed them up, and forced them to 'clear' out after a short struggle. This happened in the Free State, as well as Natal. The Boers now *trekked* in earnest to the Transvaal.

'The Transvaal at this time was almost inaccessible to an English army, because of the distance from the coast in which it lay; therefore the Boers were not only able to hold their own, but also to harass the English in the neighbouring Colonies so as to force England to solemnly recognise their independence at the Sand River Convention. After the Sand River Convention, the Boers lived at peace with England for many years. But they still had to struggle on against native tribes, poverty, and the internal dissensions usual to a nation in its infancy and in course of formation. At last a time came when the hardy Boers were sorely pressed, what with no market for their produce, a President not in sympathy with their simple ways and manners, and native wars. In the meanwhile England, or rather certain Jingoistic Englishmen, began to see what a mistake was made when England allowed an independent state to grow up on the borders of its own possessions in South Africa, the more so as England had already been forced by avarice to do an unjust act to the Free State, by forcing that independent State to give up its most valuable possession—the diamond fields—for a paltry consideration. And gold having begun to be discovered in the Transvaal, it seemed to be the best policy to take full possession of the Transvaal before further discoveries of gold took place, which might necessitate the same course of action which was pursued in the case of the diamond fields. Besides, a trick of that kind does not generally succeed twice; therefore something new must be tried this time, and the best plan would be to take possession of the whole country on some pretext or other. When an excuse is sought to do an unjust thing, such an excuse is easily found. Now that the Boers were so hard pressed, what could be more in conformity with England's usual policy of succour and protection of weak countries than relieving the

Boers of any further trouble of forming their State on a firm basis by annexing the Transvaal? This was done in a manner unworthy the traditions of a country like England.

'Sir Theophilus Shepstone, England's tool and emissary, sent a letter to the Transvaal Government, in which he requested a conference to discuss certain matters in which the States and Colonies of South Africa were alike interested, amongst which was the threatening attitude of the natives in the Transvaal, stating, in a passing sort of way, that he was bringing an escort of a few gentlemen and twenty-five border policemen from Natal; and as he was sure that there would be no objection to his coming, he would not wait for a reply, but would start at once.

'Of course no reasonable objection could be made to his coming, so he was received in a friendly manner. What was the surprise of the Government when Sir Theophilus, after a pretext of discussing matters, formally annexed the land in the name of the Queen? Of course protest was made, but no heed was given to it. What were the Boers to do? They had no wish to fight mighty England; so it was decided to try all peaceful ways to endeavour to get their beloved country back. Deputation after deputation was sent to England, praying the Queen to give back their own. But it was all in vain. England would not easily give up territory once obtained.

'At last, at a great meeting of the people, it was decided to fight, and, if need be, *die*, for their independence. War was declared. The result all the world knows. The Boers fought bravely and fairly, and through God's blessing, the cause of justice was victorious. England, after the loss of several battles, professed to see the justice of the claims of the Boers at last. A truce was called, and England promised to accede to the wishes of the Transvaalers on terms to be decided at a convention to be held at Pretoria. The Boers were disbanded and sent home rejoicing at having achieved their independence. The convention was held. But alas for England's good name, now that the Boers had gone home and had once more settled peaceably to their occupations, she would not give up all she had taken. She had taken the Transvaal as an entirely free and independent country. Now, after her latest promises, she would not give back more than a shadow of that former independence possessed by the Transvaal. England must retain the suzerainty of the country, with a right of veto on the foreign policy of the country. The Boers loved peace. They accepted these terms, hardly realising what a yoke they placed upon their necks in so doing After some years it was seen that the country could not be *free* while England retained the suzerainty of the Transvaal. The British Government was approached on the subject. A new convention was drawn up in 1884 and agreed to, by which the suzerainty was withdrawn. Now came a time of prosperity to the country. Gold was discovered in various places. Wealth poured into the country. A large population of Englishmen grew up in the gold-digging centres. Once more an Ahab desired to possess the vineyard of his neighbour. Not content with reaping the fruits thereof, the Englishmen living on the goldfields wished to have full possession of the whole country. Agitation and conspiracy was rife. The result has been seen in the events of the first few days of January of this year. Although these events have been distorted shamefully, yet you must know enough to glean the true facts of the case from what you have heard.'

'Although you have put it in a very few words, yet you have put it so plainly that you have enlightened me on many points which were dark to me before. Past events, as stated by you, make the crime against your country even blacker than it appeared to be before. But what about the complaints of ill treatment and oppression laid by the Uitlanders against your Government?'

'Oh, that is easily disproved. But I see signs of the

company dispersing. I am afraid we have paid our host and his guests a poor compliment by keeping our conversation all to ourselves. But if you will do me the honour to come to my quarters to-morrow evening and have a cup of tea or something stronger, if you prefer, with me, then I shall show you a very capable article from some English paper, which was taken over from the paper in question by *The Press*. This article, by facts and figures, disproves the Uitlander grievances much more capably than I could do offhand. What do you say?'

'With pleasure. I should like nothing better than to continue our conversation when we have more leisure. You may expect me. At what hour shall we say? Will seven o'clock do?'

'Finely; that is settled then.'

After this the conversation on politics was dropped, and Steve and his new acquaintance joined in the general conversation.

CHAPTER XXVII

A LOOK INTO THE FUTURE

THE following evening found Steve's new acquaintance, true to his promise, seated at a table with our hero, partaking of a cup of tea and biscuits. After tea, Steve brought forth a box of his favourite Dutch cigars. The genial old Scotchman did not wait long to press Steve to continue their conversation of the night before, which seemed greatly to interest him. So, both being comfortably seated in a couple of easy-chairs, Steve proceeded to read the cutting of which he had spoken the night before, and we shall make no apology for reproducing it, as it will prove of interest to those readers who have heard of the *Uitlander* grievances (?) but have never heard the other side of the matter.

As you will see, it is a letter written to the editor of the *London Daily Chronicle* and taken over by the *Pretoria Press*. This is it:—

'The following important and timely communication on Transvaal affairs has been addressed to the editor of the London *Daily Chronicle* and appears in the leading journal under date the 1st inst: When the *Times* in one and the same issue, that of the 27th inst., publishes among the telegrams that most remarkable letter from Mr Schreiner, late Attorney-General to the Cape Colony under Mr Rhodes, on the cause of the attempted rebellion at Johannesburg, and publishes under the head of "The Colonies," the statement that it was "the intolerably bad administration of President Kruger's Government," I think it is the duty of those who know what they are writing about to set the public at rest as to what were and what were not the real causes.

'For the *Times* it should have heen enough that the

FIRM AND ENTHUSIASTIC ADMIRER

and follower of Mr Cecil Rhodes, his trusted Attorney-General in two Administrations, distinctly and almost brutally, three weeks after the rebellion, when in possession of all the facts—facts which we shall know in all their detail in three weeks time—declares the rebellion to have been "due to a body of commercial speculators, the machinations of the Chartered Company, to a minute but powerful body of speculators in concert with financial plotters outside," and much more to the same purpose. Mr Schreiner has nothing to say about the intolerably bad administration of President Kruger having been the cause, and he would not have been slow to put this reason forward if he in conscience could have done so. But

THE MANIFESTO OF MR CHARLES LEONARD

says so. Yes, and it is about the manifesto that I wish to set the public right once and for all; and my claim to write on this subject is not to be disputed, as the oldest continual resident at Johannesburg, from its very inception until six months ago, intimately conversant with men and with measures during the whole of that period. There is no doubt much to be blamed in the past and much to be improved in the future. I am not a defender of the Kruger *régime à outrance;* but the faults that have been committed and the omissions that are laid to its charge are the natural consequence of the rapid and

VIOLENT TRANSITION

from a State devoted to pastoral pursuits to the most intense mining and industrial pursuits, invaded by the plutocracy. But neither the faults nor the omissions are such as to have at any time, or in any country, justified even armed resistance.

'Never was the like of such a manifesto put forward as a justification of rebellion, and the length of it—four closely-printed newspaper columns—is in itself its condemnation. If the leaders had a cause, the justice of which required such wordy explanations, they had no just cause to put before their followers. In the most serious charges, the misappropriation of Government moneys, we have terms like "it is stated," "it is said," "we hear," "we believe," and scandal which was

FORGOTTEN SEVEN YEARS AGO

is raked up to justify recent events.

'The reasons brought forward in the lengthy manifesto can be conveniently divided under two heads—material ones; corruption, mal-administration, and the fiscal policy strangling the mining industry; and political: one is the government of the country by a small faction of

Hollanders, the language grievance, the educational grievance, and the franchise grievance.

'To begin with the first section. I cannot deny that the enormous temptations held out to some subordinate officials by men who, having in an incredibly short time acquired immense wealth, and who drowned every scruple in their desire to increase the same, have caused these men to fall; but from intimate knowledge I deny that corruption in the Transvaal

EXTENDS TO THE HIGHEST OFFICIALS

or to any appreciable number of officials. I ask, however, Mr Editor, whether the financial system which has brought corruption in its train into the Transvaal can be allowed in its turn to appeal to English sympathy and to put forward this corruption as a justification for placing the lives of thousands of peaceable men, women and children to the hazard of the sword? If Pretoria has been tempted, it is Johannesburg which has held out the tempting hand.

'The next point is, that the Government by granting concessions and monopolies, and by its fiscal policy, is endeavouring to strangle the mining industry. Now, it is a fact, though perhaps a curious one, that most of these

CONCESSIONS HAVE BEEN GRANTED

to the Ecksteins, the Neumanns, and their friends; and that, although these interests have often been clever enough to obtain them ostensibly in some other name, they actually hold the largest interest in them, viz., the water and lighting concessions in Pretoria, the tram concession in Johannesburg, the cement, iron, National Bank and Mint concessions in Pretoria. These same interests advanced the Government a few years ago £50,000 for the object of purchasing Swaziland concessions. It was stipulated by them that these moneys should be repaid as soon as Swaziland was incorporated with the Transvaal, and that as a bonus they should receive the water, lighting, and tram concessions in all the principal towns in the Transvaal. The

DYNAMITE CONCESSIONS

is the next point of attack, and even in this they had a share. The statement is made, that this Government monopoly imposes upon the mining industry an intolerable burden, insomuch as the Government having the right to charge 90s. a case for dynamite, it can be supplied at 30s. I go into the figures of this business, because there is here a concrete case, from which your readers can judge for themselves the credibility of other statements in the manifesto. The Government does not charge 90s. but 85s. per case, and I cannot give a more convincing proof that it cannot be supplied at 30s., than the fact that the De Beers Company, a powerful financial and monopolistic company, where there is no charge incurred for storage, distribution *del credere*, etc., pays more than 60s. per case delivered in Kimberley.

'Add to that price—Additional railage to Johannesburg, storage, distribution over an area of forty miles of reef and over a hundred companies, *del credere* and collection commission, besides some import

DUES TO THE TRANSVAAL,

and it becomes clear what use has been made of the Government monopoly in powder and explosives for purposes of agitation. To give an even more graphic illustration. I extract from the last annual report of the Crown Reef Company (the only company in which the use of explosives is separately accounted for), the fact that out of a total working cost of 30s. 2⅜d. per ton, the actual cost of all explosives was 1s. 2½d. per ton; the unbearable burden justifying revolution!

'Now, as to the other taxation said to strangle the

mines. There is no country in which the personal taxes are lighter. I challenge anyone, be he the richest or poorest, to show me that he pays more than £5 per annum of personal taxes in the Transvaal. And as for direct taxes levied on the mines, I just extract from the

LAST ANNUAL REPORT

to hand the following:—

'Crown Reef Gold Mining Company produced last year in gold £420,106, 19s. 6d., has distributed last year in profits £96,912, 2s. 5d., has paid to the Government for rents, licences, and all other rights and privileges last year £1191, 9s. 10d.

'Robinson Gold Mining Company produced last year in gold £651,928, 5s. 3d., has distributed last year in profits £346,628, 12s. 6d., has paid to the Government for rents, rates, and licences £395, 11s. 8d.

'New Chimes Gold Mining Company produced £93,013, 15s. 11d.; paid profits, £32,485, 16s. 3d.; paid rates and licences, lumped in the balance-sheet together with insurance premiums, £664, 16s. 5d.

'The Transvaal Coal Trust produced 266,945 tons of coal last year; all Government taxation amounted to £53, 1s.

'The Consolidated Land and Exploration Company, of which the Ecksteins are the largest holders, owns over 250 farms of about 6000 acres each; all the taxes, including absentee tax, amounted to £722, 2s. 6d. last year.

'Now for the

INDIRECT TAXATION.

All machinery for mining purposes is subject to only 1½ per cent. import dues; the term machinery is stretched by the Government to its uttermost possibilities to meet the mining industry, and it is made to include f.i. sheet lead, cyanide, etc. All other articles not specially rated are subject to an *ad valorem* duty of 7½ per cent., the Cape Colonists pay an *ad valorem* duty of 12 per cent. Specially rated articles affecting the white miners, such as tea, coffee, butter, rice, soap, sugar, are in most cases subject to lower, and in no instance to higher, duties than in the Cape Colony, f.i.

	CAPE COLONY.	TRANSVAAL.
Butter,	3d. per lb.	5s. od. per 100 lb.
Cheese,	3d. ,,	5s. od. ,,
Coffee,	12s. 6d. per 100 lb.	2s. 6d. ,,
Rice,	3s. 6d. ,,	1s. 6d. ,,
Soap,	4s. 2d. ,,	5s. od. ,,
Sugar,	6s. 3d. ,,	3s. 6d. ,,
Tea,	8d. per lb.	5s. od. ,,
Guns,	£1 per barrel.	10s. od. per barrel.

'The article maize,

THE PRINCIPAL FOOD

of the Kaffirs, pays in the Cape Colony 2s. per 100 lb., and in the Transvaal 2s. per 100. Periodically, through droughts, locusts, or other causes, prices for this commodity rise rapidly, often from 10s. 6d. to 26s. 6d. per bag, variations which are only slightly affected by the import duty. Nevertheless, the Government has in every instance of excessive prices abated the duty for the time being.

'The only other tax affecting the mining industry is the Pass Money of 1s. per month per native; and the moneys resulting therefrom are handed by the Government to the Johannesburg Hospital, an excellent institution, exclusively established for the use of Johannesburg and its mines.

'I think every reasonable mind will absolve the Government from the charge of endeavouring to strangle the mining industry.

'And now as to

THE CHARGES CALLED POLITICAL,

Hollanders, I take it, are as much Uitlanders as is Mr Phillips or any other Englishman; they have this one advantage, that they speak the language of the country, while 95 out of every 100 English in the Transvaal decline to acquire it. But what are the facts? The President and all the members of the Executive are South African born, so is the Minister of Mines, so is the Treasurer-General, the Auditor-General, the Postmaster, the Surveyor-General, so is the Commandant-General, the Chief of Police; so was, until three months ago, the Attorney-General, so is the Mining Commissioner of Johannesburg, and so are all the Landdrosts (equal to your magistrates) throughout the country, with one exception only. Of the judges of the High Court two are South African born, two Hollanders, and one Scotch.

'The only other official of high standing who comes from Holland is

THE STATE SECRETARY,

Dr Leyds, and that he is an extremely able and distinguished man his worst enemies will allow.

'A census taken throughout the Civil Service has shown that eighty-three per cent. are South African born, and seventeen per cent. Uitlanders. Naturally, the latter are selected from those who can speak the language of the country.

'Before I come to the other three grievances, I must set right the grossly exaggerated figures which are given in the English Press as affecting the population in the Transvaal.

'Mr Rhodes, in his cabled letter to the New York *World*, gives them as 100,000 English against 14,000 Boers! Now the

ACTUAL FIGURES

from quite recent compilations are :—

Total inhabitants, ...		226,028
Of which Transvaal born, .	150,308	
And Uitlanders of all nationalities, ...	75,720	
Of these again are English, .	41,275	
And of all other nationalities, including those from Cape Colony and Natal, . .	34,445	

'These figures, which are correct, make the absurdity of the political claim clear, but more clear still if you deduct from the 75,720 Uitlanders the 60,000 who dwell at Johannesburg and its mining district; if you eliminate that one town from the total, you have the Boers numbering ten to one against the Uitlanders throughout the country. And would you have a country ruled in language, franchise and education by one mining town.

'To prove the correctness of the above statement you have only to consider that there are on the

MILITARY REGISTER

over 25,000 Boers. Every one of them is married, and most of them have children, the average being over four children, which gives the 150,000 souls.

'Of these fully two-thirds do not understand English. It is reasonable then to claim that the official language, that official documents, shall be the language spoken by two-thirds of the people, or do the women and children count for nothing? But although the official language by law is Dutch there is not a single Government office in which there is not English or German spoken to those who cannot speak Dutch. In the Courts in the witness-box the judges frequently shut their eyes to the use of the English language, and in the lower Courts English is invariably spoken by English litigants.

'Also as to the education the manifesto makes gross misstatements. Though the State schools are, of course, Dutch, and the ordinary State-aided schools are Dutch, the

GOVERNMENT HAS ALWAYS AGREED

to give to all English schools exactly the same aid as to the latter, provided they will gradually, in the higher classes, introduce the State language, so that in the lowest classes only English is spoken, while in the highest class Dutch is to be the medium. The Germans in Johannesburg have and pay for their own school, the English claim to have their schools, in which, as Mr Lionel Phillips expressed it in his speech, Dutch may be taught, perhaps, if there was a "little time left," maintained at Government expense.

'And now to the last point, that of the franchise. That a *settled* and *loyal* population cannot for ever be refused a reasonable voting power I am the last to deny. But is the Johannesburg population settled and loyal? Can you wonder that the Boers have their grave doubts? Where are all the men from the Transvaal who have made their fortunes there? The Beits, Taylors, Neumann, Bailey, the English, Barnato, Dunnings, and all the others? Do they throw in their lot with the Transvaal? Not at all; they live in London; spend their money there, regard themselves as English, and do not want to be anything. The very same men who now

CLAMOUR WITH BAYONETS

fixed for the franchise, cover the addresses presented to the High Commissioner when he comes into the Transvaal with thousands of signatures as "Her Majesty's most loyal subjects." Can you wonder at the Boer if he cannot conceive the dual loyalty which claims to swear allegiance to the Transvaal without abandoning that to England?

'Can you wonder if he points to the doings of 1896 as his justification for the refusal to grant the franchise indiscriminately, points to the men who have called in the enemy, the Chartered Company, into the country, and under the dastardly pretext, too, that the Boer was threatening to murder women and children, when the Boers were quietly at their farms, while Johannesburg had for the last six months been arming its thousands of men with smuggled rifles and guns?

'Can you seriously

WONDER AT THE BOER,

who knows only one loyalty to his country, that of leaving wife and child, plough and land, aye, and his life, too, in the defence of the independence of his beloved land? And are these qualities held so cheap in this nineteenth century that stock-jobbers and adventurers and their legal advisers may safely sneer at them and find the approval of the great English nation? I trust not.

'Is the decision of peace or war of continents to be left in these hands? is what I would like to know as

'A TRANSVAAL UITLANDER OF TEN YEARS' STANDING.'

'*Jan.* 31.'

After Steve had finished reading the extract, he sat looking at his guest thoughtfully for a moment, who seemed buried in thought. After a while, the visitor turned to his host and said,—

'Are those facts given in that letter based on truth?'

'Mainly so; the only fault is that he is too mild; he could put it much stronger in favour of the Government, without exaggeration.'

'Humph, this is a different tale entirely from the one told in Leonard's manifesto; and from what I have seen and learned here, I am inclined to believe this one in preference to the other one. But let us take it for granted that this one is correct, and leave the question of the past alone for a moment, I want you to look into the future for a few moments, and tell me what do you and your countrymen look forward to as the probable future of South Africa?'

'There are various views held. There are those who wish for peace at any price, and who would be content to leave matters as they are, viz., to keep what we have, and let England keep what she has. But this will only last while England allows us to peacefully keep possession of our country. But, should England press us, these would join the other party without a moment's hesitation.'

'And what are the views of the other party?'

'Well, it has never been defined. It is merely a leaven permeating the thoughts, words and deeds of the party. It is a strong patriotic feeling in the breast of every true and thoughtful Afrikander, a desire to build up a strong and united South African nation and a strong and united South Africa.'

'And how do you propose to bring this desirable union to fruition?'

'As far as I have been able to think it out, it can only come to pass in two ways.'

'And those two ways are?'

'Either to fight for it, or to get it peacefully. If we can get it peacefully, it would do England more good than harm. England must have seen that the universal desire of all South Africans of any merit, English or Dutch, are tending towards Republicanism. It is true that there has been a great deal of friction between English and Dutch in the past, but the events of this year have brought over nearly all of the English *South African born* people of the colonies to the same view that has all along been held by the Dutch, viz., that the Imperial factor serves only to keep this friction alive, and that when South Africa is entirely free that this, race hatred will die out, and that, instead of having, as at present, an Imperial and a Republican party, we shall only have the more desirable Liberal and Conservative parties, both parties possessing Englishmen as well as Dutchmen amongst their members. As I have said, South African Englishmen have recognised this fact, and all thoughtful South African Englishmen are beginning to desire a Republican South Africa as much as the Dutch. Now, if England is wise enough to recognise this fact, and wise enough to act upon it in time, she has only one thing to do, viz., to call a meeting, or congress, of leading politicians from all the states and colonies of South Africa. And this is what she should propose:—

'If I give up the whole of South Africa to you, to form an entirely independent South Africa, will you,

'Firstly, give me the same commercial benefits I now enjoy?

'Secondly.—Will you give my ships, commercial as well as ships of war, the same shelter and protection as well as the same coaling facilities in times of peace or war as now enjoyed by them?

'Thirdly.—Will you enter in solemn treaty to be England's friends in both peace and war?

'Fourthly.—Will you guarantee that you shall never allow yourself to be annexed by any other power?

'Fifthly.—Will you give me the most favoured nation treaty in all respects, which would amount to England enjoying the same benefits as now without any of the responsibilities or worries she now has, and what would South Africa reply to such a proposal?

'They would be only too glad to obtain their independence and freedom while remaining at peace with and the friend of England, and they would accept with joy?'

'But should England refuse to give the whole of

South Africa their freedom on these or any other terms, what would then happen? Do you think that you would deliberately fight for it?'

'Yes.'

'Do you mean to say that the whole of, or any part of, South Africa would rise up against England and demand that she should vacate South Africa or—fight?'

'No, these things do not happen in that way, as a rule. It will simply happen that one of these days, in the course of the petty persecutions against the two Dutch representatives, which is always going on to a greater or less extent, that the Republicans will put their foot down and refuse to accede to some unjust demand made on them by some Jingoistic British minister, the consequence of which would be a war, the end of which would be a united South African Republic, with or without foreign aid. Either that would happen, or—the utter extinction of the Boers.'

'Do you think the last is at all likely to happen?'

'If it is God's will, *then* it will, otherwise not?'

'Quite true! but from a worldly point of view, what are the probabilities of the South Africans winning their independence?'

'A Joshua will arise, who will unite the different races and peoples by a common sympathy. He will cause the two contending parties or races to trust him—he will form a link uniting the two together. Once united with a common desire of Freedom and Independence, and a leader worthy to be trusted by all, the battle will be more than half won. With the people of South Africa once united, they can resist any army that England may send against them. England's power lies in her navy. The South Africans won't go to seek her on the sea to fight her. They will simply wait for any and every army sent against them on land, and by various means, which comes to those fighting for liberty, will demolish those armies. They will simply keep out of the way of the ironclads when necessary, and keep on holding the land for years if need be, until out of sheer weariness England shall grant them peace. This is should they have no further aid than their own people. But should one or more European or American powers take up their cause, the end will be sooner and more easily obtained.'

'Would you or your Government then call in European aid?'

'I could not say what might or might not happen, but I do not think it improbable that aid might come unasked, and should we find ourselves hard pressed, we might find ourselves simply forced to accept foreign aid.'

'And do you think there is really much chance of a Joshua fulfilling the Herculean task of uniting the various races of South Africa.'

'It would not be such a Herculean task after all. The thing is almost half done; the events of this year have almost completed the task; it only wants the right man to complete it entirely. What we want is a man who would be trusted by all parties—a man who would do everything unselfishly, who would leave *self* out of the question entirely, and whose only desire would be to advance the interest of *land* and *people*.

'And do you think there is any probability of such a man being found?'

'I have great hopes. The material for great and noble men is plentiful in South Africa. I believe when the want is felt for such a man by the people, the man will be found.'

'I can see you have thought much on the subject. If you had the choice of the two means of obtaining your independence, which would you choose?'

'I would certainly choose the peaceful one. For then the country would not receive the great check to progress which she would receive after such a terrible war, as would be the result in case we fought against England.

Once we have obtained our independence by fighting for it, our prestige as a people would be far greater than when obtained by peaceful means. But besides the bloodshed and material losses after such a war, we should for many years have England for an enemy, and we would still have a small party of Jingoistic Imperialists in the country. While, should we obtain our independence peacefully, we would have England for a friend and the Imperialist in South Africa would not feel the bitter hatred against the Republicans as was the case when the Transvaal had obtained her independence after fighting for it. A hatred, the evil effects of which are felt to this day.'

'Yes, you are quite right. I think, both for the sake of South Africa and England, it would be far better if the problem were solved peacefully. England would be no worse off than she now is if she were to give up the country on the terms proposed by you; while you would have the satisfaction of being independent. As to the race hatred felt after war, history has shown its evil effects—witness France and Germany.'

'And I do not see why this peaceful solution should not be obtained. The only obstacle is the misrepresentation of South Africans by parties interested. And then we have people who declare that the Dutch in South Africa must be extinguished, politically, at least, at any sacrifice, even that of principle.'

'Yes, I understand. You refer to the Jameson Raid and those concerned in it. But I hardly condemn the raiders as much as I do those who approved it, who should know better. I can tell you I feel ashamed of being a Britisher when I read, for instance, Alfred Austin's poem. It is a shame that a man who implies such *want* of principle should hold the position of Poet Laureate to the British Crown.'

Steve smiled and said,—

'That reminds me that I have another extract which I would like to show you. It is a parody on Austin's poem, published by the Orange Free State *Express*.'

'I should like to see it?'

'It ought to be read together, so if you will allow me, I will read you Austin's poem first, and then the parody. Listen :—

'JAMESON'S RIDE'

ALFRED AUSTIN

'WRONG! Is it wrong? Well, may be:
But I'm going, boys, all the same.
Do they think me a Burgher's baby,
To be scared by a scolding name?
They may argue, and prate, and order;
Go, tell them to save their breath:
Then, over the Transvaal border,
And gallop for life or death!

'Let lawyers and statesmen addle
Their pates over points of law:
If sound be our sword, and saddle,
And gun-gear, who cares one straw?
When men of our own blood pray us
To ride to their kinsfolk's aid,
Not Heaven itself shall stay us
From the rescue they call a raid.

'"There are girls in the Gold Reef City,
There are mothers and children too!
And they cry, 'Hurry up! for pity!'
So what can a brave man do?
If even we win, they'll blame us;
If we fail, they will howl and hiss.
But there's many a man lives famous
For daring a wrong like this!"

'So we forded and galloped forward,
As hard as our beasts could pelt,
First eastward, then trending nor'ward,
Right over the rolling veld;
Till we came on the Burghers lying
In a hollow with hills behind,
And their bullets came hissing, flying
Like hail on an Arctic wind!

'Right sweet is the marksman's rattle,
  And sweeter the cannon's roar,
But 'tis bitterly bad to battle,
  Beleagured, and one to four.
I can tell you, it wasn't a trifle
  To swarm over Krugersdorp glen,
As they plied us with round and rifle,
  And ploughed us, again—and again.

'Then we made for the Gold Reef City,
  Retreating, but not in rout.
They had called to us, "Quick! for pity!"
  And he said, "They will sally out."
They will hear us and come. "Who doubts it?"
  But how if they don't, what then?
Well, worry no more about it,
  But fight to the death, like men."

'Not a soul had supped or slumbered
  Since the Borderland stream was cleft;
But we fought, ever more outnumbered,
  Till we had not a cartridge left.
We're not very soft or tender,
  Or given to weep for woe,
But it breaks one to have to s'render
  One's sword to the strongest foe.

'I suppose we were wrong, we were madmen,
  Still I think at the Judgment Day,
When God sifts the good from the bad man,
  There'll be something more to say.
We were wrong, but we aren't half sorry,
  And, as one of the baffled band,
I would rather have had that foray
  Than the crushings of all the Rand.'

'Now listen to the parody, here it is:—

JAMESON'S RAID

WRONG is it? Most wickedly wrong!
  That treacherous raid, some call *ride*,
Of Jameson, Maxims, and rover throng;
  Though *noblemen* rode by his side.

They may argue, and hunt for excuses,
  To prove their intention was good,
Common sense now it is that accuses
  And proclaims their intention was *loot.*

Let lawyers and statesmen ponder,
  To prove that their action was right ;
Van den Berg, MacDonald, Van Tonder,
  Lost their lives in the wantonest fight.
When the jobbers wrote secretly, 'help us'
  'In our scramble for more and more gold,'
Jameson's answer it ought to have been thus :
  'British honour I'm bound to uphold.'

There are babes in the Gold Reef City,
  There are boys and maidens and wives,
And the cowards, that knew no pity,
  Imperilled those innocent lives.
Had they done what their duty demanded,
  We would never have heard of the raid ;
Had but counsels of prudence commanded,
  Constitutional ways were their aid.

But Jameson's band scampered forward,
  As hard as their horses could pelt,
First eastward, then westward, then nor'ward,
  Meandering over the veld,
Till the sons of the land they invaded
  With courage, the offspring of right,
The usurpers with bullets persuaded
  They had to surrender or fight.

There was heard the dread Maxim's rattle
  And thundering cannon's loud roar,
But Jameson found in this battle
  His match in the Transvaal Boer.
can tell you it wasn't a trifle,
  That search for a hole to creep through
While the Boers plied unerring the rifle,
  Taught the raiders to die or to do.

They made tracks for the Gold Reef City,
  Expecting their jobber friends out,
But those cowards, whom brave men pity,
  Had noticed their plot 'up the spout.'

They distinctly could hear the guns rattle,
They could help. Did they ever try?
No. They left their poor dupes to do battle,
To be driven about, and to die.

The raiders had supped, drank and slumbered,
And were fully prepared for the fray;
They knew that they were not outnumbered,
But their conscience caused them dismay.
They're not very considerate or tender,
But their hearts sunk down to the boot,
And they had to accept a surrender
In lieu of gold, glory and loot.

I'm sure they were wrong—worse than madmen,
And I think at the Judgment Day,
When God sifts the good from the bad men,
For themselves they'll have little to say.
They were wrong, but they are not sorry,
They've caused innocent blood to flow,
And the men who joined such a foray,
Unrepentant, to Satan must go.

GERT DIKKOP.

Basterland, Feb. 1896.

After Steve had finished reading, the smiling and laughter-loving Scotchman burst into a hearty laugh.

'Very good; very good indeed; ha, ha!' he laughed. 'I should like to see Austin's face if he should read this; ha, ha! It certainly has the merit of *truth* which Austin's poem lacks.'

After some further conversation Steve's guest left him, giving him a hearty invitation to dine with him the following day.

CHAPTER XXVIII

LOVE AT LAST

WE have endeavoured to keep romance and love stories out of this book. We have nearly succeeded, but in order to complete our work, we find that love will intrude itself, if it is only in the last chapter. It is not our fault, we have done our best, but our hero, like all other heroes, has gone and done it. He fell in love. With whom? Why, my dear reader, it cannot be difficult to guess. We have not introduced many ladies into our story. We have only introduced two who would or could be a fit mate to our young friend. The first one was the sister of the poor young fellow who was killed by lightning. But we honestly declared, from the moment of introducing her, that Steve was not going to fall in love with her. So there is only one left. We have not tried to deceive the reader in the least. When we knew that Steve was not going to fall in love, we told the kind and indulgent reader so honestly. We did not deceive the reader, but Steve deceived us. He never told us that he was going to fall in love. When we heard of it, it was an accomplished fact. It happened in this way. Steve got a fortnight's holiday. What was he to do? He thought for a moment, then jumped up and said aloud, astonishing his friends who were with him at the time.

'Oh, I have it, a good idea!'

'A good idea?' queried Keith. 'Where did you get it from?'

'Never mind; I am going to act up to it, too. I have a standing invitation from the Mijnheer Meyer to pay him a visit, and I think I cannot do better than give Black Prince a sight of his old home again.'

There now, gentle reader, the cat is out of the bag; you know now with whom Steve fell in love surely.

And Steve did act up to his *idea*. He took Black Prince to see his old home again. When he arrived at the door of the well-appointed farmhouse, he did not see anyone about. He dismounted and knocked at the door. The door was opened by—no, not Miss Meyer, but Jankie, the old Hottentot, who was Steve's first acquaintance on the farm. *He* did not recognise Steve.

'Is the baas in?'

'No, sir, but the young missus is in. The old baas and the old missus have driven over to Baas Rantenbach's farm, but will be back this evening. The two young baases are also out, but will be back to-morrow.'

Steve felt a little embarrassment when he heard that only Miss Meyer was in. However, he decided to make the best of it until the old man returned.

'Tell the young *nooi* that I would like to see her.'

'Yes, sir. Will you come into the sitting-room? I will tell the *nooi* that you are waiting there.'

Steve walked in, and had hardly sat down when he saw a vision of beauty walk into the room, which surprised him, as it was most unexpected. He had only seen Miss Meyer before, when greatly agitated, and when the light was faint and indistinct. Now that he saw her in the bright daylight, he saw a young girl, with a sweet, smiling face, in whose bright eyes shone the light of great intelligence; she was tastefully but simply dressed. Her form and face appeared to him simply perfect. Her long light hair was hanging in a wavy mass down her shoulders, while a halo of sunny tresses surrounded her glorious forehead. But what pleased and attracted him most was the *Soul* he saw shining through her expressive countenance.

'Surely this is the sweetest creature that ever I saw,' was the thought that flashed through his brain during the moment that elapsed before she spoke. He was standing with the light on his back. She came up and tried to make out his face, but seemed puzzled.

'Can I do anything for you, sir? My father is not in now, but will return this afternoon. Shall I tell the boy to put your horse in the stable?'

'If you will be so kind, I shall be much obliged to you, Miss Meyer. Poor creature, he is a bit tired; it is a long time since I have ridden him so far,' he said, smiling.

As Steve spoke, she looked at him inquiringly, as if she half recognised him but was afraid to make a mistake. She turned to the door and told Jankie to take the horse round to the stable, then came back and asked in the usual Afrikander way,—

'May I ask who you are, sir?'

'Don't you know me, Miss Meyer?'

'I thought I did, but I am not quite sure. When I look into your eyes and hear your voice, I am almost sure I know you, but that beard confuses me. The one I take you for had no beard when last I saw him.'

'No, Miss Meyer, I had no beard then; but since that day I have never shaved, because your mother thought me an enemy because my face was shaved.'

'So you really are—'

'I am the one that was in grief and despair, and to whom an angel came and touched me on the shoulder and said, "God has heard your prayer." That angel came in your form, and gave me the most beautiful and best horse in the country, when I would have given my all for the ugliest old moke to be had.'

'Oh, Mr Joubert, is it really you then? I thought it was you the moment I saw you, but, as I said, the beard confused me I am so glad to see you again. My father has long expected you, as he said you had promised to pay us a visit. But don't call me an angel again; I am all flesh and blood, and prone to sin, and you will tempt me to become proud if you thus flatter me, and pride is sinful.' And as she spoke the blood she spoke of flushed rosily in her face, as if to prove her assertion of being flesh and blood.

What need to say more. The thing was done. Each felt drawn to each. Each felt that each had met a kindred spirit, and each soon felt that each loved each other; and when Jankie came in half-an-hour later to tell his *Nonnie* that Master Willim's black stallion had come back, he found the two talking and smiling as if they had known each other for years. When old Mijnheer Meyer came home, he gave Steve a princely welcome, and the old lady, in spite of her former distrust of him, soon learned to love him as a son; the more so as he had grown a beard since last she had seen him. She detested a man who shaved.

And when Master William came home, he gladly renewed his former friendship with Steve, while his younger brother rivalled him in his attentions to their guest.

Before Steve's holiday was over, everything had been decided upon. They were to be married in a month's time. The month was to enable Steve to give his employers a month's notice to leave, as old Mijnheer Meyer had given him and his betrothed the Pretoria farm belonging to the family.

. . . .

The wedding was over. Steve took his beautiful young bride for a trip to his old home in G——, to see his mother and sisters. His mother was greatly pleased that her son had taken such a good and beautiful young wife.

As Steve received, as the wedding portion of his wife, a farm, with house, furniture and everything complete, and as his wife, like all daughters of well-to-do farmers, possessed her own flock of sheep, her own little herd of cows and bullocks, besides horses, etc., Steve found himself a fairly well-to-do young farmer. He now felt himself in the position to indulge to his heart's content in the pleasures of tree-planting, gardening, farming and bee-keeping, which had always been his special hobby.

With a good and beautiful wife, a well-stocked farm, and by selling the greater portion of his mining shares—a good capital to work his farm—Steve has every promise of a happy and prosperous life before him. What his future *will* be we cannot say. With his intense love of country, he is sure to go in for politics, and with the freedom he now enjoys as an independent farmer, he will

S

have leisure enough to enter into the political arena. If the opportunity offers, he is sure to do something for his country yet, and the reader may yet hear of him again as a leader of his people. We shall bid him and the reader now good-bye.

THE END

LONDON: DIGBY, LONG & CO., PUBLISHERS,
18 Bouverie Street, Fleet Street, E.C.

www.ingramcontent.com/pod-product-compliance
Lightning Source LLC
Chambersburg PA
CBHW021046030726
47496CB00006B/1709
* 9 7 8 3 7 4 4 7 5 5 1 8 4 *